Alfred P. Swineford

History and Review of Copper, Iron, Silver, Slate

And other Material Interests of the South Shore of Lake Superior

Alfred P. Swineford

History and Review of Copper, Iron, Silver, Slate
And other Material Interests of the South Shore of Lake Superior

ISBN/EAN: 9783337176600

Printed in Europe, USA, Canada, Australia, Japan

Cover: Foto ©ninafisch / pixelio.de

More available books at **www.hansebooks.com**

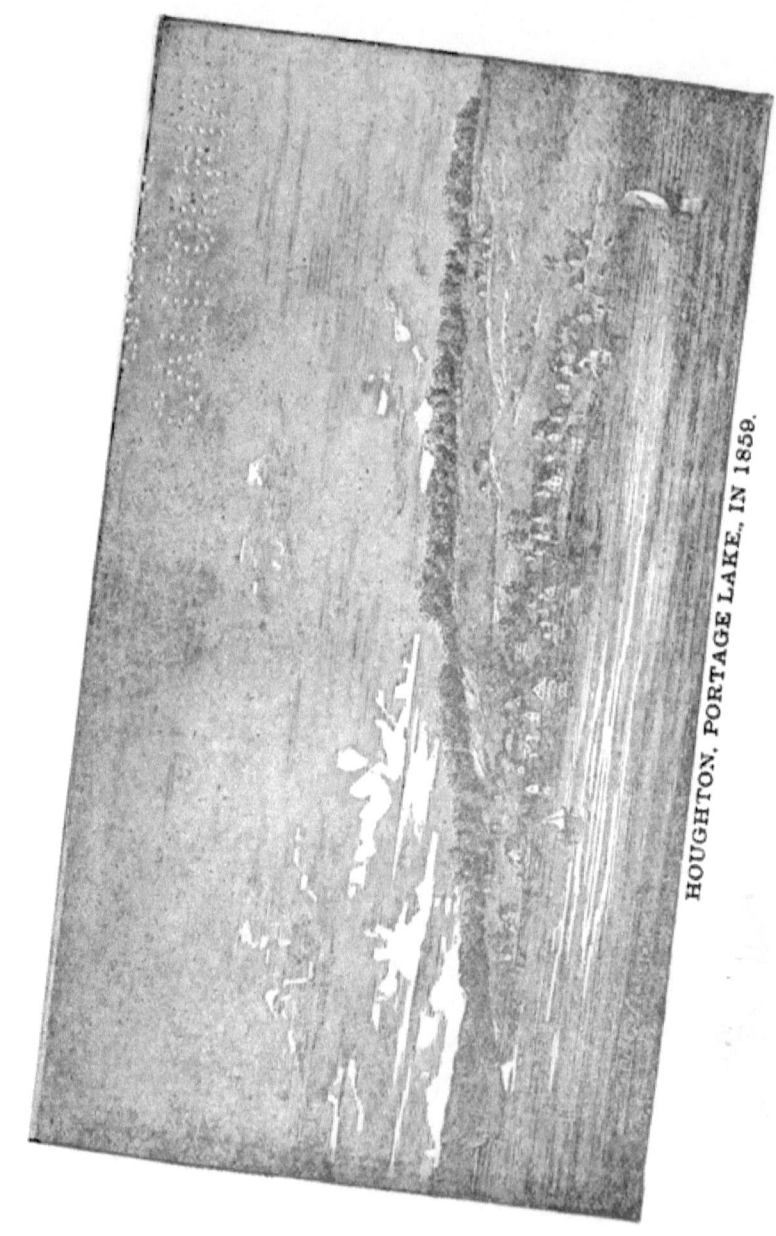

HOUGHTON, PORTAGE LAKE, IN 1859.

HISTORY AND REVIEW

OF THE

COPPER, IRON, SILVER, SLATE

AND OTHER

Material Interests

OF THE

SOUTH SHORE OF LAKE SUPERIOR.

A. P. SWINEFORD.

MARQUETTE, (L S.) MICH.
THE MINING JOURNAL.
1876.

ENTERED ACCORDING TO ACT OF CONGRESS, IN THE YEAR 1876, BY
A. P. SWINEFORD,
IN THE OFFICE OF THE LIBRARIAN OF CONGRESS, AT WASHINGTON.

PREFACE.

THIS volume has been compiled for the triple purpose of preserving the history of the Lake Superior region, to attract attention to its unparalleled mineral resources, and, if possible, to put enough money into the pocket of its compiler and publisher to compensate him for what might otherwise be a labor of love.

In this connection I desire to return my sincere thanks to Hon. John H. Forster, one of the earliest among the pioneers of the copper region, for a very nearly complete history of the discovery and development of the copper interest, and at the same time, to beg his pardon for having so elaborated his valuable paper as to impair, in some degree, the style and harmony of his composition.

I am also indebted to Jacob Houghton, A. R. Harlow, and Hon. Peter White, for much valuable information, aside from the former's very interesting paper on the "Ancient Copper Miners of Lake Superior." The geology of the Iron District, by Chas. E. Wright, M. E., though brief is exhaustive, and written in words that are within the comprehension of others than scientists. It is pronounced the ablest and most reliable paper upon the subject that has ever been written.

For himself, the author claims no other credit than that which may justly be accorded for having made the best use he could of information derived from others—that part of the book relating to copper, being, so far as he is concerned, little else than a compilation.

Marquette, March, 1876.   A. P. S.

MINERAL RESOURCES OF LAKE SUPERIOR.

EARLIEST DISCOVERIES AND RESEARCHES.

The Jesuit Fathers were the first in modern times to intimate to the world the existence of native copper on the shores of Lake Superior. In the seventeenth century—more than two hundred years ago—impelled by a burning zeal for the salvation of souls, these devoted and intelligent Frenchmen, cross in hand, pushed boldly out into the savage wilderness of the great Northwest. These men were something more than mere zealots; they were good geographers, topographers and naturalists; they were apt observers, and possessed the skill and industry necessary to render their discoveries of value to mankind. Among other things, they carefully noted, as they navigated the great lake in their frail canoes, copper lying on the shores and in the possession of the superstitious savages; but it is doubtful whether these holy Fathers understood much about geology, or whence the float copper came. The Indians seem never to have made practical use of this valuable metal, but regarded the copper in their possession as something sacred. At a very late day, since mining became an industry on the lake, the same superstitious reverence prevailed. In this respect they were far inferior in intelligence to that pre-historic race known as the ancient miners. Of the works of this unknown people more hereafter.

The first published account of the existence of copper and other minerals on Lake Superior, is to be found in "Lagarde's" book, which appeared in Paris in 1636; it contained many things which would be of interest to the general reader at this time, but we shall have to be content with a few brief quotations. All the information concerning the existence of copper and other minerals on Lake Superior given by this early writer, appears to have been obtained from the Indians, and it would seem that he was not himself well versed in mineralogy. He says, referring to the south shore of the lake: "There are *mines* of copper which might be made profitable if there were inhabitants and workmen who would labor faithfully. That would be done if colonies were established. * * * About eighty or one hundred leagues from the Hurons there is a mine of copper from which Truchement Bruslé showed me an ingot, on his return from a voyage to the neighboring nation." This book, it must be remembered, was published thirty years before the advent of the Jesuit Fathers, Allouez, Mesnard and Marquette, and the language of the author is such as to encourage the belief that there existed at the time to which he refers copper *mines* that were actually being wrought by the Indians, or, perhaps, by a last remnant of the "ancient miners;" otherwise why should he have used the word "mines?" Nor could he have seen an *ingot*. It is much more probable that his "mines" were undeveloped lodes, and the "ingot" a mere boulder—the ancient miners must have been extinct thousands of years before, according to archæologists. "It is," says he, "pretended, also, that near Saguenay, gold, rubies, and other precious stones are found. I am assured that, in the country of the Souriquois there are not only mines of copper, but also of steel; also certain blue transparent stones, which are as valuable as turquoises." He also says that "among the rocks they found stones covered with diamonds attached to the rocks—some of them appearing as if just from the hands of the lapidary, they were so beautiful." He was not sure, however, that they were fine, but they "were very handsome, and would write upon glass." And: "it seems that one might find mines of iron and many other minerals, if one would take the trouble of searching, and go to some expense. There is an abundance of limestone and other materials required for building."

In the *Relacion de ce qui s'est passe dans le pays des Hurons*, there is much information concerning the "Lac Superieur." The *Relacion* for 1659-'60 gave an account of one of the Jesuit fathers "residing in the lake which we call Superieur." "It is enriched on all its borders by mines of lead almost pure, and of copper all refined in pieces as large as the fist, and great rocks which have whole veins of turquoises."

In a small duodecimo volume of less than two hundred pages, published in Paris in 1640, by Pierre Boucher, the following mention of Lake Superior is made:

"There are mines of copper, tin, antimony and lead." Can it be that the author visited the tin discovery on the north shore, afterwards found and *lost again* by Detroit parties? "In Lake Superior there is a great island which is fifty leagues in circuit, in which there is a very beautiful mine of copper; it is found also in various places in large pieces all refined." Is it not probable that the "beautiful mine of copper" referred to by this writer was the ancient mine now being re-opened by the Minong company? It is barely possible that the exodus of the ancient miners may have been so recent at that time as to leave fully exposed the pure masses that are now being taken out of ancient pits by Mr. Davis. If the works of the ancients are so clearly discernible at this late day, it is not impossible that the scene of their mining operations, may at that date—two hundred and fifty years ago—have presented more the aspect of a lately developed mine than that of one long abandoned.

In the *Relacion* for 1666-'67, in a chapter entitled, "*Journal du Voyage du Pere Claude Allouez dans le Cais 'des Outaouacs*'" are to be found these passages:

"The savages respect this lake as a divinity, and make sacrifices to it, on account perhaps, of its magnitude, for it is two hundred leagues long and eighty leagues wide; or on account of its goodness in furnishing them with fishes, which nourish all these people where there is but little game. There are often found beneath the water. pieces of copper all formed, and of the weight of ten and twenty pounds. I have seen them many times in the hands of the savages, and as they are superstitious, they keep them as so many divinities, or as presents from the gods beneath the water, who have given them as pledges of good fortune. On that account they keep the pieces of copper enveloped among their most precious furniture. There are some who have preserved them for more than fifty years, and others who have had them in their families from time immemorial, and cherish them as household gods.

"Sometime since a large mass of copper, like a rock, was seen with the point projecting out of the water. This afforded passers by an opportunity of cutting off pieces. Nevertheless, when I went by there it was not to be seen. I believe the storms, which are here very violent and like those on the ocean, had covered the rock with sand. Our savages wished to persuade us that it was a divinity, and had disappeared, for some reason which they did not mention."

"*De la Mission du Sainte Esprit a la Pointe de Chagaoumigond dans le Lac* Tracy *ou Superieur—Chapter XI, des Proprie tez et Raritez*. We find in Dr. Jackson's report, made to the Secretary of the Interior in 1849, the following translations:

"The lake has nearly the form of a bended bow, of more than eighty leagues in length. The southern side represents the string, and a long tongue of land which springs from the south shore, and projects upwards of twenty-five leagues into the lake near to its middle, is the arrow." (The writer, of course, refers to Keweenaw point, and his illustration of the form of the lake was apt and truthful, though he does not seem to have had an accurate knowledge of its length.) "The northern coast is bordered with frightful crags, which are the termination of that prodigious chain of mountains which take their rise at Cape Tourment, above Quebec, and extend to this place, traversing more than six hundred leagues in extent, and losing themselves at the farther extremity of the lake. There are very few islands in the lake, and they occur mostly on the northern side, near the shore. This great expanse of the waters gives room for the winds, which agitate the lake with as much violence as they do the ocean."

On page 26, of the same work, is a chapter entitled, "Mines of Copper which are found on Lake Superior:"

"Up to the present time it was believed that these mines were found only on one or two of the islands; but since we have made a more careful inquiry we have learned from the savages some secrets which they were unwilling to reveal. It was necessary to use much address in order to draw out of them the knowledge, and to discriminate between the truth and falsehood. We will not warrant, however, all we learned from their simple statements, since we shall be able to speak with more certainty when we have visited the places themselves, which we count on during this summer, when we shall go to find the 'wandering sheep' in all quarters of this great lake. The first place where copper occurs in abundance, after going above the Sault, is on an island about forty or fifty leagues therefrom, near the north shore, opposite a place called Missipiconatong.

"The savages say it is a floating island, which is sometimes far off and sometimes near, according as the winds move it, driving it sometimes one way and sometimes another. They add that, a long time ago four Indians accidentally went there, being lost in a fog, with which this island is almost always surrounded. It was long before they had any trade with the French, and they had no kettles or hatchets. Wishing to cook some food, they made use of their usual method, taking stones which they picked up on the shore, heating them in the fire, and throwing them into a bark trough full of water, in order to make it boil, and by this operation cook their meat. As they took up the stones they found they were nearly all of them pure copper. After having partaken of their meal they thought of embarking, fearing to remain lest the lynxes and the rabbits, which are in the place as large as dogs, would come and eat up their provisions, and even their canoe. Before leaving they collected a quantity

of these stones, both large and small ones, and even some
sheets of copper. But they had not gone far from the shore
before a loud voice was heard, saying in anger, 'who are
these robbers who have stolen the cradles and playthings of
my children?' The sheets of copper were the cradles, for
the Indians make them of one or two pieces of wood—a flat
piece of bark with a hoop over one end—the child being
swathed and bound upon the flat piece. The little pieces of
copper which they took were the playthings, such pebbles
being used by Indian children for a like purpose. This voice
greatly alarmed them, not knowing what it could be. One
said to the others, it is thunder, because there are frequent
storms there; others said, it is a certain genii whom they
call Missibizi, who is reputed among these people to be the
god of the waters, as Neptune was among the pagans; others
said that it came from Memogovissiousis—that is to say, sea-
men, similar to the famous Tritons, or to the syrens, which
live always in the water, with their long hair reaching to
their waists. One of our savages said he had seen one in the
water; nevertheless, he must have merely imagined that he
did. However, this voice so terrified them that one of these
voyageurs died before they reached land. Shortly after a
second one of them expired; then a third; so that only one
of them remained, who, reaching home, told all that had
taken place, and died shortly afterwards. The timid and
superstitious savages have never since dared to go there for
fear of losing their lives, believing that there are certain
genii who kill those who land there; and within the memory
of man no one has been known who has set foot on that
shore, or even coasted along its shores, although the island is
within sight, and even the trees are visible upon another
island called Achemikonan.

"There is both truth and error in this story, and this is
probably the explanation: These savages were poisoned by
the water which they boiled with red hot copper, which by
the intensity of its heat gave off its poison, etc. It is not a
poison which acts immediately, and on one as soon as it will

on another, as happened in the case of these Indians. It may be that when they were taken ill, they more readily imagined they heard a voice; perhaps an echo, such as are very common among the rocks which border this island; or, perhaps, they made this fable since, not knowing to what to attribute the death of these Indians. When they said it was a floating island it is probable they may have been misled by the vapors which surround it; they being rarified or condensed by the variable action of the sun's rays, made the island appear sometimes near and sometimes far off. It is certain, however, that it is a common belief among the Indians that there is a great abundance of copper on the island; but they dare not go there. We hope to begin our discoveries upon it this summer.

"Advancing to a place called the Grand Anse, (Great Bay,) we meet with an island which is celebrated for the metal which is found there, and for the thunder which takes place, because they say it always thunders there, (Thunder Cape.) But farther towards the west, on the same north shore, is the island most famous for copper, called Minong, (the good place,) Isle Royale. This island is twenty-five leagues in length; it is seven leagues from the main land, and sixty from the head of the lake. Nearly all around the island, on the water's edge, pieces of copper are found mixed with pebbles, but especially on the side which is opposite the south, in principally a certain bay which is near the northeast exposure to the great lake. There are shores '*tous escarpez de terre glaize*,' and there are seen several beds or layers of copper, one over the other, separated or divided by other beds of earth or rocks. In the water is seen copper sand, and one can take up in spoons grains of the metal big as an acorn, and others as fine as sand. This island is almost surrounded with islets, which are said to be composed of copper, and they are met with even to the main land on the north. Advancing to the head of the lake, and returning one day's journey, by the south coast, there is seen on the edge of the water a rock of copper which weighs 700 or 800 pounds, and is so hard that steel can hardly cut it; but when it is heated it cuts as easily as lead. Near Point Chagaoumigong, where a mission was established, (Lapointe,) rocks of copper and plates of the same metal were found on the shores of the islands.

"Last spring we bought of the savages a sheet of pure copper two feet square, which weighed more than 100 pounds. We do not believe, however, that the mines are found on these islands, but that the copper was probably brought from Minong, or from other islands by floating ice, or over the bottom of the lake by the impetuous winds, which are very violent, particularly when they come from the northeast.

"Returning still towards the mouth of the lake, following the coast on the south, at twenty leagues from the place last mentioned, we enter the river called Nantounagan (Ontonagon,) on which is seen an eminence where stones and copper fall into the water, or upon the earth; they are readily found. Three years since, we received a piece which was brought from this place which weighed a hundred pounds, and we sent it to M. Talon, at Quebec. It is not certain exactly where this was taken from; some think it was taken from the river; others that it was from near the lake and dug up from the soil.

"Proceeding still further, we come to the long point of land which we have compared to the arrow of the bow (Keweenaw Point;) at the extremity of this there is a small island which is said to be only six feet square, and all copper.

"We are assured that copper is found at various places along the southern shore of the lake. All the information we obtained from others it is not necessary for us to detail; but it seems necessary that more exact researches should be made, and this is what we shall endeavor to effect. If God prospers our enterprise, we shall speak next year with more certainty and knowledge."

The *Relacion* of 1670-'71 contains the remarks of Pere Ablon. On page 91, he gives an account of the copper mines: "We would remark, by the way, that copper is found in all parts of this lake, although we have not as yet sufficiently exact knowledge, for want of thorough explorations; nevertheless, the plates of this metal which we have seen, weigh each a hundred or two hundred pounds, and much more. The great rock of copper of 700 or 800 pounds, and which all the travelers saw near the head of the lake, besides a quantity of pieces which are found near the shore, in various places, seem not to permit us to doubt that there are somewhere the parent mines, which have not been discovered."

These accounts are from the letters or reports, of the Jesuit missionaries; Rene Mesnard having been, so far as is known, the first white man who visited this region. He left Quebec on the 28th of August, 1660, and on the 15th of October of the same year reached the head of Keweenaw Bay (L'Anse,) having coasted along the south shore in a frail birch-bark canoe. Spending the winter among the Indians at that point, the following spring, accompanied by only a single Indian, he started for Chaquamegon Bay. He took the route through Portage Lake; while the Indian was carrying the canoe across the Portage to Lake Superior, the good father wandered into the woods, and was never seen again. That was the story told by the Indian; but it is far more probable that he fell a victim to Indian treachery. Father Claude Allouez was the next to follow, reaching Lapointe on the first of October, 1665, where he established a mission. After him came James Marquette and Claude Dablon, who established a mission at Sault Ste. Marie, in 1668. The first map of Lake Superior was drawn by Allouez and Marquette in 1668, and was published in 1672. They named the lake "*Lac Tracy Ou Superieur.*"

In 1688, Baron Le Houtan published a book of travels in Canada. He had followed in the footsteps of Allouez, and describes many of the objects spoken of by the latter. After describing the lake, and the people who dwelt upon its shores, he closes by saying that "upon it we also find copper *mines*, the metal of which is so firm and plentiful that there is not a seventh part base from the ore."

In 1721, De Charlevoix visited Lake Superior and crossed from the falls of the St. Louis river to the Mississippi, exploring that river to the Gulf of Mexico. His published account is much more minute than that given by those who preceded him, entering, as he does, more into details concerning the resources of the country through which he passed. Speaking of Lake Superior, he says: "Large pieces of copper are found in some places on its banks, and around some of the islands, which are still the objects of a superstitious worship among the Indians. They look upon them with veneration, as if they were the presents of those gods who dwell under the waters; they collect the smallest fragments which they preserve, without, however, making any use of them. They say that formerly a large rock of this metal was to be seen elevated a considerable height above the surface of the water, and as it has now disappeared, they pretend the gods have carried it elsewhere; but there is good reason to believe that in process of time the waves of the lake have covered it entirely with sand and slime; and it is certain that in several places pretty large quantities of this metal have been discovered without being obliged to dig very deep. During the course of my first voyage to this country, I was acquainted with one of our order, (the Jesuits,) who had been formerly a goldsmith, and who, while he was at the mission of *Sault De Ste. Marie*, used to search for this metal, and made candlesticks, crosses, and censers of it; for this copper is often to be met with almost pure."

In 1765, Capt. Jonathan Carver, starting from Mackinac, coasted to Green Bay in company with some fur traders, then ascended the Fox river through Lake Winnebago, to the portage between that river and the Wisconsin, and thence descended the latter to the Mississippi. From there he proceeded up the Mississippi to St. Anthony, where he remained with the Indians until the spring of 1767, when he retraced his steps to the Chippewa river, and made his way up that stream to an Indian village of the same name. From there he crossed over to a head branch of the St. Croix, descended this branch to a fork, and then ascended another to its source. On both of these rivers, he says, he discovered "*mines of virgin copper, which was as fine as that found in any other country.*" From the head waters of the St. Croix his route was to the sources of a river which he named Goddard's River, was most probably the Bois Brule which he descended to Lake Superior. He says in his publication that the Ontonagon river is "remarkable for the abundance of virgin copper that is found on and near its banks, a metal which is met with also in several other places on this coast." "I observed," says he, "that many of the small islands, particularly those on the Eastern shores, were covered with copper ore." His book was, justly perhaps, regarded by many as a second edition of Gulliver's travels, and it is certain that the subsequent explorations of the country through which he passed failed to confirm the truth of many of his statements, which appear to have been merely the creations of a vivid imagination. That he visited the places he describes there is no good reason to doubt; that he discovered "*mines of copper*" on the Chippewa or St. Croix no one is now willing to believe. He may have seen a few boulders, and from their presence took it for granted that they came from "mines" near by, but which really had no existence. Such boulders are occasionally found far removed from any known lodes of the ore or metal, but their only significance is to confirm belief in the glacial theory. However, the publication of his book of travels produced such a sensation in England that a copper company was at once formed for the purpose of developing the mines Carver claimed to have discovered. This was in 1770. The company engaged in their arduous and doubtful enterprise with great spirit and enthusiasm.

The details of the operations and failure of this company have been preserved in a book published by Alexander Henry, entitled "Travels and Adventures in Canada and the Indian Territories between the Years 1760 and 1776." Henry was the earliest English traveler who visited the shores of Lake Superior of whom we have any account. Mr. Henry was an adventurous gentleman. He escaped the dread fate of others at the Mackinaw massacre; was an Indian captive and carried into the Rocky Mountains; was a fur trader, and, after the ancient miner, was the first mine superintendent on the lake. He was also the historian of this first mining enterprise, and in his book gives an account of a trip made by him along the south shore of the lake in 1765, which shows that he was here in advance of Carver. He says:

"On the 19th of August, 1765, we reached the mouth of the Ontonagon river, one of the largest on the south side of the lake. At the mouth was an Indian village, and three leagues above, a fall, at the foot of which sturgeon at this season were obtained so abundant that a month's subsistence for a regiment could have been taken in a few hours. But I found this river chiefly remarkable for the abundance of copper which is on its banks and its neighborhood, and of which the reputation is at present more generally spread than it was at the time of my first visit.

"The copper presented itself to the eye in masses of various weight. The Indians showed me one of twenty pounds. They were used to manufacture this metal into spoons and bracelets for themselves. In the perfect state in which they found it, it required nothing but to beat it into shape. The Piwatie, or Iron river, enters the lake to the westward of the Ontonagon, and, hence, as is pretended, *silver was found while the country was in possession of the French.*

"On my way back to Michilimackinac, I encamped a second time at the mouth of the Ontonagon river, and now took the opportunity of going ten miles up the river with Indian guides. The object for which I most expressly went, and to which I had the satisfaction of being led, was a mass of copper of the weight, according to my estimate, of no less than five tons. Such was its pure and malleable state, that with an axe I was able to cut off a portion weighing a hundred pounds. On viewing the surrounding surface, I conjectured that the mass, at some period or other, had rolled from the side of a lofty hill which rises at its back."

In 1770, Henry built a sloop of forty tons, at Point Aux Pins, and in the spring of 1771, with a party of miners, sailed on a voyage of discovery around the lake, finally landing at the mouth of the Ontonagon, in the fall of that year, where they built a house. Having pitched upon a spot for the commencement of operations, and arranged everything for the accommodation of the miners during the winter, he returned to the Sault. He says:

"Early in the spring of 1772, we sent a boat load of provisions, but it came back on the 20th of June, bringing with it, to our surprise, the whole establishment of miners. They reported that in the course of the winter they had penetrated into the face of the hill, but on the arrival of a thaw, the clay on which, because of its stiffness, they had relied, and neglected to secure by proper supporters, had fallen in; that from the detached masses of metal, which to the last had daily presented themselves, they supposed there might ultimately be reached a body of the same; but they could form no conjecture of its distance, except that it was probably so far off as not to be pursued without sinking an air shaft; and, lastly, that the work would require the hands of more men than could be fed, in the actual state of the country.

"Here our operations ended. The metal was probably within our reach, but if we had found it, the expense of carrying it to Montreal must have exceeded its marketable value. It was never for the exportation of copper that our company was formed, but always with a view to the silver, which it was hoped the ores, whether of *copper or lead*, might in sufficient quantity contain."

According to Dr. Houghton, "Henry began his operations at Miner's river, in the upper gray sandstone; and, also, on Ontonagon river, near the mass of native copper, at which point a shaft was commenced and carried about forty feet through a reddish clay, at which point the red sand rock was reached." Why Henry failed is obvious to any practical miner of to-day.

Later on, from time to time, scientific and treaty making expeditions were conducted up the chain of lakes, and thence across to the head waters of the Mississippi. Governor Cass, Mr. Schoolcraft, Colonel Long, U. S. A., and others, men eminent in affairs and scientific acumen, early in the present century, gave to the world in graceful and instructive narrative the sum of their observations and discoveries.

In an humbler sphere, perhaps with more selfish aims, the great fur trading companies were largely instrumental in bringing the lake region into notice. The Hudson Bay, Northwest and American fur companies had extended their almost regal sway from the lakes to the Polar regions, from the Atlantic to the Pacific ocean. Penetrating the great trackless wilderness, ransacking those boundless solitudes, the contemplation of which now fills the mind with wonder and awe, the hardy hunters and trappers, the *voyageurs* and *couriers du bois*, pursued their adventurous calling. Neither heat nor cold; nor toil, nor hunger, nor savage foe, nor mountain heights, nor boundless plains, nor swollen torrents, nor tempestuous lakes, nor labyrinthian swamps stopped these enduring continental rangers. The practical knowledge of the countries traversed acquired by these men of the woods, was great, and although the policy of the fur trading monopolies was close and repressive, yet it was not possible to wholly prevent some portion of that knowledge concerning those vast, richly endowed solitudes reaching the outer world. At a later day, these *voyageurs* — of the rank and file — became useful aids in the exploration and settlement of the Upper Peninsula. Many of our respected French citizens, of to-day, were of this class.

Notwithstanding the very considerable measure of knowledge gathered from all of the above-mentioned sources, yet it must be confessed that even at so late a period as 1840, that knowledge seems not to have spread far or wide. The general public regarded the great Northwest as through a glass, darkly. We extract a paragraph or two, from the Detroit *Free Press*, to illustrate this point; these extracts also fix the date of the first bill for an appropriation for the St. Marie ship canal:

WASHINGTON, April 21st, 1840.

This day in the senate, the bill granting to the State of Michigan 100,000 acres of land to aid her in the construction of a canal around the falls of Ste. Marie, came up again on third reading. Mr. Norvel and others, advocated the bill. Mr. Clay, of Kentucky, took occasion to speak of the work as one beyond the range of the remotest settlements in the United States, or in the moon. Senator Norvel advocated the bill mainly on the ground that the completion of the canal would stimulate the fisheries of Lake Superior, estimated to be worth one million of dollars per annum. The honorable Senator added, "In the country bordering on the southern shore of Lake Superior, copper ore and other minerals are believed to exist in abundance."

It remained for Dr. Douglass Houghton, the first and ablest State geologist of Michigan, to make such careful exploration of the south shore of Lake Superior as to clear up the mists of tradition, illuminate the subject and attract the attention of the people of the United States and of Europe to the new mineral fields of North America. Dr. H. first visited Lake Superior in 1830, with Gen. Cass. While at the mouth of the Ontonagon, the whole party went up the river to see the famous copper rock referred to by Henry. The year after he came back with the Schoolcraft expedition, which was sent out by the general government for the purpose of ascertaining the sources of the Mississippi. Having prepared himself with chisels, he again visited the copper rock, and cut off and took away some specimens, which are still retained in the family. In cutting off the specimens he broke two of his chisels, which he left on top of the rock. While making his first geological survey in 1840, he again visited the rock, and found his broken chisels just as he had left them, nine years before. His first report to the legislature. in 1841, after ten years of explorative toil, produced a great impression. In 1844, Dr. Houghton took a contract from the general government to make the linear surveys on the lands bordering Lake Superior on the south, *combining them with the geological survey.* This system was his own—the rapid, careful, minute manner in which the surveys were conducted under it, is the best evidence of its wisdom.

Dr. Houghton was ably and faithfully assisted in his surveys by Messrs. Wm. A. Burt, Bela Hubbard, C. C. Douglass, Wm. Ives, S. W. Hill, Mr. Higgins and Jacob Houghton, Jr.

In the autumn of 1845, while on his last expedition for the season, when approaching Eagle river in a small boat, a sudden storm arose, and before his frail bark could find a safe landing place, on the iron-bound shore, it was capsized and all on board perished, save one man. The whole country was shocked at the announcement of this tragical event, and science mourned for one of its brightest ornaments. Aside from personal considerations, his death was to be deplored; many of his field notes were lost with him, and the treasures of his well stored mind were irreparably beyond recall. His final report, which he was prepared to make, could never be given to the world. Mr. Bela Hubbard completed the contract which Dr. Houghton had entered into with the United States Government. Mr. Hubbard and Wm. A. Burt, Esq., subsequently made interesting and valuable sub-reports of their operations.

Dr. Houghton was small in statue, blue eyed, with light hair; temperament exceedingly active and nervous. He was hardy, bold and daring, even to rashness; he endured the toil, hardships and privations of a life in the rough wilderness with unconquerable resolution. He was a leader among men. Said one of our upper peninsula representatives in an address before the members of the legislature of 1875: " Here let us pause—for DOUGLASS HOUGHTON is a name which no citizen of Michigan, and certainly no Lake Superior man, can pass without a tribute; unspoken, perhaps, but none the less stirring, deep and pure in the bottom of his heart. The world has now but just turned from the pageant which followed to an illustrious tomb, the scarred and weather beaten frame of that great man, Dr. Livingstone, who gave up his life to his God, humbly kneeling by his rough couch in the wilds of Africa, where no other white man's foot had ever trod, in magnificent solitude. We have here no enormous London, no rich and cultured people, bowing in enthusiasm before the thrones of intellect, science, genius and heroism; no titled hereditary lords and sovereigns, in funereal train; no vast and sombre monumental pile, where rest in peace the ashes of the mighty dead. We are a rough, practical, money making race; seldom, in our busy life can we pause to ponder on the goodness of a by-gone friend; and we shudder to think how soon the stream of life will close over our heads after we too have followed. But we have great, warm, working, western hearts, which the icy waters that were *his* winding sheet cannot chill, and they shall be our Westminster Abbey —DOUGLASS HOUGHTON's mausoleum." His remains were not recovered until the spring of 1846, when they were taken to Detroit by his brother, Jacob Houghton, Jr., for interment. The same spring the writer of this encamped at Eagle river, and observed a plank nailed to a hut with the following rude inscription: "Douglass Houghton wrecked Oct. 13, 1845." This is the only monument that the people of Lake Superior have yet erected to the memory of one of their earliest and best benefactors.

In the year 1846-7, Dr. Jackson was commissioned by the United States Government to make further geological surveys. He appeared on the lake with a large party of interesting young men. He spent some time in visiting the working mines and in collecting mineralogical specimens. He employed as assistants Messrs. Foster and Whitney, who had been in the country one or two years—acting as geologists, we believe, for private exploring parties. About mid-summer, Dr. Jackson sailed for Isle Royale, accompanied by Professor Foster, John H. Mullett, surveyor, and others. The object of the expedition was a brief examination of the island, but as no vessel came for the distinguished party, it was detained there many weeks. Their observations were confined to the immediate shores of Rock Harbor, and a study of the piscatorial inhabitants of that charming inlet.

In 1848, Doctor Jackson was superseded by Messrs. Foster

and Whitney, and the valuable report which they gave to the world is evidence enough of the able manner in which they discharged their duties. In 1873, Professor Foster, LL.D., published an interesting work entitled Pre-Historic Races of the United States of America. He died in Chicago in 1874. Professor Whitney has since become eminent as state geologist of California.

In the summer of 1842, a treaty was made with the Chippewa Indians, by Robert Stewart, which was ratified by the Senate at the next session of Congress. By this treaty, all the country east of Fond du Lac, including the islands in Lake Superior not previously acquired, was ceded to the United States. Immediately after the ratification of this treaty, applications were made for permits to explore and dig for copper ore, within the limits of the territory thus acquired. Hon. David Henshaw, of Boston, was then Secretary of War, and he not only gave these applications favorable consideration, but through his influence Boston capitalists were enlisted in the prosecution of the first mining enterprises; and ever since then Boston has been largely identified with the development of the Lake Superior copper interest. She is interested in, if, indeed, she does not control, all the larger mines; and her investments have all been returned with interest, though the money may, in some instances, have gone into the pockets of others than those who made the original investment.

Caught in the whirl of excitement which pervaded the country the writer of this, in the spring of 1846, found himself one of a packed crowd on a small steamer commanded by Eber B. Ward, late millionaire of Detroit, bound for the copper mines. He reached the Sault in due time, and found that old trading post transformed into a very lively city of white tents filled with gay adventurers. A wagon road led across the portage; baggage and freight were transported to the head of the falls on carts. A few small schooners and the propeller Independence, which had been hauled over the portage, constituted the Lake Superior fleet. The side wheeler, Julia Palmer, was that year hauled over. We embarked upon the schooner Swallow, and spread our blankets in the main hold, on top of the freight. We sailed, and six days thereafter made our first landing at Presque Isle, near the now beautiful and enterprising city of Marquette, then among the things to be. On that rocky peninsula we met some Cornish miners at work on a small vein of pyritous copper associated with sulphuret of lead. Some beef cattle which we had brought for these miners were thrown overboard and left to swim, in the ice cold water, to the shore. On the seventh day out from the Sault the vessel reached Copper Harbor.

Copper Harbor is a good, rock-bound haven, and has always been esteemed by navigators as a harbor of refuge on that stormy coast. It is a beautiful sheet of water, and enlivened as it was in the summer of 1846, by numerous canoes, Mackinaws and sloops, darting to and fro, it formed a lively picture. These small vessels belonged to the copper explorers. Opposite the mouth of the harbor is seen the wreck of the fur trading brig Astor, her ribs bleaching upon the inhospitable rocks. Located at the head of the bay is the Brockway House. Father Brockway, the genial landlord of that inn, still resides in the copper country; he has dwelt in the land continuously, displaying great adhesiveness and endurance; may his shadow never be less! Two of his daughters, who are emphatically Lake Superior ladies, "to the manor born," were married in the country, namely, Mrs. Farwell and Mrs. J. N. Scott. Nearly opposite Brockway's is Porter's Island, a bit of rock, upon which was built the "government house," the residence of that high and potent individual, the U. S. agent, who reigned over the copper land, countersigning permits and dispensing favors of a consular nature. The then occupant was Major McNair, a large, dignified Pennsylvanian, with Freeman Norvell, now of the Spurr Mountain iron mine, as secretary. Near the eastern end of the harbor, a little way back from the shore, was situated, upon the margin of lake Fanny Hoe, the small stockade called Fort Wilkins, it was screened from the winds by a native grove of poplars, birch and fir. One company of infantry was stationed at the fort under the command of Captain Alburtis. In the fall of 1847, the troop was ordered to Mexico, and the gallant captain was decapitated by a cannon ball, in front of Vera Cruz. Charlie Brush—the good, genial, hospitable sutler of the post —who among the old pioneers will ever forget his unremitting kindness! He has been dead many years.

In the summer of 1843, Walter Cunningham who had been appointed Special Agent for the mines on Lake Superior, in company with some twenty persons, landed at Copper Harbor, where he established his agency. This agency remained at Copper Harbor until the spring of 1846, when it was removed by Gen. John Stockton to Sault de Ste. Marie, with assistants stationed at Copper Harbor, at the mouth of Ontonagon river, and La Pointe.

About that time Col. Charles H. Gratiot, with a company of miners from Gratiot's Grove, arrived at Copper Harbor, and also a company consisting of Thomas Carrol and others, from Vinegar Hill, Wisconsin. This last company immediately proceeded up the lake as far as Ontonagon river. They here found James K. Paul and Nick D. Miniclier, who had reached there some time in the month of March, having crossed the country by land from Plattville. Paul and Miniclier were the *first* miners who came into the country, for the purpose of mining, after those under Henry, in 1771. They had come to take, and were in possession of the copper rock, which they had succeeded in removing to the mouth of the river. It was sold by them to Julius Eldred, and afterwards seized by the government and taken to Washington, where it still remains.

The policy of the general government at this time was not to sell mineral lands, nor allow pre-emptions. These lands were not controlled by the general land office, but by the War Department. As before stated, an agent of the War Department was stationed on Porter's Island, with his corps of engineers and draughtsmen. Permits, as they were called, were issued in Washington. These permits at first covered nine square miles, but were finally reduced to one square mile. This permitted you to enter upon any lands not otherwise claimed; you were allowed one year for exploration, and three more years to mine, with the privilege of two renewals of three years each, making the whole term ten years. The Department required returns to be made to the Mineral Agency, giving an account of the work performed and mineral raised, and a payment to the mineral collector, at the rate of twenty per cent. mineral value. The term of the grant or lease, was presumed to be ample to enable the fortunate holder thereof to realize immense gains, such wealth as would lead him to regard as mere bagatelles the mine plant and other improvements which would revert to the government. Afterwards commissioners were sent to appraise the mineral lands and fix a money value on them. Five dollars per acre, if our memory serves us, was the valuation. Later, all lands were subject to pre-emption except mineral lands. Finally, all lands, without exception, remaining unsold, (save school and canal lands) were thrown open to pre-emption, and could be had for one dollar and a quarter per acre. Lands held under permits required personal occupancy. These permits were issued in vast numbers, still there was much wire-pulling used to secure these invaluable documents, the mere possession of which was enough to make a man happy and affluent. It was the business of geologists, surveyors and explorers to hunt up eligible land upon which to plaster the permits. The country was prospected thoroughly for this purpose, but at last an actual examination of land suitable for "locations" was abandoned as too slow, and the work of locating was done in the office, on the maps. One of the consequences was, that when the owners came to examine their properties, guaranteed to be rich in copper and silver, the lands were found to be out under the lake, or down among the lower Silurians. A powerful magnifying glass was an indispensable instrument to an expert explorer It took but a few grains of copper to insure a good vein. Geologists, and the practical miner from Cornwall, assured us that that was enough to start on. One had only to "sink" on the vein to be rewarded, in due time, with an abundant yield. Since that day there has been much "sinking" done but not always with the results predicted. Many of our readers will remember how it used to be necessary to salivate a mineral specimen in order to bring out its beauty.

We learn from a valuable book, entitled, "Reports on the Mineral Region of Lake Superior—published in 1846, by Jacob Houghton, Jr., and T. W. Bristol," that there was made on the south shore of Lake Superior upon permits issued from the War Department at Washington, and applications to the Mineral Agency at Copper Harbor from August, 1844, to November, 1845, 595 locations. As this business was most active in 1846, it is safe to assume that from first to last more than 1,000 locations were made.

Many of these locations were worthless, and perhaps a majority were never occupied as mines, at least, not until many years afterward, and then by other parties; the lands fell back into the hands of the general government for disposal at some future day.

We are very certain that the Ste. Marie Falls Company has not realized its humble aspirations. We quote from prospectus: "This company has secured four islands in the Falls, as desirable locations for erecting stamping mills, etc." Think of the Calumet shipping 800 tons of rock per day to the Sault, for treatment!

In the earlier times, when permits were in vogue, a man was hired at twenty dollars a month and provisions, and sent far into the woods to hold possession of a claim. By the side of some brook he erected out of poles and cedar bark the rudest of huts; some hemlock boughs, thrown upon the ground, formed, with the aid of a pair of blankets, a couch; a fire in the middle of the hut served for warmth and cookery. The smoke was expected to escape through a liberal hole in the roof, but it did not always satisfy expectation; on the contrary it persisted in remaining inside; this was good in the mosquito season, and, strange to say, the human occupant of this tabernacle did not seem to mind it—only he smelt smoky to one of delicate olfactories. In winter, when this rude habitation was covered with snow, but for the smoke issuing from the peak, one would mistake it for a natural mound, or large boulder. The fire in this lodge was never allowed to go out; in the ashes stood an iron kettle, always simmering with delectable bean porridge, hot; this porridge, and bread baked in the ashes, constituted the " baked meats " all the year round; a cup of tea or coffee, pure, served to enliven the repast; a pipe of " soul-soothing tobacco" was a constant companion. After several years of seeming wasted life —and certainly it was a terrible life, to spend a long, dreary winter in one of those lonely hovels—the necessity of watching locations was done away with. Then, perhaps, the original locators, having abandoned their claims, the watchers became squatters, and some of them in time realized handsomely from the sale of lands to mining corporations. They deserved all they got.

Upon the first threatening of winter in the autumn of 1846, all fair weather birds, all high governmental dignitaries, all who cared not to brave the rigors of the climate, sought more genial climes. Those who remained, settled down to the regular work of mining, or to watch developments, so as to be ready for new enterprises when the whelming snows should have disappeared, on the return of summer.

The people whom the winter of 1846-7 found residents in the isolated wilderness in which the mines were situated, were wholly dependent upon each other for society. The mails, brought by dog trains, once a fortnight, through a trackless wilderness of three hundred miles, afforded the only intelligence of what was transpiring in the outer world. These mails were eagerly looked for, but they were uncertain and disappointing. The mail-carrier, if he found his dogs overloaded *en route*, had a facile way of easing them; he simply had to hang a bag or bags of mail matter upon a tree and leave them, in most cases, to winter. Unfortunate, indeed, was the person whose letters happened to be in the suspended mail bags. During a period of seven months the writer of this did not draw one prize in the mail lottery, but in the month of June he received, at least, half a bushel of letters. The mine locations were few and far between, but there was much visiting, locomotion being performed on snow-shoes. Hospitality was unlimited, unbounded; when you came you were welcomed with open arms—when you went away, your departure was a matter of regret. The best that a limited larder could supply was spread before you—pork, beans and bread—take your choice. A joint of fresh beef was the choicest of luxuries, and could only be had when an overworked ox gave out, and it was required to sacrifice him upon the altar of necessity. The visitor always carried his blankets strapped on his back; the hospitable log cabins receiving him seldom had the luxury of a spare bed. Yet, with all these aids to social enjoyment, the denizens of the remote locations in the forests found the winter to "drag its slow length along" rather wearily. After the close of navigation, for weeks upon weeks, there was nothing but clouded skies and ceaseless falling of snow; no bright ray of sunshine darted through the noonday gloom; the days were short and the nights proportionately long; Jack Frost, reigning supremely, penetrated everywhere, hushing in the silence the babbling brook and flashing lake, and smothered every voice of nature in a deep pall of snow; the deep forests, stripped of their summer apparel, and, with the lesser growths buried out of sight, presented a cold, bare, melancholy picture, not at all conducive to a buoyancy of spirits. Often, after a great snow storm accompanied with high winds, locomotion, even on snow-shoes, was impossible. In these days of well-broken highways and railroads, and thick clustering towns and cities, the northern regions washed by Lake Superior are robbed of the terrors of the pioneer days.

Copper Harbor was the great depot and rallying point of copper hunters; here the innumerable exploring parties prepared for the woods, and hence departed in quest of hidden

mines of copper and silver. The country was penetrated far
and wide by these sanguine De Sotos, and the dense forest
ransacked up and down. Probably at no time while the
aborigines held sole possession of the territory, had the woods
been so populous. Camp fires blazed upon a hundred shores,
and the most secluded and rocky recesses awoke to the echoes
of shout, song and story. After weeks of arduous toil, coast-
ing in small boats many a league of stormy shore, pushing
their way through tangled underbrush and almost impenetrable cedar swamps; carrying packs of provisions, tools and
blankets on their backs; fording, or rafting on streams, and
exposed to all the storms of heaven, tortured by mosquitoes,
black flies and sand flies, and often suffering from thirst and
hunger, worn, ragged, unshorn, tanned like Indians, these
indomitable explorers would return to Copper Harbor, and
pitching their tents in a cool place by the side of the waters,
indulge in a period of rest and recreation. The "Boys,"
were sometimes a little wild; but the spirit of adventure was
abroad and the restraints of civilization feeble. That same
unconquerable spirit since those days has led men to sweep
across the continent without pause, no barrier preventing
this side of the golden shores of the Pacific. Many of our
earlier pioneers were found later among the throngs which,
with undaunted hearts, climbed the far-distant Sierra Nevadas
and rushed down the opposite slopes to seek their fortunes in
the gulches and canyons of California. By some, fortune and
fame were secured; others only found graves to cover broken
hearts, while a few, after years of toil and hardship, gravi-
tated back to the old camping grounds of Lake Superior.
The excitement which began in 1844, reached the culminat-
ing point in 1846. Delegations from the four quarters of the
globe came to spy out the land—scientific men, capitalists,
members of Congress, Senators, Governors, agents for land
and mining corporations, business men, pleasure seekers, and
a host of young men who had their fortunes to make. Many
of these gentlemen remained in the country, or have been
identified with it ever since and have exercised a powerful

influence over its destinies. John N. Ingersoll, Esq., editor and proprietor, issued the first copy of "*The Lake Superior News and Mining Journal*" from the Astor House, Copper Harbor, in the summer of 1846. The appearance of this sheet produced a sensation. Ingersoll still lives at Corunna, full of honors. The paper was afterwards removed to Sault Ste. Marie, and from thence to Marquette, where it is still published by the author of this book.

The Copper, or Trap Range, extending from the extremity of Keweenaw Point to the Porcupine Mountains, is about 140 miles long, and has a width varying from one to six miles. There is another sub-district within the state of Michigan, known as Isle Royal. This whole territory, now become famous throughout the civilized world under the name of the Copper Mines of Lake Superior, was the broad and wild domain upon which our people set themselves to work, with indomitable energy and courage, to hew out a new empire, and achieve fame and wealth as miners. Mining on a grand scale was a new occupation to the American citizen. He who views the whole ground in this year of our Lord, 1876, we think, cannot justly deny that our people have acquitted themselves well. The earlier pioneers had a Herculean task to perform; a fact which those who have come after should not forget.

Burt's solar compass—then a recent invention—was highly appreciated by those who had seen it; but its merits were not generally known. Parties who desired to locate on unsurveyed lands, knowing the uncertainty of the magnetic needle in the copper and iron regions, were perplexed, and wondered how they should be able to run straight lines. A learned gentleman at last solved the question—to his own satisfaction, at least. Basing his theory upon the assumed fact that, at a certain distance above the earth, the local attraction would cease to have any effect upon the needle, he proposed that a surveyor (he must needs be the reverse of corpulent) should take his compass, climb the highest tree, and from the top sight to some other tree in the distance;

then come down, proceed to the tree noted, climb it and make another observation; and so on to the end of the survey. Whether the learned gentleman ever obtained a leather medal from any scientific society, has not transpired.

EARLY NAVIGATION.

The American, British Northwestern and Hudson Bay Fur companies, prior to the year 1829, had on Lake Superior, employed as traders, the following named vessels: Discovery, Invincible, Otter, Mink and the Recovery. They were respectably sized schooners, of from 20 to 100 tons burthen, and all built, it is quite certain, on Lake Superior. The respective years of their building are not known, but as some had long been in service, their construction would seem to date back very early in the nineteenth, if not even to the closing days of the eighteenth century. The Invincible was wrecked on White Fish Point, prior to the year 1823, and the Discovery lost in an attempt to run the rapids in Sault Ste. Marie river. What became of the Otter is not definitely known, but in the records of the war of 1812, there is an account of the capture of a vessel above the Sault by the U. S. brig Niagara. As it would be impossible for the brig to ascend or make the passage of the river at that time, the inference drawn is, that the capture was effected by means of boats sent out from her for that purpose. This vessel was, in all probability, the Otter, as all the rest are accounted for, and her known history terminated at that time. Further, and what is still more conclusive, the records above cited state that in the attempt to run the prize over the rapids she was wrecked and lost. The Mink, our informant states, "laid her bones in the bay on the Canadian side, just above the rapids." The Recovery belonged to the British Northwestern Company, and on the breaking out of the war of 1812, great fears were entertained for her safety. It is stated as a historical fact, that in one of the deep, narrow bays on the north-east end of Isle Royale, which was then within British jurisdiction, the vessel was secreted, and her spars being taken out, she was entirely covered over with boughs of trees and brush-wood, and there lay until the termination of hostilities, when she was brought out from her hiding place, and again put in commission. She remained on the lake till 1829, in which year she made a safe run over the falls into Lake Huron. She was a schooner of about 90 **tons, well built of spruce, pine** and tamarack, and finely **fitted and furnished in every** particular. **She** was bought of the Hudson **Bay company** by Merwin & Giddings, of Cleveland, in the same year **(1829) and taken to** that city by her owners, who afterwards **sold** her **to some parties** in Canada, and she ended her days **on the** lower **lakes.** It is also known that Bayfield, in the years 1822-23, **used** a small vessel of about 20 tons, while engaged in making a survey of Lake Superior. The vessel used by him, however, may have been the Mink, **furnished** by the Hudson Bay company.

From the year, 1829 to 1835, there was a lapse in the navigation of Lake Superior, during which no vessels of any considerable size were known to be upon her waters—only the common *batteaux* and canoes in use by the Indians, French, and traders of that early day.

In the year 1835, George W. Jones, of Cleveland, constructed above the Sault, for the American Fur company, the John **Jacob Astor,** a schooner of 113 tons. In **August of** that year she was fitted out and made her first voyage, under the command of Capt. Charles C. **Stanard, with the following** officers: John **Webster,** first mate; **John J. Stanard, second mate;** and Capt. John McCargo, pilot. Capt. C. C. Stanard sailed the Astor until the close of navigation on Lake Superior in the fall of 1842.

In 1843, Capt. B. A. Stanard took command of the Astor, and sailed her during the seasons of 1843 and 1844. She was wrecked at Copper Harbor while under his command, Sept. 20, 1844. "Stanard's Rock," an almost indiscernible projection, lying nearly on a level with the water, and extremely dangerous for vessels, **was** discovered by Capt. C. C. Stanard in **August,** 1835, while on his first trip up the lake in command **of the** Astor. Its location was determined as nearly as possible with the instruments then at hand, which consisted merely of a common mariner's compass and a "chip log and line," by Mr. B. A. Stanard, in the summer of 1844. This opportune discovery, no doubt, has been of great advantage in perfecting reliable marine charts of the coast, and preventing disasters to shipping.

The schooner William Brewster, 75 tons, was built for the American Fur company at Sault Ste. Marie in 1838, and was sailed by Capt. John Wood until the fall of 1841, when she was laid up in ordinary at La Pointe. She was again fitted out in the summer of 1842 by Capt. B. A. Stanard, brought down to Sault Ste. Marie and run over the rapids. From thence she was taken to Detroit, and ended her days on the lower lakes.

The schooner Algonquin, 50 tons, was built at Black River, Loraine county, Ohio, by Capt. G. W. Jones, in the summer of 1839. She was owned by the firm of Converse & Mendenhall, and was taken to the Sault in the fall of that year, hauled over the portage and made ready for navigation of the lake in the spring of 1840. She was commanded first by Capt. Rockwood, and subsequently by Capts. Goldsmith, Smithwick and McKay.

In 1839, the American Fur company built a small schooner of from 15 to 20 tons at La Pointe, called the Madeline, for the purpose of collecting fish from their stations along the west shore of Lake Superior, and upon Isle Royale, and bringing them to La Pointe for shipment to the Sault. She was under the command of Capt. John Angus, and was lost at Isle Royale the same year. The schooner Siskiwit, of about 40 tons, was built by the same company soon after at La Pointe, to supply the place of the Madeline, and sailed under the command of Capt. John Angus. She went ashore at Isle Royale in 1841 or 1842, but was subsequently gotten off and repaired by Capt. John J. Stanard, and laid up in ordinary at La Pointe; but she was again fitted out in 1845, and navigated the lake during the summer and fall of that year, under command of Capt. B. A. Stanard. She was laid up on the close of navigation, at the Sault, and her after career is not known.

The Canadian schooner Whitefish, about 40 tons, was built by the Hudson's Bay Fur company at the Sault, in 1838, and was sailed by Capt. Lamphen. She was still in service up to a very late date, but it is hardly probable that anything remains of her at present.

In 1845 the following named vessels were hauled over the portage at the Sault, and made their appearance on Lake Superior: schooner Chippewa, 20 tons, Capt. Thomas Clark, master and owner; schooner Florence, 20 tons, hauled over the Portage on the Canadian side by Antrim & Keith, commanded by Capt. David Keith; schooner Swallow, 80 tons, was hauled over on the American side and tried her fortunes on the lake, under command of Capt. Smithwick; schooner Merchant, 80 to 90 tons, was hauled over and made her first appearance on the lake under command of Capt. Moore. The Merchant was lost in 1846 or 1847, under the command of Capt. Robert Brown, with all hands on board, and no vestige of her was ever found. Next in order came the schooner Uncle Tom, (Mrs. Harriet Beecher Stowe's) 90 tons, under the command of Capt. John Angus. She, like the others, failed to make the anticipated fortunes of her owners, and was subsequently run over the rapids, and ended her days on the lower lakes. The schooner Fur Trader, about 60 tons, made her appearance the same year (1845) under command of Capt. Calvin Ripley, master and owner. The propeller Independence, Capt. P. Averill, was hauled over in the summer of 1845, and made one trip during the fall, to La Pointe. She returned to the Sault and was laid up for the winter. During the summer of 1845, the schooner Napoleon was built at the Sault, and commenced the navigation of the lake under command of Capt. John Stewart. The Napoleon was overhauled in 1849, and changed to a propeller. She continued running on the lake until the completion of the St. Mary's Falls ship canal, when she was taken to the St. Clair Flats and used as a tow boat until taken out of service. In the fall of 1845, the steamer Julia Palmer, 240 tons, was brought to the Sault and laid up for the winter. In the spring of 1846, she was drawn over the portage, and during the season was under command of Capt. John J. Stanard. She was laid up in the fall, and thus ended her career, except, perhaps, that she was subsequently towed to Waiska Bay, and there converted into the foundation for a wood dock. Subsequent to 1846, the schooner Ford, Capt. Parker, steamer Sam Ward (master unknown) and propeller Manhattan, Capt. J. Spaulding, were hauled over the portage and successfully navigated the lake until the finishing and opening of the St. Mary's Falls ship canal.

In 1846, the steamer Julia Palmer—an old-fashioned, turtle-shaped side-wheeler—was the popular vessel in the Lake Superior fleet. The propeller, Independence, was her only steam competitor for the public favor. In calm weather, with a full head of steam, the Independence could make four miles an hour, easily. She was finally destroyed at the Sault, by the accidental explosion of her boiler. The Julia Palmer was a staunch sea boat; she had been tried severely on Lake Erie, and was destined to still severer trials on the great northern lakes. Late in the fall, deeply laden with freight and passengers, she sailed from the Sault for Copper Harbor. Before she could reach her destined harbor one of those fierce, westerly gales, accompanied with snow, common to Lake Superior in the fall, struck her. Bravely did she buffet the winds and waves, but she could not make head against them; she drifted off into the middle of the lake, and then her fuel gave out; she fell into the trough of the sea and was at the mercy of the elements; consternation fell upon all on board; the waves dashed over and through her; ice accumulated rapidly; the sick passengers were hurled from side to side of the cabin; she sprung a leak; the pumps were started; the freight was thrown overboard; but the water gained on the pumps, and the passengers were compelled, all through a dark, stormy night, to bail with buckets, or anything else that would hold water. By the most strenuous exertions they kept her afloat, for thirty-six hours the boat drifted helplessly; at last, as if guided by a Providential hand, she drifted into a snug, rock-bound harbor in an island on the north-east shore of the lake, in Canada. The anchor was dropped, and a period of rest and respite was granted. But the question was soon propounded: How are we to get away from this desolate coast, without sail or fuel? Winter was at hand, and what was to be done must be done quickly. The crew and passengers were armed with axes, (fortunately there was a supply on board intended for the mines,) and sent ashore to cut wood. After hard work, sufficient fuel was provided to run the boat to Copper Harbor; the anchor was tripped, and in a few hours the exhausted and happy passengers reached the desired haven. Ever after they entertained a wholesome fear of the great lake when aroused by the terrific, snow-laden gales of November.

THE FIRST WORKING COMPANIES,

organized for the mining of copper, silver, and iron, were managed by boards of Trustees; were incorporated under the laws of different States, and issued such numbers of shares or stock certificates, as suited the convenience of each individual set of incorporators. One company, for example, issued 1200 shares, par value one hundred dollars; another 3000 shares, par value ten dollars. The largest number of shares that we can remember was 6000. It was not until some years later, that the state of Michigan enacted the wise and salutary general mining laws now on the statute-books, fixing the number of shares of each organization at 20,000, with par value of $25 per share. These laws were afterwards amended so as to permit actual working companies to consolidate, and thereby virtually increase the number of shares. More recently, the law was so amended as to permit the organization of mining companies upon a basis of $2,500,000, divided into shares of the par value of $25 each. They are also permitted to acquire and hold 50,000 acres of land, instead of being limited to 10,000 acres, as formerly.

The practical miner, whether of American birth or foreign

extraction, at the very outset of his work found a new and marked feature in the veins which were to be subject to exploitation. Native copper, in a chemically pure state, in large masses, and in great quantity, was an anomaly. The celebrated copper mines of Cornwall, Germany, and Chili—the chief sources of copper supply for the world, so far—produced only the ores of copper, sulphurets, and oxides. It will be seen, moreover, that the difficulty which arose, incidental to the mining, dividing into convenient forms for handling and smelting, was new and perplexing. But the skill of the Cornish miners, and the philosophic minds of such men as John R. Grout, Esq., finally overcame all obstacles.

For several years after mining had become a regular business and while explorations for new veins continued, nothing was considered of any practical worth except true, or fissure veins. Such was the impress made by books; such were the ideas imported from Europe by alien miners; (and the first valuable discovery of copper in place, in fissure veins, confirming the whole,) it was not strange that men should believe in nothing else. This mistaken notion caused much blind groping for years, great waste of means, and the abandonment of many valuable properties, and a persistence in the working of others utterly worthless, because of the existence thereon of thin seams filled with chlorite, serpentine or spar. The great and famous contact vein which was the basis of the Minnesota mine; the lodes containing mass and stamp copper, like the Pewabic, and the conglomerate belts, all running with the formation, (and not across it like fissure veins,) such as the mammoth Calumet and Hecla consolidated company is working upon, subsequently corrected the ideas erroneously entertained as to the mineral sources of the country.

We will now, beginning in point of time with the year 1846, pass in hasty review the working mines of note—making mention of the men and managers of the time, so far as we may be able to do so—then give a brief account of new discoveries and developments, on the Trap Range, and

Isle Royale; trace the growth of new districts and villages, with mention of the prominent men of the country down to the present time.

In the year above mentioned a mine had been opened by the Pittsburgh, Boston and Copper Harbor Company, on a fissure vein a few rods east of Fort Wilkins; several tons, perhaps 40, of black oxide of copper had been raised from the shafts and cuts. But the mine was speedily abandoned, and the miners and appliances had been transferred to another location, owned by the Company, lying a few miles southwest of Eagle river, whereon a wonderfully rich vein of mass copper had been discovered—since known as the Cliff mine.

West of Copper Harbor was a mine which we mention to bring out the fact that one George N. Saunders, the notorious rebel sympathizer and wire-puller during the late war, was the superintendent thereof. There was another mining company operating near the Harbor—the Isle Royale—of which Mr. Cyrus Mendenhall was superintendent.

BOHEMIAN AND LAC LA BELLE COMPANIES.

These two companies were operating on locations situated on the south side of the Range near Lac La Belle. The mining was confined to small fissure veins, charged with yellow and gray sulphuret ores. Mr. Simon Mandlebaum was the superintendent of the former, and Major Alexander H. Sibley of the latter. In their log cabins by the beautiful lake, these gentlemen dispensed a princely hospitality to all comers. They have been largely interested in copper and silver mines from that day to this, and have done very much to aid in the development of the country. Work on these mines was suspended in 1847, to be resumed again about the year 1864-'5, at which time, a village on the immediate lake shore was begun, smelting works erected, the Harbor opened to large class vessels, aided by an appropriation from the general government of 100,000 acres of land, and a good wagon road built out to the other mines. A few years later the work was suspended, the attention of the proprietors being engaged by the rich discovery of Silver Islet on the north shore. Mr. A. C. Bishop was the last superintendent.

From the Indian trail leading from Copper Harbor to Eagle Harbor and Eagle river, one had access to several locations—small clearings in the woods—whereon mining, in its incipient stages, was being conducted. The Messrs. Bernard were in charge of a party near Copper Harbor on the west. At Agate Harbor, the New York and Lake Superior Company was operating. Mr. Edward Learned was president of this company, and Mr. C. G. Learned was superintendent. The Northwest Company were mining in the bluff back of Grand Marais Harbor. Mr. Bailey, now one of the *patriarchs* of Keweenaw county, was first in charge. Horace Greeley was a trustee. Mr. Stoughtenburgh, the tall New Yorker, was, a little later, the superintendent. Quite a handsome show of small mass copper was discovered in the open cut, at the mine. This mine has never risen into importance.

EAGLE HARBOR.

The Eagle Harbor Company were working quite a large force of miners. The harbor is a natural one and convenient of access; there were several good buildings at the west end of the bay, nestling among the pines. The mine is near the village and lake shore; it was one of the most promising yet opened. A mass was in sight, which was estimated to weigh 75 tons, almost pure native copper. The vein projects under the lake; from a boat, out in deep water a mass of copper could be seen protruding from the rock bottom. (*Query!* is this the mass Father Allouez saw?) Subsequent workings in this mine did not justify early promise. At this day the Eagle Harbor location—a nine-mile tract—is considered a valuable undeveloped property.

Copper Falls Company, location situated west of Eagle Harbor, had Mr. Joshua Childs as its superintendent. It is one of the oldest mines on the lake, and is now operating. In 1846, it was in a flourishing condition. They were working on a fissure vein (Owl creek?); in an open cut, near the surface of the ground, a handsome mass of native copper, several yards long, was exposed. There was no machinery available to enable the miners to hoist it out; Mr. Childs was puzzled to know how to remove it, or cut it into convenient pieces for removal. A saw was tried, but did not answer the purpose. Copper Falls mine has been worked for 30 years with varied success, but we believe has never QUITE been recorded among dividend paying mines. It has been a source of wealth to individuals. The operations have been upon the fissure vein and the "Ash Bed," a lode producing only shot and fine copper—stamp work. Ball's celebrated steam stamps and washers were first introduced here. During its long career, Copper Falls mine has been under the management of several able men, namely: Messrs. Childs, Petherick, the man of figures, Hon. Sam'l W. Hill, A. P. Thomas and Mr. Emerson. When quite a lad, Mr. John Simpkins was clerk at this mine; this gentleman became an influential, wealthy copper broker, and was director in several successful mining enterprises.

Northwestern Company. — Working on a location lying south-east of Eagle river. The mass vein showed considerable mass copper. Mr. Jacob Houghton was superintendent.

Lake Superior Company. — This is the pioneer company of the region: location situated 1½ miles south of Eagle river. Mr. C. C. Douglass is superintendent. There were about 20 buildings on the location. Seventy men were at work. Several shafts had been sunk on the vein to a depth of 125 to 150 feet. A horse-whim was used to hoist water and mineral from the mine. The ore raised from the mine was valued, to wit:

"A ton of ore, delivered in Boston, yielded as follows:— Of Silver, $568; of Copper, $200—DR. JACKSON."

This is truly a wonderful mine! It was stated that the Shares had sold for $1200 each. Whole number of Shares, 1200. This mine had in operation a small stamp-mill and a saw-mill, run by water-power, the first concerns of the kind, erected by a mining company, in the country. In 1847, Mr. Corry)l succeeded Mr. Douglass as Sup't. In after years this company took a new name, the Phœnix. It is an active and productive mine at this day — but the main work is now on a fissure vein under the greenstone.

Eagle River.— On the sand hills, near the lake, and the mouth of a small stream into which it is hard work to force a small boat, is a cluster of rude cabins — dwellings, stores, and shops — this is Eagle River. Deacon Johnson, afterwards long-time resident at Ontonagon, kept a good hotel in his log cabin. Enterprising Uncle John Atwood, in 1847, built a large frame warehouse on the lake shore. This hale, hearty old pioneer is still ready with a smile and warm shake of the hand to welcome his friends at L'Anse, where he now abides. In his sphere, he has done well in the building up of the country. Phil. Morrison was a resident of Eagle River. Mr. John Senter has resided there from very early times, and has been largely instrumental in promoting the prosperity and advancement of Keweenaw. James Crawford, a well-known character, Dr. Alexander, Porter Hitchcock, the Leopolds and Austrians, and Col. Wright were also residents of the village. Eagle River is the port through which the mines of that vicinity have received their supplies and exported their mine products. The Cliff mine has maintained a dock and warehouse there. The village became a lively business centre.

The Pittsburgh and Boston Company.—This company had been operating at this point about two years; quite a con- a nine mile tract; the works upon it were situated about five miles southwest of Eagle River. It had opened a grand fissure vein, under some high, picturesque cliffs, which was wonderfully rich in native copper and silver. They had siderable log village clustered in the clearing, under the shadow of the cliffs. Messrs. Hussey, Avery, Howe, Petit and Scudder—household names in the copper region—were trustees. Dr. Petit was the superintendent for a brief period. He will be vividly remembered by all old settlers. Mr. John Hays was another active gentleman connected with the Cliff and many other enterprises. Capt. Jennings was one of the earliest superintendents of the Cliff. There were others holding the same position whose names cannot be recalled. Mr. John Slawson occupied the position ably for many years. During its prosperous days the "Old Cliff" divided to its stockholders $2,280,000. Drs. Senter and Heaton were the distinguished resident physicians and surgeons at the mine for a long period. Hon. E. J. Hulbert was the mine engineer who engineered the famous perpendicular snaft down through the greenstone. Capt. John Gundry, Capt. George, Capt. Carnsew and Capt. Benetts, were able underground men. Mr. Augustus Coburn, afterward an influential citizen of Ontonagon, passed the winter of 1846-'7 at the Cliff mine. A few years ago the old company suspended work, and let the mine fill with water. The whole property was subsequently purchased by a gentleman resident in Boston for $100,000, and Mr. Farwell, long well known as the able manager of the Phœnix mine, was placed in charge. He, with his characteristic energy, started the pumps, removed the water, resumed mining, and, to-day, may congratulate himself that the good old mine has again arrived at almost a dividend paying point. All honor to him! The "Old Cliff" is truly a historical mine. During the dark days that followed the excitement of 1846, and during other dark days, which from time to time fell upon the copper region—the "Cliff" was a sure and steadfast reminder that copper mining *could* be made profitable in the upper peninsula. It was always a strong, moral force—encouraging new hopes and enterprises.

Dr. Avery was a wealthy Methodist clergyman, and resided in Pittsburgh. He was associated with Dr. Hussey, James M. Cooper, Thomas M. Howe, and some Boston gentlemen, as a stockholder and director in the Pittsburgh and Boston company. Several assessments had been levied and paid; another was called for or talked of. Considerable copper had been mined and shipped, but the cost of mine improvements, purchase of machinery, etc., had absorbed all the earnings, and more with it. The Boston stockholders were dissatisfied, and refused to contribute anything more in the way of assessments, and there was every prospect that the mine would have to be abandoned. At this juncture, Dr. Avery stepped forward, made a thorough examination of the mine, and called a meeting of the board for consultation. At this meeting the doctor expressed his unwillingness to abandon the mine, and, "gentlemen," said he, "I have lying in the bank just $83,000, eighty thousand of which is at your disposal, if you will use it to continue the work, and give me a mortgage on the mine property as security." The offer was accepted: work was continued, and in less than eighteen months the money was repaid from the earnings of the mine, and a goodly surplus divided among the shareholders. But for this action on the part of Dr. Avery, the mine would have been abandoned, and the development of the copper interest delayed for years. In the dark days the old Cliff stood as a beacon light to the despondent operators throughout the district; its failure would have been followed by a general collapse, and the mineral wealth of Lake Superior would have been everywhere regarded but as a punctured bubble.

North American Company.—This company was operating just west of the Cliff on a fissure vein. Gurdon Williams and Henry J. Buckley, of Detroit, were, respectively, President and Secretary of this company,—well known Michigan men. Honest John Bacon was the superintendent. This company had made quite a start in the woods, but were exploring, rather than mining. In the winter of 1846-'7, Judge Bacon struck quite a large mass of clean copper in the vein or adit. He was so much elated that he, in hot haste, mounted his snow-shoes and started for Detroit,—to buy more stock. Think of this heavy, corpulent man tramping 300 miles through an unbroken wilderness to Green Bay, in mid-winter,—a journey that required from four to six weeks hard work ! Before the Judge reached Detroit, the mass came to an end, or in the elegant language of the country,—*Petered.* The North American has had a varied career, but it has never reached a point of success. Captain Joseph Paull was, at one time, the superintendent. The property was afterwards sold to the Pittsburgh and Boston company.

The *Albion Company.*—This company held several locations. Two or three miles west of the Cliff we found active operations going on under Mr. Wm. H. Stevens, the "Professor." Mr. Stevens is well known in the copper region as an active, energetic man, a mine manager and stock operator of shrewdness, whose footsteps may be traced from the extremity of Keweenaw Point to the region beyond the Ontonagon. The company was testing fissure veins, and hunting for more under the greenstone cliffs. Several snug log houses had been erected, and quite a large number of miners were at work. Tom Taylor was clerk—a man of great parts. Later, Mr. Rickard and Captain Richard Edwards tried their hands at this mine. They also superintended a branch mine of same name, situated near the village of Houghton; this location subsequently became the Columbian, then, by consolidation, the Shelden and Columbian. The old Albion finally took the new name of Manhattan, and is quiet at this time. Captain Rickard was at one time superintendent of the Isle Royale mine, Portage Lake. He came to the lake in June, 1850, and remained at the Albion until the latter part of January, 1851. In February, 1851, he preempted the south-east quarter of section 10, Town 57, Range 32—the first pre-emption made in the upper peninsula. The land office was then located at Sault Ste. Marie, and leaving Eagle river sometime in March, he reached the Sault on the 12th of April, being the first to file pre-emption papers with Register Backus—a fact shown by the records. He retired from the country in 1858, and settled in New York city. But he has always taken a warm interest in this upper country, in which he owns large interests. He is a gentleman much respected for his ability and integrity.

Captain Edwards removed with his family at an early day (1853) to Portage Lake, and settled in the now village of Houghton. Having acquired considerable wealth, he died in the year 1868, lamented by the whole community. He was a gentleman of much shrewdness and sagacity, high-toned, and possessed of great amiability of character. He was a good citizen, and those who knew him best loved him most.

Fulton Company.—Working on a location a few miles south-west of the Albion. A few log cabins had been erected and a few miners were at work on a thin fissure vein, showing some native copper, found in a low knob of trap. Mr. Kennedy, of New York city, a sanguine, whole-souled gentleman, was the superintendent.

Ohio Trap Rock Company.—Working on a location on headwaters of Trap Rock river, south-west of Fulton; sinking a shaft on a vein of serpentine; no copper. McGiffin, superintendent.

New York & Michigan Company.—This company own 16 locations, one of which was an *iron ore* bed. Messrs. John R. Grout and C. C. Douglass, general agents. Mining for copper at junction of trap and sand-rock with 8 men; found considerable fine copper — stamp work. John H. Forster, superintendent. This property is now called St. Louis.

Douglass Houghton Company.—Mining by driving an adit under the falls, on a branch of Trap Rock river, about two miles from Torch Lake and Calumet stamps. Some fine copper exposed. Lavalette Douglass in charge.

Portage Lake.—A party belonging to a Pittsburgh company spent the winter of 1846-'7 in a rude hut on Wheal Kate mountain. There was a small clearing, or boat landing, near the present Quincy Stamps. Some exploring had been done on the hill side, below the present Quincy mine. Elsewhere the beautiful wooded shores of Portage lake were in a state of nature.

Mr. Ransom Shelden, the *Father* of the Portage lake mining district, came to the lake in the summer of 1846, but he passed the winter at L'Anse. He built a large frame warehouse and dwelling at the mouth of Portage river in 1847, and settled there with his family. L'ANSE was an old missionary settlement. On the west side of the bay the venerable Father Baraga, afterward bishop of Marquette, resided with his Indian flock—a good shepherd of the fold. On the east side was the Methodist mission, under the care of Rev. Mr. Pitzel, a worthy, young man. Then "old man" Jackson was beating the anvil; then Maj. Beedon taught the natives civilization, and all the arts; Capt. James Bendry cruised on the lake during the summer and ran a saw mill during the winter.

It was in the month of October, 1846, that we, for the first time, passed over Portage lake. This remarkable sheet of water, which fills a gorge cut boldly through the trap range, where the range is six hundred feet high, and which nearly severed Keweenaw Point from the main land, the connecting isthmus being only two miles wide, (since pierced by the Portage Lake and Lake Superior Ship Canal—making Keweenaw Point to-day, in fact, an island,) has been for centuries, perhaps ages, the highway of travelers. The ancient miners doubtless navigated its waters, and many a peaceful or warlike band of savages have availed themselves of this short-cut in their migrations or forays. This grand portage saved a detour around stormy cape Keweenaw of 110 miles.

The scenery bordering the lake was exceedingly beautiful, especially so at the narrows through the highlands, at points where Houghton and Hancock now stand, and westward and northward. Our cheerful Canadian boatmen, singing as they rowed, would often rest upon their oars in order to enjoy the quiet, brilliant panorama. The native forests in primitive grandeur, starting at the water's edge, slope up precipitously toward the sky, presenting a great variety of pleasing shades and colors, from the soft neutral-tinted maple, the lemon-colored birch and poplar to the dark green of the pine, hemlock and fir. Here and there, there is a bit —a patch—which has been touched severely by the first frosts of autumn; upon it is a brave display of scarlet, orange and gold. The mountain ash, which flourishes in this high northern latitude and loves the water, is seen here and there, with its red berries clustering among the green leaves, and the soft maple, its delicate foliage blushing "rosy red" more intensely than any of its sisters, under the rude assault of master Jack Frost. The surface of this narrow lake is perfectly smooth, and reflects back each overhanging declivity. The color of the water is that of brandy—a tinge acquired from the seepage from cedar swamps and beaver dams. An intense quietude pervades the scene—the only sound which falls upon the ear is the cadence of our oars, or the echo of our own voices coming back faintly from the muffled wooded shores. At one or two points only were to be seen "signs" of vandal man. A few trees had been felled and space cleared sufficient for a small encampment. And this was at a point which is now the busy mining and commercial centre of Portage.

To-day—1875—the reverse of this picture is presented, and a more stirring locality cannot be found in the country. The busy, picturesquely situated villages of Houghton and Hancock, with their outlying suburbs; the giant stamp mills, which make the earth tremble with the heavy thud of ponderous hammers; the air dark with smoke, and the water discolored with rejected sand and slime, once beautiful crystalizations of calcite and feldspar; the fiery furnaces of the copper smelting works, when the copper from the mines, once tortured and beaten under the stamps, is again subjected to volcanic heat that it may become more pure and fit for use; the numerous manufactories, with their noisy rattling and banging; the fleet of steam and sail vessels that might navigate the ocean, lying at the docks, where once the bark canoe noiselessly glided under overhanging forests; and, latest innovation of all, there goes rushing up the hill-side a locomotive with a train of cars—all of these things, and more that could be mentioned, go to make up a picture instinct with life and characteristic of this age of progress. And while we write it is announced that the lake, 60 feet deep, has been spanned by a bridge 1,600 feet long. The old ferry, like the dog-train, succumbs to progress. We trust that Mr. John Martin, the pioneer ferryman, may reap new honors in some other field. The time was when John's old yawl boat was gratefully appreciated, and a quarter given "to cross the ferry," cheerfully.

Silver Mountain, a conical trap knob, which arose out of the level plain some ten or fifteen miles west of L'Anse, had been worked by a party of miners. They drove an adit into the base of the knob on a vein, but we who visited the works after they were abandoned in the fall of 1847, could find not a trace of silver. The miners left two comfortable log houses, well furnished, to rot down. In those days there were men called "wreckers;" men who made a business of levying upon the personal property left at abandoned mines. One of these "wreckers," who is still a resident of Portage Lake, visited Silver Mountain after it had been abandoned, built a raft, and loaded upon it the anvil, bellows, steel, etc., and set sail down the Sturgeon river. Ten miles below the mountain the river passes through Otter Lake. While crossing this lake, the raft parted, the whole of the " wrecker's" booty went to the bottom, and he and his men narrowly escaped drowning. It is but just to say that the incident served a good purpose in that the gentleman was never afterwards known to engage in a similar enterprise.

The headwaters of the Elm, Misery, and Flint and Fire Steel rivers were pretty thoroughly explored in 1846. Julian Magill was the only superintendent who can now be recalled to memory.

Ontonagon.—We describe Ontonagon village as first seen in the summer of 1846. The river of the same name, is one of the largest streams on the south shore of Lake Superior; it is one hundred yards wide at the mouth, and carries eight feet of water over the bar. A short distance above the mouth, the stream expands, forming a wide basin, or bowl, with an island in it. The east bank is from six to eight feet high; quite a level plain sweeps off to the eastward, offering a good town site. A few acres are cleared, but some oaks have been spared. Two buildings occupy the open space, namely, Jim Paull's cabin and the Mineral agency. The last named is a good log structure, costing $1,500. Mr. Paull's cabin is about eight feet by ten, with a door, but no window and low roof. This is the *hotel* of the place, *par excellence;* chief entertainment, whisky, tobacco and Jim's stories. Mr. Paull is a *character* hailing from Old Virginia, a generous, honest, fearless, backwoodsman. Ontonagon is the rallying point on the west for copper hunters. Sunday is the day when the crowds, pouring in from the woods, there most do congregate. A wild, nomad set truly! Whisky is then fearfully punished and punishes in return. *Bar fights* are common. The little clearing swarms with people. The white tents gleam up and down on the banks. Gambling is the amusement of those who do not fight. At such times Mr. Paull has much business on hand with the drunken half-breeds. He is equal to the occasion. He had a rencontre with inebriated John Champaign. Old John was a powerful half-cast, gentle as a lamb when sober, but a devil when in liquor. Already drunk, he presented himself at Jim's bar and demanded more whiskey. He was refused. Thereupon he challenged Mr. Paull to fight. The southern blood was up in an instant. Jim leaped over the counter, seized a spade and made a pass at John's head; the blow glanced and struck Captain Graham and nearly brought him down. Meantime John darted a knife at Jim's abdomen, but only the waistband was cut. Now Jim raised the spade again and brought the edge *thug* down upon John's head. He sank to the ground without a moan, quivering like a stricken ox. The place ran red with blood, and John was dragged off the scene by the hair of his head. He was around all right, next day. Paull, afterward, in graphically relating the story of the fray, would say, "I *tuck* him the second time."

Poor Mr. William Schlatter was a denizen of Ontonagon at this time. He was a gentleman of fine education and possessed great talent as a draughtsman; but he was the bond slave of whisky—WOULD have it, somehow. Among our camp stores was a bottle of pungent physic. One day, when the tent was empty, Mr. William stole cautiously in, in search of whisky. He eagerly clutched the bottle of physic and drank freely thereof before he discovered his mistake. The consequences may be imagined, not described. The poor gentleman was afterwards frozen to death on the hill back of the Quincy mine. When discovered, he was lying meekly on his back, with his hands folded on his breast, and his hat placed reverently by his side. He had chosen a spot where the branches of the trees opened so he could see the stars. He died bravely, looking into the heavens! The old pioneers will remember him.

Col. A. B. Gray, attached to the mineral agency, afterward Chief Surveyor on Mexican Boundary Survey, and, later still, a Col. of Confederate Engineers, killed on the Mississippi river, once went with Mr. Paull after a big mass located by an Indian geologist somewhere in the region of lake Agogeebic. The party sailed mysteriously from Copper Harbor and landed at Iron River, and then took to the woods, guided by the Indian. On the evening of the third day the guide announced that they were near the mass, but they didn't see it. He had lost his reckoning; they would find it on the morrow without fail. They tramped all the next day and reached the spot where the mass had been. But the evil Manitou had carried it off! Was angry with white man! The lively little Colonel threatened to shoot the lying Indian; Mr. Paull proceeded to castigate the gay deceiver, who, divining trouble, ran into the woods and was seen no more. Travel worn, out of provisions, our deluded ones started for the nearest water, and finally came out at L'Anse—with their faith in Indian geologists much shaken. Col. Gray related this story to the writer, under the genial skies of Mexico, in the old homes of the Aztecs of the Gila—that mystic people who may have been the same race as the "Ancient Miner" who worked at the mass of copper discovered by Mr. Knapp in the ancient diggings at the Minnesota Mine. Who knows? Paul still resides at Ontonagon, and takes great pleasure in relating how he found the copper rock and scared off Eldred and his Indians.

CUTTING UP A MASS OF NATIVE COPPER.

DE NUEVO A LA LUZ

The copper boulder noticed by the earliest travelers was the cause of many strong delusions. Dr. Houghton saw and described this mass, as lying in the westerly fork of the Ontonagon river, twenty-six miles from its mouth. Houghton and Bristol say, "this mass was removed by Julius Eldred, and after considerable pieces had been cut from it, was weighed in New York, and found to weigh 3,708 pounds net avoirdupois." (They were mistaken. The honor belongs to Paull, who found and removed the rock, and afterwards sold it to Eldred, as before stated.) The writer of this sketch finds in his note book the following memoranda:—date, summer, 1846. "I saw on a rude raft, tied up near the mouth of the river, a slab-like mass of pure copper several feet in length, worn smooth and spotted all over with silver. This float was found up the river in the drift; it is a great curiosity. Many are the conjectures as to whence it came. Dr. Jackson thinks it came on an iceberg from Isle Royale. Why?" Who found this mass, and brought it out, the writer has no data for ascertaining.

About a mile up the river, Mr. Cash had opened a farm on the west bank of the river; he finally made it a success. This pioneer resided in Ontonagon county until the day of his death, about four years ago. He was a useful and much respected citizen. Colonel Whitllesey, the distinguished geologist and writer, a graduate of West Point Academy, explored the Ontonagon region very thoroughly in 1846-'7. Southeast of Ontonagon, on the Range, there was a vast amount of exploring done and, at points, regular mine work was begun. At the *Algonquin* mine, quite a clearing had been made, and a force of miners were at work on an epidote lode showing considerable copper. Mr. Bushnell was superintendent of this company. The surface of the whole country was wild and broken, and there were many out-crops of Trap,—a favorable condition for exploration.

Up the river, on the east bank, some miners were working on an epidote vein which yielded considerable bunch copper. This point was near the afterward famous Minnesota mine.

Iron River.—Exploring parties had penetrated the region drained by this river, and locations were made. The Porcupine mountains were also thoroughly explored and located, though unsurveyed. Nor did the bold copper and silver mine hunters pause at the limits of the State of Michigan; they pressed onward to the head of the lake and thence, following around the north shore, explored the deep bays and islands of that rugged coast, and, after weeks of dangerous navigation, in frail boats, they finally rested at the falls of Ste. Marie.

This completes our hasty and imperfect sketch of the first crusade, so to speak, and the beginning of permanent mine industry and actual settlement in the Copper mines of Lake Superior.

It remains for us to sweep with the utmost rapidity over the canvass which the local events of thirty years has crowded. In the space allotted, it would be impossible to do justice to this teeming period. We dare attempt only the briefest mention.

The closing down of the winter of 1847-'8, brought gloom and despondency. The "Cliff" was really the only bright spot in the whole horizon.

The discovery of the great Minnesota lode in 1847, near the Ontonagon river, was a memorable and salutary event. It gave a new impetus to mining, revived hope in despondent breasts, and inspired confidence in all. It was the beginning of a new era in progress and discovery. This grand mine, for many years, produced mass copper in great abundance; much native silver was also raised. During its active career this mine divided among its stockholders nearly, if not quite, $2,000,000, we believe.

Mr. Knapp, we believe, was the first superintendent. Messrs. Roberts and Townsend were, for a decade or more of years, the sagacious managers or agents. Captain William Harris acquired here an enviable reputation as chief mine captain. Very many gentlemen, since prominent in the copper mines, acquired their experience at this mine. The National and Rockland were immediate neighbors on the same lode. In this community we found in 1847 the following named gentlemen: Drs. Flanner and Osborne, Messrs. I. N. Wright, Thomas Buzzo. Sutton, Webb, Richards, Chenoweth, Hoyt, F. G. White, Mr. Anthony, Mr. Sanderson. Mr. Cooper, of Pittsburgh, was a conspicuous figure in the National, as he was in the Cliff and many other enterprises. All along the range, both east and west of the river, mining operations were, for a time, active. Of the names that we can now recall, we note those of Messrs. A. C. Davis, S. S. Robinson, L. M. Dickens, W. H. Stevens, Captain Hardie, Mr. Sales, Hon. W. E. Dickinson, Mr. Roberts, Captain Martin, Mr. Buzzo, Sr., Mr. Spaulding, Mr. Coburn, all chief mine mangers or proprietors. The flourishing village of Rockland sprang up under the nurture of the Minnesota and National. Messrs. Benjamin T. Rogers, Phelan, Johnson and Judge Alan were prosperous citizens of that town.

Ontonagon village, the county seat and sea port of the county, grew rapidly and became the handsomest town on Lake Superior, before Marquette arose to claim precedence. The people were refined and enterprising. Among the good citizens. Mr. Lew Dickins, one of the *oldest* of the pioneers, Mr. Paull, Mr. Coburn, Mr. Sales, Mr. Cash, Mr. Jones, Honorable Jay A. Hubble, present member of Congress from the Ninth District of Michigan, Mr. Mercer, Mr. Close, Mr. Carson, State Senator Willard, Mr. Condon, Mr. Holland, Mr. Beaser and Mr. Devereaux, were conspicuous names. Thomas F. Mason was pecuniarily interested in the Minnesota mine. He visited the country at an early day, and has many claims to the rank of a pioneer. He has occupied important and controlling positions in the Quincy and several other mines. Mr. Horatio Bigelow, also, in all the copper counties, has filled acceptably, many responsible directorial and financial positions. Our space will not permit of even a passing notice of the numerous mines that have flourished in Ontonagon county. The abatement of the copper yield of the Minnesota and National, among other causes, has placed the county under a cloud. But its mineral resources are great, and we think the time is not distant when some new discovery, or a more favorable set of circumstances, will make that district once more prosperous and happy. The very best mining countries have had their ups and downs, and so it will ever be.

Ancient Mine Works.—All along the Trap Ranges ancient mining works are numerous. The first discovery of one of them was, according to Dr. J. W. Foster, made in the winter of 1847-'8, by Mr. Samuel O. Knapp on the Minnesota Company's grounds. One pit opened by Mr. Knapp, is thus described. "When he had penetrated to a depth of eighteen feet, he came to a mass of native copper, ten feet long, three feet wide, and nearly two feet thick, and weighing over six tons. On digging round the mass, it was found to rest on billets of oak, supported by sleepers of the same material. The wood, from its long exposure to moisture, was dark-colored and had lost its consistency. It opposed no more resistence to a knife blade than so much peat. The earth was so firmly packed as to support the mass of copper. The ancient miners had evidently raised it about five feet and then abandoned the work as too laborious. The number of ancient hammers he took from this and other excavations, exceeded ten cart loads. They were made of greenstone and porphyry boulders. Selecting a stone of the desired size and form, the ancient miner cut a grove, arched it so that it might be secured by a withe, and thus wielded as a sledge hammer."

The instances of similar works elsewhere are too common and well known to be dwelt upon. There is scarcely a productive vein or lode in these districts, that did not show traces of ancient works. Mr. Hulbert found them at the Calumet, leading down to the conglomerate belt. Hon. Samuel W. Hill, some two years ago, discovered pits and trenches on Isle Royale of great magnitude and of surpassing interest. He states that those works exceed in extent all other works of the kind heretofore seen in the copper region put together. The Minong mining company, Mr. A. C. Davis, Supt., is successfully operating in a system of those pits, which covers a space 400 feet wide and $1\frac{1}{2}$ miles long.

An army of ancient miners must have wrought there many years.

Float copper is also of common occurrence; it often leads to the discovery of veins in the immediate neighborhood The largest pure mass found in modern times was cut up by Mr. Jacob Houghton, Agent of the mine on the Mesnard Mining Company's land, near Hancock. It weighed eighteen tons. It was found in the woods, and was covered with moss. It had been worked at by the ancient miner. Much charcoal was found under it; its top and sides were beaten smooth; marks of stone hammers were apparent. All projections, every bit of copper that could be pounded off had been carried away. The ancient man then left the pure, noble mass, doubtless feeling a supreme disgust at his inability to remove the treasure.

This mass had evidently been forcibly torn from its bed, 50 feet distant—the Epidote lode—by an iceberg. Subsequent mining disclosed its original bed, or matrix.

PORTAGE LAKE COPPER DISTRICT.

This district, at the present time the most prominent, did not attain to much note prior to the year 1860. Mr. Ransom Shelden, who now resides at Houghton, as we have already stated settled at Portage Entry in 1847. For a time he traded with the Indians, but his summers were spent on the Range in exploring. Although not a mineral expert, or highly educated, he acquired a good practical knowledge of the vein phenomena of the country, multiplied field-notes and, in the course of time with the assistance of capitalists, he succeeded in purchasing many sections of mineral lands of value, which ultimately placed him and his partner, Mr. C. C. Douglass, among the largest and wealthiest landed proprietors in the upper peninsula.

In 1852 he removed to the Quincy mine and lived in a small log house on the hill side. In 1854 he removed to Houghton, built the log house which stands across the street from his present mansion, and the old log store which stands opposite Smith & Harris' store. In 1857, Houghton contained, by count, 40 buildings including shanties. It is now a flourishing village of 3,000 people, and is the county seat.

In the decade, 1850 to 1860, Portage Lake mine industry was of slow growth,—with many pull backs and clouded with doubt and uncertainty, and not very highly esteemed by the magnates of the Cliff and Minnesota. On the south side of the lake mining at first was most active. The Isle Royale, Portage, Huron, Shelden and Albion, were wrought with more or less vigor. Three of these companies had constructed small stamp mills on the lake shore. C. C. Douglass managed the Portage and other properties—J. H. Forster, for a brief term in 1857, was Supt. of the Portage. Mr. Rickard was at the Isle Royale, afterwards Mr. Dickinson and Mr. Hopkins, and later still, Mr. Eschweiler and John Mabbs. Captain Edwards was at the Albion, and had constructed a saw mill near his family residence. Mr. Shelden was active in mine operations on both sides of the lake. Under the management of Mr. Sam'l W. Hill, the "old warhorse" of Houghton and Keweenaw counties, with Messrs. Thos. M. Mason and John Simpkins as directors and financial men in New York, the QUINCY MINE, in 1860, had emerged into the position of a first-class mine. Mr. Hill was assisted by Mr. Nathaniel Simpkins, clerk; Capt. Hardie, chief mine captain; Mr. Quinn, Mr. Duncan, and the Pattersons, with Mr. Scheurman, Stamp mill Supt. The Messrs. Emerson, civil and mine engineers, were for many years connected with the mine—Mr. Luther Emerson is there still. Professor George Emerson is now filling the chair of civil and mine engineer in the University of Missouri, at Rolla. Mr. S. S. Robinson succeeded Mr. Hill as Supt. in 1860. In 1861-'2 the Quincy reached a dividend paying point, which it has maintained ever since—having divided to its stockholders $1,890,000. The deepest shaft in this mine is about 1,800 feet. Mr. Corey is the present agent; Mr. Clift, mine Capt.; Quinn, 2d.

Pewabic and Franklin Companies.—These companies are contemporaneous with the Quincy, and are working on the same lode. They were opened by Mr. Chas. H. Palmer and

Mr. Wm. B. Frue, and placed upon a favorable footing. In 1857, we saw Captain Frue hauling out masses of copper at the Pewabic, from open trenches on the lode, with oxen. From Oct., 1860 to 1865, these mines were under the management of John H. Forster, agent, assisted by captains John Gundry, John Ryan, I. P. Hodgson, J. C. Hodgson and John McCrystal. E. I. Loring, Esq., of Boston, was Treasurer, and Chas. Emery, Sec'y. These mines, during the term mentioned, paid handsome dividends—(the Pewabic, $270,000; the Franklin, $160,000,) besides adding largely to the mine plant and liquidating a large indebtedness. Messrs. Chas. Wheeler, James Blandy, John Blaine, John Rice, Carlos Watson, Henry Lewis and Chas. Smith were clerks. The Pewabic and Franklin each had four heads of Ball's stamps, and separate tram-roads leading thereto. Mr. Cleaves was Supt. of the latter, and Mr. W. T. Forster of the former mill. The Franklin company introduced the first locomotive seen in the copper mines, and the first skip car. Mr. Johnson Vivian is at present agent of these mines.

The copper smelting works on Portage Lake were begun in 1860 by Col. Brigham, of Boston. Mr. John Williams was chief smelter and agent for several years. Mr. John R. Grout, the very able chief manager, has brought these works to a position of high excellence and effectiveness not exceeded by any other works of the kind in the world.

Whereas the counties, or copper districts of Keweenaw and Ontonagon were mainly distinguished for their great fissure veins which produced native copper in masses, often of enormous dimensions and great purity, the Portage Lake district is almost destitute of true fissure veins, (the small cross-courses found thus far, being destitute of copper in paying quantities,) and has relied exclusively upon stamp lodes for products and success. There are several of these lodes of prominence, namely, the Isle Royale, Pewabic, Hancock, South Pewabic or Atlantic, Allouez Osceola and Calumet. These lodes run with the formation, that is, about 33 degrees east of north; all are amygdaloidal in character, except the

Calumet Osceola and Allouez, which are conglomerates, and yield from two to five per cent. mineral. Most of the mines working upon these lodes or belts, raise some heavy copper in irregular masses, technically called " mass and barrel work." This kind of mineral is freed from rocky impurities by means of sledging or hammerings, and is then sent direct to the smelting works for treatment. But at least 70 per cent. of the mineral raised from these mines is what is termed stamp rock. The conglomerate belts are almost exclusively stamp rock. Occasional rounded boulders are found in the matrix, containing so large a percentage of copper and of such considerable size that they are sent direct to the smelt house.

The stamp rock is the finer grades of native copper—from the size of a walnut, buck-shot, bird shot, down to the finest flour—combined with the vein-stone, or matrix of the lode. It is associated with a great variety of beautiful minerals, such as calcite, quartz, phreite, table spar, laumonite, chlorite epidote and soft brown amygdaloid. In the conglomerate the copper is the cementing material which binds the boulders, pebbles and sand together in a hard, tough mass. After being mined, the reduction of the stamp rock to what is called mineral fit for reception at the smelting works, necessitates the use of powerful machinery, known as stamps or stamp mills. Hence we find on Portage Lake many mills of this character, of enormous proportions and great execution. The mills of the Calumet & Hecla company on Torch Lake, for example, with seven heads of steamp stamps, treat no less than 800 tons of hard copper-cemented rock each twenty-four hours, reducing said rock to fine sand and slime. The sand and copper as they flow from under the stamps, which by the most violent pounding conceivable, have forced a dissolution of particles, long wedded in the mine, fall upon Collum's patent washers and finishers. These washers, in great numbers, neatly adjusted, and moved by the great engine of the place, and with nicely graduated streams of water flowing through them, separate the copper from the waste sand; the copper, by its own gravity, settling in the bottom of the wired jiggers, or falling into boxes through Asmus' self-dischargers, while the sand, flowing over the aprons of the jiggers, fall into launders or sluice boxes, and is conducted by a rush of water into the lake or other place of deposit.

The mineral, assorted and numbered, is placed in barrels and sent to the smelting works to be converted into ingots, cakes and bolts ready for market. Well dressed mineral will yield about 80 per cent. ingot copper.

A large quantity of water is used in the various processes at one of these mills—say from 1,500 to 2,000 gallons per minute. A powerful pumping engine is attached to most mills, and this large volume of water is forced to the top of the mill, in some cases 40 to 50 feet high.

A mill of the character above described consumes from fifteen to fifty cords of mixed wood every twenty-four hours, or bituminous coal in relative proportion, according to number of tons of rock treated. Hence, a large mill with its two gangs of operatives, its wood choppers, teamsters and general supply men, affords occupation for quite a numerous community.

The monthly cost of operating such a mine as the Calumet & Hecla, in all departments, including a railroad five miles long, is about $100,000. The monthly product of ingot copper is about 800 tons—worth about $300,000.

VILLAGE OF HANCOCK.

This place was laid out in 1858. The first store erected was by that enterprising firm, the Leopolds. At one time Hancock was destroyed by fire. It is now a very flourishing, enterprising town, growing rapidly. It speaks for itself. President Holland's narrow gauge railroad terminating at this point is the latest triumph in this district. The days of Indian trails and dog trains are indeed gone!

We deeply regret that the prescribed limits of this paper cannot be exceeded. We would like to make further mention of the Portage district—of its older and newer mines—its many local enterprises—and its industrious, go-ahead, generous, cultured people. We must content ourselves with saying that prior to 1866, the Huron mine had attained prominence under the agency of Mr. E. J. Hulbert. Also, that the South Pewabic and Adams (now Atlantic,) were discovered, opened and equipped, having four of Ball's largest stamps, by agent William B. Frue, assisted by Messrs. David Hodgson, John Rice, William Ryan, William Noble, Henry Lewis, Joseph Ames and William T. Forster. The mine is now managed by Mr. Robert. Finally, the greatest discovery made in the district was about the year 1866—the *find* of the great Calumet conglomerate, by Mr. E. J. Hulbert. It would be like attempting to paint the lily to describe this mine. Mr. I. N. Wright is the chief agent at the head of this mammoth concern.

The Osceola, on the Calumet lode, is a promising new mine, Hon. F. G. White, agent.

The Allouez is another new concern on the Allouez lode. Capt. William Harris, agent.

As intimately connected with the mines, we mention the Portage River Improvement. This work began in the fall of 1859; was opened to navigation in the summer of 1860. The money to build it was contributed by the local mining companies and Messrs. Shelden and Douglass. Mr. W. W. Williams was the contractor, Mr. John H. Forster, engineer.

PORTAGE LAKE AND LAKE SUPERIOR SHIP CANAL.

This work, predicted by Mr. Wm. A. Burt, a generation ago, was finished in the year 1873. About seven years were consumed in its construction. It is $2\frac{1}{4}$ miles long, 100 feet wide, with heavy breakwaters on lake Superior, and cost several millions of dollars. The Messrs. Avery & Wells were contractors and proprietors. J. N. Greene, C. E., planned the work, and began it. Mr. John H. Forster was engineer thereon during the administrations of Gov. Baldwin, and for two years under Gov. Bagley. These canals have added greatly to the commercial importance of Portage Lake.

Before the Portage River improvement was made, and prior to 1860, Portage lake was difficult of access. At the earliest time, the lake steamers used to land passengers in small boats, at the portage; a portage of two miles had to be made, most of the way through a tamarack swamp, and then the traveler was rowed in a small boat, to Houghton. In 1857, steamers began to run to Portage Entry. They anchored in the roadstead, and landed freight and passengers upon scows, which were towed into the river and up the lake by small tugs. There was only three feet of water on the bar at the mouth of the river. Several days were consumed in discharging a steamer, and if a storm came on, the boat had to cut and run to L'Anse, and there await favorable weather. The arrival and departure of steamers at the Entry was a matter of much uncertainty, and passengers were often detained there several days, in consequence. Many will remember vividly the days of waiting in Edgerton's log cabin in the swamp, in mosquito time, with scarce a rood of dry land to stretch one's limbs upon. The bill of fare did not outrival Delmonico's, and the softest bed to be procured was a blanket spread upon a pine puncheon. Cards and whisky were the only and questionable resources from utter misery. We are afraid that the amount of profanity evolved then, under trying circumstances, was sufficient to demoralize the neighboring community of bull frogs, for many generations.

Capt. James Bendry, as commander of the slow-sure tug, Pratt, was a prominent figure in those waters. He could steer his vessel over the mud flats and through the sinuous river, just as well asleep as awake. During the busy season he never undressed, or laid down for weeks, and the little sleep he got was while standing at the wheel; the Pratt, like a thing of life, going where she had a mind to. Like a mud turtle, she rather affected a soft, oozy point to run her nose upon. Passengers were generally fortunate if they reached Houghton the same day of their departure from the Entry, a distance of fourteen miles—such were the delays and dangers of navigation. The delights of this voyage were greatly augmented when Captain Bendry was towing a scow loaded with a thousand kegs of powder, alongside his brave tug. The scenic effect was increased if your journey was protracted into the dark night; for then the millions of sparks from the wood fuel could be seen pouring out of the flue, and falling in showers upon the powder. Passengers speculated, the while, as to the probabilities of a speedy transfer to another world, but the jolly captain never lost his *aplomb*, or showed the white feather—and what's better, he never blew up; for our old friend is still an active and useful citizen of Baraga. When he does receive his final marching orders, he will be sadly missed. Mr. Carlos D. Shelden also commanded the rival steamer, Princess.

The very latest water-way improvement is the ship canal,—about two miles long, cut through the marshes between Portage and Torch lakes. This work was finished in September, 1875. It was executed by E. T. Williams & Co., with their powerful dredges. The entire cost was about $100,000; this sum was furnished by the Calumet & Hecla Mining Co. The largest steamers and coal-laden vessels on the lake, now discharge at their docks on Torch lake, the lake terminus of their railroad.

We record here the names of such mining-men as we can recall,—not previously mentioned,—who have wrought in the Portage district, many of them on the list of pioneers, namely: Messrs. R. J. Wood, A. B. Wood, H. Q. F. D'Aligny, C. E., Jacob Houghton, Mr. Crofts, Mr. Hague, Mr. Worminghouse, Mr. Swift, Mr. Bennetts, the Pryors, Austin Mabbs, Captain Moody, Graham Pope, Alexander Pope, S. L. Smith, Wm. Harris, John and Richard Hoar; captains Dunn, Northey, McDonald, Roberts, Beesly brothers, Reid, Goodell, Asmus, Wallace, Cox, Chas. H. Palmer, Jr., Fleige, Snell, Dr. Fuller, Dr. Rhodes, Dr. Carpenter, Dr. Tompkins, Dr. Robbins, T. J. Brown, T. M. Forster, Joseph Edwards, Wm. Hendrick, Ross, Ellenbecker, Sullivan, E. S. Forster, Winlock, Cowles, Wright, Hooper, Robinson, Todd, Ferguson, Tracy, Daniel, Fleming, Richard Uren, H. H. Mildon,

T. W. Edwards, John Mildon, Jeff Day, J. Q. McKernan, and E. F. Douglass.

In *Keweenaw County*, since 1854, the Central Mine Company has been working on a magnificent fissure-vein, which has produced extraordinary masses of native copper. This mine is situated under the greenstone, about midway between Eagle River and Eagle Harbor; it has long pursued the even tenor of its way; it has been eminently prosperous—a beacon light in the land. Under Mr. Mills, as president, and Mr. Petrie, as superintendent, and Mr. Dunstone, mine captain, it has occupied a most enviable position for years. It has divided among its stockholders one million dollars.

The Phœnix (old Eagle River) is a promising mass vein to-day, brought out by F. G. White, late superintendent.

ISLE ROYALE.

This "Lone Isle of the Sea," has been the theatre of active mine operations during the last two years. Under the supervision of Messrs. Hardie and Cole, the Island mine has been partially developed upon a conglomerate belt, near Siskirvit Bay.

THE MINONG MINING COMPANY OF DETROIT,

was organized December 16th, 1874, with a capital of one million dollars. It owns 1,455 acres of land in sections 22, 23, 26, 27, 34 and 35, township 66 north, range 35 west, lying at the head of McCargo's cove, on Isle Royale. These lands are traversed by heavy metalliferous belts and transverse veins, carrying copper, elevated one hundred and fifty feet above the lake, and distant but an average of half a mile from the cove, which is about two and a half miles long and one thousand feet wide, forming a perfectly land locked harbor. The exploration on this property, previous to the organization of the company, was induced by the discovery of a very large amount of ancient mine work, which had been done at some remote period in the past, the date of which was antecedent to the traditions of the Indians, and by a race who worked only with stone hammers and fire. The cleaning out of sections of the transverse veins they had worked to the depth of twenty-five feet, gave fine specimens of barrel copper, and in the opening of a pit sixteen and a half feet deep on the belt, there were found boulders of copper, and one mass, weighing 5,720 pounds, bearing ancient hammer marks, and evidently too heavy for those people to carry away. The Minong Company did not commence work until about the middle of June last; they had to construct every thing to work with, having but the dense thicket of brush and timber at their first landing. They have worked from that time to the middle of November, a daily average of forty men, and have shipped to Detroit 54,287 pounds of mass and barrel copper, and adding to this the 5,720 pound mass, spoken of above, which came from the same open cut, they have 60,007 pounds, producing 88 per cent. of ingot, leaving at the mine over three hundred tons of very rich stamp rock. They have also erected a substantial dock, store, warehouse, and agent's, boarding and tenement houses sufficient to accommodate seventy men and families for the winter. This work, with its promising results, has satisfied the stockholders of the value of their property, the working of which will be by an increased force, and by the addition of machinery for stamping and hoisting, thereby insuring regular products and with more economy. The business office of the company is located at Detroit, and the following gentlemen are the officers for the ensuing year:

Directors—S. G. **Wight, John** Belknap, **C. M. Garrison,** Charles Root, George W. Gilbert, **Hiram** Walker, **I. B. Wayne.**

President—S. G. **Wight.**

Secretary and Treasurer—C. **M. Garrison.**

Sometime between 1850–55 mining **enterprises were** conducted **on** the Island **on** Rock Harbor. ·**Several** buildings were erected, including a stamp mill. **Mr. C. C.** Douglass was at one time a superintendent there. But later the whole island was deserted, **not a living soul** remaining. We trust that this rich island will soon **become a** prosperous mining **centre.**

In the summer of 1846 we saw a "half-breed" woman who had been Crusoeing on the island. She and her husband had been placed on the island in charge of property. Owing to the wreck of the brig Astor in the fall of 1845, supplies failed to reach them. Long they waited for succor, but in vain. winter came on, snow covered the ground, and ice gathered on the waters; then this lone pair were left to their fate on this savage, desolate island "out of humanity's reach." The shrieking winds, as they swept through the fir trees, and the black billows of the stormy lake, spending their sullen fury upon the rocky coasts, were the only sounds that could greet the ear during the long, long dark winter of that high northern latitude. For companionship they must depend upon each other. But, before the winter was half spent, the husband sickened and died, and the poor woman was left absolutely alone. Wrapping the remains of her dead husband in a blanket, she removed them from the hut and deposited them in the snow, where frozen solid like a pillar of ice, they were preserved until the return of spring permitted of other burial. The widow passed the long winter as best she could, subsisting upon the flesh of rabbits, which she managed to snare. Her bereavement, hardships, and the terrors of isolation, wonderful as it may seem, did not affect her health or mind. She was taken off from the island in the spring, and was happy enough when she reached the main land.

SILVER.

In the copper mines we find native silver in considerable quantities, associated with the copper in the same veins or lodes. But (unless we except the recent discoveries at Iron river,) no distinctive silver veins of value have been, as yet, discovered on the south shore of Lake Superior. At one time the so-called silver lead regions of the Huron mountains promised well; but the value of that section, with so many possibilities, must still be written down not proven. From our knowledge of the geology of the west coast of America, we are of the number who believe in the Huron mountain region. Although not a prophet, nor the son of a prophet, yet we believe that before the lapse of another decade, those mountains will cast their evening shadows upon busy mining camps.

Even in the copper district proper, why may we not hope to find native silver veins? If the occurrence of this precious metal is so common in almost every copper vein, or lode, from the extremity of Keweenaw point to the Porcupines, why may it not occur somewhere alone in paying quantities? Will some learned gentleman rise and explain?

At the old Lake Superior mine, in 1846, we saw a great deal of silver, which had been raised from a drift under Eagle river. It had been washed and rounded, and that which we saw, in a quart measure, was of about the size of hickory nuts. It was *placer* silver; it had been removed from the vein by water; tumbled about and polished and finally precipitated into a seam in the rock.

The *finds* of silver at the Cliff mine were sometimes very large. Although the miners, doubtless, carried off the largest proportion of this metal, yet the mine agent was enabled to save a good many barrels each year. We believe the largest chunk or nugget of pure native silver ever found in the county weighed eighty pounds. In the mine the silver was generally found in pockets or vuggs. Once in the night a party of miners fired their blasts, and after the smoke had cleared away they returned to their work. What was their surprise to find a small cavern opened by their shots; with his candle in hand one miner crept into the hole; his exclamations of surprise and astonishment caused his companions to poke their heads in. Here was a cavern several feet in extent, whose walls glittered with sparkling calcspar and pure white silver. It was like a fairy dream—like the palace of Aladdin. The "boys" after sufficiently admiring this exquisite cave lying one thousand feet under the ground, where no ray of sunlight had ever penetrated, set to work with picks to spoil it. Their cupidity out-weighed admiration; powder keg after powder keg of the pure silver was gathered, and hid away under stull pieces until such time as it could be carried out of the mine without detection. But the lynx-eyed mine captain, next morning saw the cave—the marks of the pick on the walls in the silver yet adhering—and demanded of the "boys" where they had concealed the treasure. They were compelled to disgorge and there remained to them only the remembrance of that gorgeous chamber. What became of the gnomes whose favorite chamber this doubtless was, did not transpire.

The Portage Lake mines, all of them, produce more or less silver. Silver-pickers are employed at most of the stamp mills to pick out the small scale silver from the copper.

The old Minnesota mine was celebrated for its silver waifs; from first to last, tens of thousands of dollars of silver must have been raised from the mine; but the honest miner, as usual, came in for the lion's share. The moral tone is that it would be wrong to steal copper, but legitimate to pocket silver.

At the present time there is a strong probability, if not certainty, that the Iron river district, in Ontonagon county, will prove to be the La Plata so long pre-shadowed by the mineral seers of the country.

Shall we ever find gold upon the south shore of the lake? is a question often asked. There is a tradition that Dr. Houghton did find it somewhere, either in the Huron mountains or in the Porcupines. But if he did so, the secret died with him. Some two years ago the writer and a friend—an expert chemist and assayer—found traces of gold in some rock sent for treatment from the Iron river section. But we were incredulous. Eighteen months later we ascertained that our specimens had been salted by a Californian, who carries about with him a small vial filled with gold dust, for the deceiving of the natives—the heathen Chinee.

In 1846, certain of the most sanguine explorers were hopeful of finding gold mines. The party to which the writer was attached was sent to explore the country lying east of

L'Anse, or south of Huron Bay, in search of copper and gold. We encamped at the Methodist mission; leaving our geologist, who was of the kind who never went into the woods, and who judged of the vein phenomena by the specimens brought to him by the practical explorer, we plunged into the woods. Before night we had crossed the Huron river and arrived at an inviting region of slate and trap rock, with strong indications of mineral. In fact, a massive vein of quartz, with some yellow ore, was discovered, cutting through a high knob. Only a partial, hasty examination could be made before night set in. It was determined to encamp near the spot, so that a thorough examination could be made next morning. Much excited over the supposed discovery of a gold bearing vein, we hurried down the slope, and camped by the side of a pool of water in a cedar swamp. After partaking of a hasty cup of tea, bread, and a bit of pork, roasted on a split stick by the fire, we sought, in the dark, to erect some sort of shelter from the impending storm. In the deep recesses of the woods, nature was quiet and calm as death; but we could hear the deep-muttered thunder in the southwest. We had but one small hatchet, and it was no easy task to procure material for the most impromptu hut. In the pitch dark, our feeble camp fire sent its rays only a little way out into the gloom. We succeeded in cutting two poles, reclining them against a giant cedar, and heaping a few boughs upon them. Then we crawled under our wigwam (there was a brace of us), which, by the way, was just spacious enough to cover our heads and shoulders, most ungenerously leaving our inferior parts exposed to the weather. Now, the thunder rolled right over our heads, and the vivid lightning, illuminating the swamp, caused every mossy trunk to resemble a weird spectre. The rain came pattering down very gently at first, but soon the burdened trees began to drop big drops upon our frail tenement, which drops finally became streams. We soon became drenched and almost afloat in a pool of water, and had to flounder out and stand up in the mud. We stirred up the flickering fire,

and amused ourselves all night heaping dead limbs upon it
and trying to keep ourselves warm. The thunder storm
passed over toward the north-east, but the rain poured down
steadily the livelong night. The profound gloom, the darkness that could be felt, the utter, helpless misery of those
long, dreary hours, in that cedar swamp, will never be forgotten. A half-drowned rat, a barnyard fowl after a rain
storm, are feeble figures to convey an idea of our appearance
when day broke. Our zeal as volunteer explorers was much
moderated; yet we returned to the quartz vein, filled our
haversack with the specimens, and started at once for L'Anse.
The rain continued to pour down, and the thick underbrush
was loaded with water, so that our tramp in was a continuous
bath, for, if the rain falling direct did not soak us enough,
the wet brush finished the business by rubbing it in.

We reached camp at noon, jaded and hungry, but we had
courage enough left to place our bag of gold specimens
triumphantly at the feet of our learned professor of geology
and mineralogy. After skillful manipulation with the blow
pipe and acids, he pronounced our quartz, quartz; our yellow
mineral, iron pyrites. Thus ended our first gold discovery.
So disgusted were all concerned, that we broke up camp and
sailed for Copper Harbor. Here our geologist left us. The
next time we saw the learned gentleman he was keeping
a corner grocery in San Francisco, in 1849. A two years'
exploration with pick and shovel, in the plains of California,
taught us the appearance and value of the yellow dross, in
more senses than one.

GENERAL REMARKS.

The old adage, all is not gold that glitters, has an application to the copper mines of Lake Superior. All the mines
are not Calumets or Cliffs. There are many idle mines in the
region — and there have been many lamentable failures.
Why is it so? Many are the causes of disaster and failure.
We cannot stop to enumerate them all; we will merely
allude to some of them.

In the first place, when the country was first opened to mining, the geology of the range was little understood, and the contents of veins were different in form from what had been seen in other countries. The old miner from Europe was about as much at loss how to manipulate the native copper as the veriest tyro of native growth. Many mining ventures, therefore, came to nought for want of sufficient knowledge.

In the second place, all veins or lodes that are productive at one place, or for a short distance, are not equally so throughout the entire length. Hence, mines opened upon well known veins or lodes of repute, in their extension may find the vein rock so poor that the amount of copper raised will not cover expenses.

In the third place, the length of the portion of vein or lode owned or worked by a company, though the mine may be rich, is insufficient to warrant large expenditures for mine plant and machinery. Hence a narrow, contracted policy of operation, which soon ends in the closing of the mine. A consolidation with neighboring mines, similarly situated, would be an effectual remedy in such a case, and if followed in many instances that could be adduced, would insure successful mines.

In the fourth place, many stamp lodes of good percentage of copper are idle to-day, because the managers have not had the boldness or capital sufficient to provide adequate stamp machinery.

And lastly, undoubtedly there has been opened, in speculative times, mines based upon lean and hungry lodes, without merit of any kind, and whose fate it was to absorb and dissipate all the capital ever ventured in them.

We deem these statements, made in all fairness, due to the copper mines and to strangers and legislators who visit the country.

The copper mines of Lake Superior do not very much differ from any or all mining districts. Mining for the more valuable metals has always been speculative in character and always will be to the end of time. It is in the nature of things. Wherever there is much uncertainty and occasional enormous gains—prizes — in any enterprise, there will be found the spirit of speculation—if not gambling. One big bonanza like the Comstock lode excites whole communities, and peoples deserts. One big conglomerate mine like the Calumet & Hecla fires the imaginations of all, and the waste places of the Trap range teem (like dragon's teeth) with other conglomerates, which shall rival the successful Calumet.

The business of copper mining on Lake Superior has passed through many and great vicissitudes. Doubt, uncertainty and gloom have more than once enshrouded the land. Yet even when the tide of prosperity had run to the lowest ebb, it has been met by an incoming wave which has carried this industry to a higher point than it had previously attained. The country is now blessed with a large, prominent and rapidly increasing population, whose homes and interests are affixed to the soil; a large capital has accumulated, and as the value of the mines, forests and fisheries is now assured beyond peradventure, there is little reason for the apprehension of great calamities and sweeping reverses in the future.

One of the darkest hours we remember for the copper mining interests, was the first year of the war on the Union. Every one supposed that the end had come—that the mines must close down—that nothing was left to do but to shoulder the musket and march to the South. Copper stocks fell to a zero point: nobody would want our copper, and it must, perforce, lie in the ground. The price of ingot copper fell to 17 cents, and the end came? No; as soon as the government found that it had work to do, a large army and navy to arm and equip, they turned to our own copper fields with eager demand for a supply of copper, which could not be safely procured from the old sources, in foreign lands. This demand greatly stimulated mining, and created active business in all kindred departments. It was not long before the price of copper attained a highly remunerative point, and before the war closed it reached the unprecedented figure of 50 cents per pound, or $1,000 per ton! This paid? Yes, indeed! But there were drawbacks to this prosperity. The demands for the army, the demands for miners and all other kinds of labor, owing to the vigorous working of the old mines and the springing up of new ones in every direction, explorations and speculative movements rendered labor scarce, independent, costly and refractory. Everything cost enormously; everybody was making money, but all wanted more. There was a great blossoming of new men—superintendents and captains of mines, promoted instanter from the ranks. It was a troublous time. Intemperance, vice and crime ruled the hour. Strikes among workmen, upon a large, combined scale, were common during the winter months, and mine officers were much exercised in their endeavors to control and regulate the unreasoning, turbulent masses. Violent assaults, maiming, and even manslaughter, were not uncommon occurrences, and he who did not go around with a good revolver was deemed foolhardy. At one time an appeal was made to the Governor for arms, and fifty stand of muskets were sent forward. Mine officers were drilled in the manual, ostensibly for the purpose of fitting themselves for service in the army, but really to be prepared to resist internal commotions. Miners and laborers were composed of several nationalities, but chiefly of Cornish, Irish and Germans. The first two classes were bitterly hostile, and often assumed a belligerent attitude in force, or would indulge in secret personal attacks, which often terminated in murder. The older pioneers will recollect the trouble which occurred at the Minnesota mine, where the Irish and Cornish contended with desperate intent. At Portage Lake these Greeks and Trojans, long before the war, occasionally arrayed their forces, armed with picks, hammers, guns and stones, and marching down the Portage hill by different paths, entered the village of Houghton at extreme ends, halted, and challenged each other to come on. "Lay on, McDuff, and damned be he who first cries hold, enough," was the cry; third parties always interfered and prevented a collision *en masse;* but later in the day, individuals and squads, infuriated by villainous Pike's whisky, would indulge in frequent bloody combats. At night the most peaceable citizens were knocked down and beaten to a jelly. At one time the Pewabic stamp mill was threatened with sack. Some offended individuals proposed to clean out that establishment one bright Sunday morning. Being warned in time, the superintendent, Mr. T. Forster, prepared for the emergency. He called in his men, armed them with chunks of stamp copper, barricaded the doors, and attached the hose to the boilers, so as to be able to deluge the assailants with hot water. He was prepared to give his foes a *warm* reception, but they did not venture down the hill; they doubtless smelt danger in the wind.

About the second year of the war, laborers became so scarce that the mining corporations determined to send an agent to Europe to induce immigration. An agent actually went to Sweden and contracted with a large number of men who finally made their appearance at Portage Lake. They were billeted off to the several companies, but nine out of ten refused to go to work or to abide by their solemn contracts made in their own country. They had reached this free and independent land without cost to themselves, and they proposed to act a freeman's part and do just as they pleased. The fact that the mining companies had expended $90,000 in their transportation, and that they were required to work at good wages, only a sufficient length of time to reimburse those who had assisted them to reach this country, was of no importance—not worthy of a moment's consideration. But one good came out of this venture at the time. Some forty of the men volunteered to fill the draft quota and were marched off to the wars, where some ill-natured ones charitably hoped they might become food for confederate gunpowder. This was the first introduction of the Scandinavian upon Lake Superior. Its later fruits may be seen to-day in the large, industrious class of this people now settled in the copper and iron mines. They are generally esteemed as good citizens.

But, with the war ended, a more orderly and peaceable era succeeded. Dull times followed, the price of copper fell; many mines suspended operations, and labor was at a discount. Hence, wise men became prudent and circumspect in conduct—they were obliged to or starve. For the last decade there has been no general strikes in the copper mines, even in prosperous times. Indeed, we should fail in duty should we neglect to state that the laboring classes at the mines are deserving of praise for the good order, industry and temperance which, as a class, they have maintained for many years. Their good example might well be imitated in many mining districts that might be named, but notably, in the coal fields of Pennsylvania and Ohio. Some of the very brightest children in the public schools are the sons and daughters of miners; and another thing must be said in commendation of these, our worthy citizens; namely, they do diligently attend to the scriptural injunction—"increase and multiply and replenish the earth." With a fine, healthy climate to aid them, their achievements in this line are marvelous.

The rise and fall of prices had much to do with the success of the copper mines. We note the fluctations for a series of years, as follows:

July, 1860 . . . . $21\frac{1}{2}$ cents per pound.
" 1861 . . . . $17\frac{3}{4}$ " " "
" 1862 . . . . $22\frac{1}{2}$ " " "
" 1863 . . . . 32 " " "
" 1864 . . . . 55 " " "

After the war the price fell to 17 cents, and copper was a drug in the market. It now sells at 22 to 24 cents.

Nothing in the copper mines of Lake Superior is more remarkable and significant than the immense progress that has been made in mining and kindred branches within the last fifteen years. The rude skid shaft lining; the rickety ladder, the awkward kibble, the clumsy chains, the whim, the wheelbarrow, the horse and cart, and the old Cornish stamps have all been superseded. In their places we find the underground tram-way; the smooth-timbered shaft laid with Trail, the man-engine to carry the men up and down the mine; the easy running skip-car which dumps itself; the wire-rope of Rœbling's best; the powerful steam pumping and hoisting engine with friction gear; the surface automatic railway which rapidly moves the car from shaft to rock-house "like a thing of life;" the vast rock-houses with steam hammer and systems of Blake's stone-breakers preparing the coarse stamp rock for further treatment at the stamps; the efficient steam railroad carrying the mine product to the distant mill; the stamp mill, an immense building filled with a maze of obedient machinery with steam stamps, each head capable of pulverizing one hundred tons of hard copper-tied rock into the consistency of fine sand and slime, each twenty-four hours, washing and separating the copper at the same time, are marvels of improvement.

This progress has been made under very trying circumstances, at the cost of infinite toil, expense and discouragements. The miners found the country a howling wilderness —remote from the centres of population and supply; half of the year it was a region buried in snow, with the only outlet, the lakes and rivers, closed by ice. If to-day our copper mines are prosperous, it is owing, under Providence, to their intrinsic worth, and the skill and indomitable energy of the people, aided by non-resident capitalists.

The outlook for the future is bright. New discoveries will be made; the country is yet in its infancy and freshness. Not a tithe of the mineral ranges has been uncovered, and there remains to the generations to come ample work and almost unlimited wealth.

The Upper Peninsula of Michigan—the Superior country—is destined to become a wealthy, populous and powerful commonwealth.

DIVIDENDS PAID.

The following table shows the amount of **dividends paid to shareholders** by the several mines which have been **profitably** wrought, together with amount of assessments and **surplus:**

Name of Company	Assessments.	Dividends.	Surplus.
Calumet and Hecla	$800,000	$9,440,000	$4,000,000
Pittsburgh and Boston (Cliff)	110,000	2,280,000	....
Minnesota	440,000	1,750,000	20,000
Quincy	200,000	1,990,000	385,000
Central	100,000	920,000	140,000
Pewabic	240,000	400,000	25,000
National	150,000	300,000	40,000
Franklin	380,000	240,000	10,000
Ridge	200,000	150,000	43,000
Copper Falls	500,000	**100,000**	45,000
Totals	$3,120,000	$17,570,000	$4,708,000

Showing for the **ten mines named, an excess** in dividends and surplus over expenditures **of $19,158,000.** Ten other mines **which have produced** a very considerable amount of copper, **but have not yet** attained **a dividend paying** basis, have **called** assesments to the amount of **$6,760,000.** The mines not enumerated in the dividend paying list, produced in 1875 a little over 4,000 tons of mineral, worth $1,500,000. Of these last named mines, some are rapidly nearing their first dividends. **The Osceola, in particular, gives** promise of a large production in the future. **The Franklin,** which paid its last dividend in 1872, is again rising into prominence, and the Atlantic, though **not yet a dividend paying mine,** ranks fourth in the amount of mineral raised.

It will be noticed **that there has been a steady increase of production** since 1867, **and especially in the** Portage Lake **district;** Keweenaw county holds **its own,** but there is **a slight** decrease **in** Ontonagon, as compared with 1873.

STATEMENT OF COPPER PRODUCT FROM 1845 TO 1874.

	Tons.
1845 to 1854	7,642
1854 to 1858	11,312
1858	4,100
1859	4,200
1860	6,000
1861	7,500
1862	9,962
1863	8,548
1864	8,472
1865	10,791
1866	10,376
1867	11,735
1868	13,049
1869	15,288
1870	16,183
1871	16,071
1872	15,166
1873	18,638
1874	22,225
1875	22,802
Total	240,060

APPROXIMATE STATEMENT OF INGOT COPPER PRODUCED, AND ITS VALUE.

	Tons.	Value.
1845 to 1858	13,955	$9,000,500
1858	3,500	1,886,000
1859	3,500	1,890,000
1860	4,800	2,610,000
1861	6,000	3,337,500
1862	8,000	3,402,000
1863	6,500	4,420,000
1864	6,500	6,110,000
1865	7,000	5,145,000
1866	7,000	4,760,000
1867	8,200	4,140,000
1868	9,985	4,592,000
1869	12,200	5,368,000
1870	12,946	5,696,240
1871	12,857	6,171,360
1872	12,132	7,774,720
1873	14,910	8,200,500
1874	17,780	8,180,800
1875	18,352	8,390,860
Total	176,174	$101,075,480

TABULAR STATEMENT OF PRODUCTS.

The following table shows the product of the Lake Superior Copper Mines in 1875:

PORTAGE LAKE AND KEWEENAW DISTRICTS.

MINE.	TONS.	LBS.
Calumet and Hecla	13,165	195
Quincy	1,763	1,315
Central (estimated)	1,150	....
Atlantic	1,089	898
Phœnix	964	140
Osceola	889	740
Cliff	824	1,341
Franklin	745	478
Allouez	850	....
Pewabic	397	1,795
Copper Falls	272	155
Petherick (estimated)	95	....
From other mines in Houghton and Keweenaw Counties (about)	250	....

ONTONAGON DISTRICT.

Ridge	200	343
Minnesota	109	400
National	73	721
Nonesuch	30	986
Flint Steel	21	1,548
Adventure	18	1,380
Aztec	10	1,410
Rockland	9	1,073
Bohemian	5	1,263
Knowlton	3	1,923
Mass	2	186
Great Western	....	640
Total	22,941	1,930
Total Product in 1874	22,225	
Increase in 1875	716	

The copper interest of Houghton and Keweenaw counties never presented a more favorable aspect than now, and it is confidently hoped and believed that Ontonagon will, ere long, assume her old time prominence as a mining region.

The Calumet and Hecla is the *great copper mine of the world*, and will, without doubt, maintain that distinction for many years to come. The Quincy and Central hold their old positions as dividend paying mines, while there are bright prospects in the near future for not a few mines whose production thus far has not been sufficient to return to shareholders the capital expended.

The gross earnings of the Calumet and Hecla for 1875 approximated *five million dollars!* Ninety million of dollars represents the actual yield of the Lake Superior Copper Mines since 1860, a period of fifteen years! Where can be found another but partially developed mineral district in the world, claiming a population of scarcely 25,000 souls, which can present such a showing!

THE ANCIENT COPPER MINERS OF LAKE SUPERIOR.

BY JACOB HOUGHTON.

Geologists now find that the antiquity of man far antedates the era assigned to his creation by the received chronology, and submit the evidences of their belief to an enlightened public sentiment. However strange these new views with regard to the origin and history of our race may appear, they cannot be disregarded. We must weigh the value of observations, and press them to their legitimate conclusions. The investigator at this day must not be trammeled, in the language of Humboldt, by "an assemblage of dogmas bequeathed from one age to another"—"by a physical philosophy made up of popular errors."— J. W. Foster.

The preparation of this paper is undertaken at the urgent solicitation of the editor of this work. The limits into which it is necessary to condense the facts, and the deductions therefrom, are unavoidably contracted. To fully elucidate the subject, and to present the comparative proofs, would require a work of many pages, and involve an amount of labor that could be given only by those who have at their disposal the time to devote to the most fascinating study of the day—the pre-historic races of man. This will be the more fully appreciated when the general statement is made, that the traces which the ancient copper miners of Lake Superior have left of the work performed by them, indicate an intelligent and industrious race—that their mining labors extended through centuries of time—that there was a general movement to the southward, through a vast number of years, of the greater portion of the people—that on the route of this transition they have left a wonderful record of their works, proving an advancing and increasing intelligence, indicated by the ancient mounds throughout the United States, and the ultimate achievement, in the erection of the massive structures of Mexico and Central America. This advancement is also indicated in the lesser arts, in the gradual improvement in the numbers, forms and embellishments of the utensils of the household, and of ornaments for the person. Therefore, treating the subject with the brevity required, the writer will make no excuse for the use of postulates, while at the same time feeling confident that sufficient connected proofs exist to warrant the assumptions that may be made.

On the south shore of Lake Superior the works of the ancient miners extend over a district of country comprising what is known as the Trap range, having a length of one hundred and fifty miles through Keweenaw, Houghton and Ontonagon counties, Michigan, with a varying width of from four to seven miles. They also wrought the copper deposits of the Trap range of Isle Royale, covering an area of about forty miles in length by an average of five miles in width. Their mining operations were crude and primitive. The process was to heat the embedding rocks by building fires on the outcrops of the veins or belts, to partially disintegrate the rocks by contraction produced by the sudden throwing on of water, and to complete the removal of the pieces of native copper by mauling off the adhering particles of rock with stone hammers. This is attested by the presence, in all of the ancient pits, of large quantities of charcoal, and of numberless hammers, the latter showing marks of long usage. That the miners had not advanced to any knowledge of the artificial elevation of water, is shown by the fact that apparently, in all cases, the pits have only been sunk to a depth where the limit of man-power in bailing out the water is reached. Between the successive pits are ridges of unremoved rock and soil, rather indicating that they were left as dams to prevent the water from passing from a pit already filled with water into one in process of being wrought.

The pits, the charcoal, the stone hammers and the implements and tools, made of copper, are the only relics left of the race that wrought these mines. Neither a grave, vestige of a habitation, skeleton or bone has been found. Among the Indians inhabiting the region, from the earliest acquaintance of the white man, neither tradition or legend remained of these ancient miners. The Indians themselves had no knowledge of the existence of copper in the veins and belts, so thoroughly had the debris of ages covered them. Their knowledge was confined to the float pieces of copper in the soil.

When considering the extent of country previously stated, over which this mining work extended, the crude and slow process of the labor and the enormous amount of work performed, it becomes evident that the work extended through centuries of time, and was carried on by a vast number of people. The largest aggregation of ancient pits yet discovered is on what is known as the Minong belt on Isle Royale. Here, for a distance of one and three-fourths miles, and for an average width of four hundred feet, the successive pits indicate the mining out of the belt (solid rock) to an average depth of not less than twenty feet. Scattered over this ground are battered stone hammers, numberless, but running into the millions.

It is not to be presumed that these ancient people were unacquainted with the advantages of the division of labor. There were undoubtedly miners, bailers of water, and men whose part it was to manufacture tools and implements out of the pieces of rough native copper produced by the miners. Others were engaged in procuring and transporting food and other necessaries of life, and still others were employed in collecting and transporting from the shores of the lake the rounded, water-worn boulders of diorite and porphyry, which were used by the miners as hammers and sledges.

Many of these stone hammers have been grooved by manual attrition or impact for the purpose of fastening them into withes or split handles, but by far the greater number are unwrought. rounded boulders which have been held in

HOUGHTON, 1875 WITH COPPER SMELTING WORKS IN FOREGROUND.

the hand when in use. Mr. A. C. Davis, now of the Minong mine, informed me that at one place, near the mouth of the Ontonagon river, he had seen quite an area of ground strewn with stone chips and broken and discarded pieces of diorite and porphyry, indicating it to have been a workshop for preparing the hammers before being transported inland.

The ancient miners made few mistakes in the selection of deposits to be wrought. In almost every instance in the places where they had carried on extensive mine work, have been wrought the successful mines of these latter days. This fact is often quoted to advance the idea that those ancient people were gifted with some mysterious knowledge by which they were able to discover and trace out mineral veins or lodes. This day, when the divining rod is lost to faith, and the mysteries of the alchemist have been opened to full light by the science of chemistry, should be too late for such a superstition. The explorers of to-day have, as aids to discovery, the dip and the traverse needles, and still the most experienced and observing of them in the reconnoisance of the surface which overlies beds of magnetic iron ore, where the needles develop the most activity, are simply enabled to approximate conclusions, and are only satisfied when a full development has been made by a system of costeaning. It may be considered improbable that the ancient miners possessed any aid approaching to the value of the magnetic needles of the present day. It is far more reasonable to assume that the ancient miners, following comparatively close upon the recession of the glaciers, occupied the country at a period before the action of the elements had disintegrated the surface of the rocks, and when the mineral veins and beds or belts were exposed to view. In this connection should be stated the fact that, without exception, the copper deposits of the country are contained between the walls of hard rocks (crystalline trap) that have served the purpose of withstanding, to a great extent, the grinding force of the glaciers. In consequence of this protection, they occupy the high points of the country, and are now covered with a comparatively small depth of soil, the product of the disintegration of the rocks themselves; while the valleys of the rivers and the lowlands bordering the lake have a greater depth of drift, probably the deposits of the receding glacial period. At the time the ancient miners were carrying on their work, under a climate milder and far more inviting than now, these high points were destitute of soil or trees, and for timber and fuel for their mining work they resorted to the valleys of the streams and the lowlands bordering the great lake—where, also, were carried on their agricultural pursuits.

The implements and tools into which the pieces of native copper thus won from the rocks were fabricated, were axes, knives, chisels, fleshers, spears, daggers, arrow-heads, awls, needles and bracelets. These tools are found scattered in wonderful profusion, from Lake Superior to Central America, and from eastern Pennsylvania on the east, to Arizona on the west. In 1870 I saw, at Pittston, Pennsylvania, several of these tools, that had been recovered from the soil in that vicinity; and in a newspaper correspondence from Arizona, in the winter of 1874-5 (Detroit *Free Press*), I was not in the least surprised to see mentioned the discovery, in that territory, of what was called by the correspondent, a copper fountain. It matters not for what purpose the article may have been used; the fact of the find is sufficient for the present purpose. These tools, however, have been found in the greatest numbers buried in the works of the mound builders throughout Wisconsin, lower Michigan, Ohio, Indiana, Illinois, Iowa, Missouri, Tennessee, West Virginia, Kentucky, Mississippi and Louisiana.

Bernal Diaz, who accompanied Cortez in his expedition of the Conquest of Mexico, says that upon entering Tuspan they found that "each Indian had, besides his ornaments of gold, a *copper* axe, which was very highly polished, with handles curiously carved, as if to serve equally for an ornament and for the field of battle. We first thought these axes were made of an inferior kind of gold; we therefore commenced taking them in exchange, and in the space of ten days had collected *more than six hundred*, with which we were no less rejoiced, as long as we were ignorant of their real value, than the Indians with our glass beads."

When Columbus, in his fourth voyage, was visited at the Guanaja islands by a trading canoe of Yucatan, the crew, according to Herrara, had "small hatchets made of copper, small bells and plates."

That the copper from which these tools, scattered over such a vast area of country, were manufactured, came from the ancient mines of Lake Superior, does not admit of doubt. Although large and numerous deposits of copper ore are scattered through Arizona, New Mexico, Mexico, and Central and South America, there is no evidence that the aborigines of this country had sufficient metellurgical knowledge or skill to reduce the ores to refined copper. On the other hand, the great Creator, for provision to the wants of that ancient race, had planted on the shores of Lake Superior the only known workable deposits of native copper in the world. The term virgin copper is well used to denote its purity. In this latter day it outranks all others in the markets of the world.

The occurrence of this native metal in segregations of various weights, enabled the ancient miner to easily follow the deposit and to readily separate the pieces of metal from the containing rock. These segregations were peculiarly adapted for the use of the forgers of the tools. The extreme ductility of the metal, due to its purity, was also a provision of great advantage to the ancient artisan. In examining the tools that have been recovered, one is involuntarily amazed at the perfection of workmanship and at their identity in form with the tools made for like purposes and used at the present day, the prototypes of the implements of our present civilization. The sockets of the spears, chisels, arrow-heads, knives and fleshers are, in nearly all instances, formed as symmetrically and perfectly as could be done by the best smith of the present day, with all the improved aids to his art. The sockets of these tools, however, are in all instances left open on one side, showing no attempt at welding or brazing. While acknowledging that the greater portion of these tools were forged from the native metal, several investigators of the subject assert that many of them were cast. Their position is principally based on the observation of certain raised marks upon the tools, which are claimed to be the marks of the joining of molds. The writer believes that the weight of evidence is against the theory of melting and casting. It is probable that the raised marks are due to unequal oxidation, or to incompleteness of fabrication. Had the tools which are made with sockets been cast, it is reasonable to suppose that the sockets would have been cast complete. Without exception the sockets are all open on one side; on the sides of the open part lips are turned sufficient for holding the handles. The presence of spots of native silver in the tools is against the theory of casting. Native silver to a large extent is present with the copper throughout the region, and always as a distinct and separate metal, occurring in macules and strings upon and through the copper. In melting for casting, the two metals would form an alloy, and as the proportion of copper would be the greatest, the silver would not be visible. In all of the relics of the mound builders there is no evidence of any vessels that would serve the purposes of crucibles or melting pots. In excavating the mounds, pieces of galena are frequently reported to have been found lying in the immediate vicinity of the copper tools, but there is no record of any lead implements whatever. When it is considered that the melting point of lead is only 594 degrees, Fahrenheit, while that of copper is 2,548 degrees, it would certainly be remarkable if the ancient race had progressed so far in metallurgy as to melt the latter, and had failed to melt and utilize the former. None of the tools are hardened; they are simply pure native copper. Any process of alloying the copper with tin or zinc for the purpose of hardening, was entirely unknown to the race.

It is an established fact, that in the Old World (a gross misnomer as applied to the age of the Eastern hemisphere, when compared with that of the Western hemisphere) man in the Stone Age existed contemporaneously with the Siberian elephant, Siberian rhinoceros, mammoth, cave bear, etc., while scientists have been loth to concede the existence of the mound builders as contemporary with the mastodon, mammoth. etc., of the Western hemisphere. The mound builders have been not rightly, assigned to the more recent Age of Bronze.

Mr. J. W. Foster, in speaking of the discovery in Illinois of a copper knife and the bone of a mastodon in the same geological formation, and separated from each other but a few miles, says: "One of two suppositions is true,—either that here has been an intermingling of the relics of two distinct ages, or that if the synchronism is established, man on this continent, as a contemporary with the mastodon, was far in advance in the mechanical arts of man, as the contemporary of the fossil elephant on the European continent.

The existence of copper tools among the relics of the mound builders has been the stumbling block in this matter. In these metal implements of man in the Stone Age in America there was only the advance over the man of the Stone Age in Europe, that was due to the obtaining of *native copper* that could be hammered and drawn out into the desired shapes without any resort to the processes of metallurgy. It was with a view to this point that I have throughout this paper endeavored to constantly impress upon the reader the fact of the purity and ductility of the native copper. It was also for this that I so fully discussed above the reasons that lie against the theory of the melting of the copper and the casting of the tools. The relics of the Stone Age left by the mound builders are the stone hammers used for mining copper, and for hammering out copper tools—axes, hatchets, fleshers, pestles for pulverizing maize, chisels, knives, arrowheads, amulets, pendants, pipes, etc.—a list of sufficient extent to warrant the claim for the mound builders of the high antiquity of the Stone Age, and *at least* of a contemporaneous existence with the pre-historic man of Europe. As proof of the contemporaneous existence in this country of man with the mastodon, the following extracts are given from a paper of the late Dr. Koch, of St. Louis, Missouri, communicated to the St. Louis Academy of Sciences:

"In the year 1839 I discovered and disinterred in Gasconade county, Missouri, at a spot in the bottom of the Bourbeuse river, where there was a spring distant about four hundred yards from the bank of the river, the remains of the above named animals. The bones were sufficiently well preserved to enable me to decide positively that they belonged to the *mastadon giganteus*. Some remarkable circumstances were connected with the discovery. The greater portion of these bones had been more or less burned by fire. The fire had extended but a few feet beyond the space occupied by the animal before its destruction, and there was more than sufficient evidence on the spot that the fire had not been an accidental one, but on the contrary, that it had been kindled by human agency, and, according to all appearance, with the design of killing the huge creature, which had been found mired in the mud and in an entirely helpless condition. This was sufficiently proven by the situation in which I found, as well those parts of the bones untouched by fire as those which were more or less injured by it, or in part consumed; for I found the fore legs of the animal in a perpendicular position in the clay, with the toes attached to the feet, just in the manner in which they were when life departed from the body. I took particular care in uncovering the bones to ascertain their position beyond any doubt before I removed any part of them, and it appeared during the whole excavation fully evident that at the time when the animal in question found its untimely end the ground in which it had been mired must have been in a plastic condition, being now a grayish colored clay. All the bones which had not been burned by the fire had kept their original position, standing upright, and apparently quite undisturbed in the clay; whereas those portions which had been extended above the surface had been partially consumed by the fire, and the surface of the clay was covered, as far as the fire had extended, by a layer of wood ashes, mingled with larger or smaller pieces of charred wood and burnt bones, together with bones belonging to the spine, ribs and other parts of the body, which had been more or less injured by the fire.

"The fire appeared to have been most destructive around the head of the animal. Some small remains of the head were left unconsumed, but enough to show that they belonged to the mastodon. There were also found, mingled with the ashes and bones, and partly protruding out of them, a large number of broken pieces of rock, which had evidently been carried thither from the shore of the Bourbeuse river, to be hurled at the animal by his destroyers, for the above-mentioned layer of clay was entirely void even of the smallest pebbles; whereas, on going to the river I found the stratum of clay cropping out of the bank and resting on a layer of shelving rocks of the same kind as the fragments, from which place it was evident they had been carried to the scene of action. The layers of ashes, etc., varied in thickness from two to six inches, from which it may be inferred that the fire had been kept up for some length of time. It seemed that the burning of the victim and the hurling of rocks at it had not satisfied the destroyers, for I found also among the ashes, bones and rocks, several arrow heads, a stone spear head and stone axes, which were taken out in the presence of a number of witnesses, consisting of the people of the neighborhood, attracted by the novelty of the excavation. The layer of ashes, etc., was covered by a strata of alluvial deposits, consisting of clay, sand and soil from eight to nine feet thick."

The preceding statements and reasonings are, therefore, sufficient for the position that the ancient miners and mound builders were contemporaneous with the mastadon, and were occupying this country at a period corresponding with the Stone Age of Europe.

The mound builders were not confined to the occupation of the country lying to the South of Lake Superior. Well attested and authenticated statements are made of the existence of the well-known artificial mounds in the valley of the Red River of the North, throughout Dakota, Montana and British Columbia. It is possible that future-explorers may trace their works still further to the northwest than investigators of this day dare predict.

It is generally conceded that during the glacial period North America was covered with ice between the Rocky Mountains and the Atlantic coast, and from the north pole nearly to the tropics. There is sufficient evidence to suggest the belief that man inhabited the tropics as early, at least, as the latter portion of the glacial period. On the recession and disappearance of the glaciers, probably accompanied with a subsidence, beneath the ocean, of a large portion of the northern continent, and followed by a modified, warm and genial climate, man, together with the mastodon, mammoth. etc., moved north and occupied the land to a comparatively high latitude. This movement, of course, occupied many ages. Subsequently there was a gradual elevation of the land above the ocean—causing a gradual change, through long time, in the temperature of the country until brought finally as it now exists. It was during the changes of this period that the copper miners and mound builders flourished. The effect of the final change in temperature, due to the elevation of the continent, was to drive this race further and further southward, until the seat and centre of their power became fixed in the Mississippi and Ohio valleys, and in the region of the great lakes. In this southward movement it is possible that the drones were left behind, and the nomadic people of the far north, and some of the tribes of worthless and shiftless Indians that it is impossible to win to industrious lives, have descended from the outcasts of the people who were the miners of copper and the builders of the mounds.

The Mexican records, as interpreted by the Abbe Brasseur de Bourbourg, are to the effect that the mound builders were finally driven from the Mississippi valley by prolonged and continuous incursions of fierce, predatory and warlike tribes which came from the west. Leaving their long occupied homes, they became dwellers in Mexico and Central America, and leading participators in the work of the early civilization that was the glory of those countries. The *beginning* of this forced migration, according to Abbe Brasseur, was more than a thousand years before the Christian era. How long prior to this was the first occupation of the Mississippi valley by this ancient people? is a question the writer will not attempt to answer. The writer, however, does believe, that in the height of their power the population of that portion of the United States occupied by those ancients, was equal in numbers to the present population of the same area. As previously stated, the mound builders were intelligent and industrious people. They followed peaceful pursuits, and their works bear evidence of the efficiency of their government. Their staple food was maize. Their works do not exist on the Atlantic coast except far to the south. Their pursuits being agricultural, they occupied the Mississippi and Ohio valleys and the Lake region as the country most suitable for those purposes,—thus being the precursors of the present race of men who, led by the same instincts, are occupying the same lands, and for the same purposes, but with an advanced civilization which is capable of making the territory once occupied by the mound builders of the Stone Age, the grain producing country for the world, and the centre of governmental power. The mound builders being driven out, their territory was occupied by their assailants. Under the sway of a nomadic and warlike people the works of the ancient race were left to decay, and their cultivated fields ran to waste. Thus, through centuries, was rest given to the soil, in order to renew fertility and prepare it for the occupation of our present race. After us—is in the future.

IRON.

The early missionaries, who were the first to announce to the civilized world the existence of copper on Lake Superior, appear not to have discovered the fact that iron ore was also one of the great natural resources of this region. In their "relacions," they refer to "mines" of copper, silver, tin, lead and antimony, but do not seem to have learned from the savages the fact that there were also mountains of iron ore. It is true that Truchement Brusle assured "Lagarde" that in the country of the Souriquois, (wherever that may have been,) there were "not only mines of copper, but also of steel," and, "it seems that one might find mines of iron if one would take the trouble of searching, and go to some expense;" but this seems to have been mere conjecture on his part. It was long afterwards that the Holy Fathers traversed the south shore of the Great Lake, from Sault Ste. Marie to Fond du Lac, and if they found iron ore, or were informed of its existence by the Indians, they certainly did not consider it of sufficient importance to speak of it in connection with their other discoveries. It is more than probable, too, that the Indians themselves did not, at that time, have any knowledge of the value, or the purposes for which iron was used—or if they did, knew nothing of its extraction from the ore, or from whence it came. At all events, it was two hundred years after the missionaries first made known the existence of copper in this region, that the whites first learned from the Indians there were also "mines" of iron as well as of copper. It is a noticeable fact that the pioneers in the development of the Lake Superior iron mines came here originally in search for copper, and with no definite knowledge of the existence of iron anywhere on the lake.

Who were the original discoverers of **iron ore on Lake Superior** (after the Indians) has been to some extent a disputed question. There have been **and are still a number of** claimants, but we believe it is an **honor which belongs not exclusively** to any one **person. The person or persons who first made** known **to the world the existence of workable deposits of** iron ore in **this region, and those who, acting upon that** information, came after them **and engaged in the laborious and almost hopeless task** of **development, are the ones to** whom the future historian **will give the meed of** praise. **The** first of these was *William A. Burt*, Deputy Surveyor under Dr. Houghton, **in 1844.**

When Dr. Houghton, as previously related in this volume, prevailed upon **the** General Government to grant an additional allowance for **the linear** surveys of the upper peninsula, **in** order that a geological examination of the district might **be** combined with it, he placed **Mr.** Burt in charge of the field **work,** giving him as compensation the whole amount **of the** government allowance, reserving nothing for **himself.**

In the summer of 1844, Mr. Burt, with **a** party **consisting of** William **Ives, Jacob** Houghton, R. S. Mellen, Harvey Mellen, James **King, and two** Indians named Taylor and Doner, was engaged in **running out** the township lines, and **making** such **geological** observations as **required by the terms of** his agreement **with Dr. H. All** the members of this party, with the exception **of Mr.** Burt **and** the **two Indians, are,** we believe, still living.

On the 15th of September the **party reached the lake, and** established the northeast corner of town 47 **north, range 25** west, about midway between the deltas **of** the Carp **and** Chocolay rivers. From thence **they** ran the township line between towns 47 and **48, and camped** at the east end of **Teal** Lake on the 18th. **The** discovery of iron ore the next **day, is** thus related by **Jacob** Houghton, Esq. :

"**On** the morning of the 19th of September, 1844, **we started** to run **the** line south, between ranges 26 **and** 27. **So soon as we reached** the hill to the south of **the** lake, the compass-man, (Mr. Ives,) began to notice the fluctuation in the variation of the magnetic needle. We were, of course, using the solar compass, of which Mr. Burt was the inventor, and I shall never forget the excitement of the old gentleman when viewing the changes of the variation—the needle not actually traversing alike in any two places. He kept changing his position to take observations, all the time saying, 'How would they survey this country without my compass? What *could* be done here without my compass?' It was the full and complete realization of what he had foreseen when struggling through the first stages of his invention. At length the compass-man called for us all to 'come and see a variation that will beat them all.' As we looked at the instrument, to our astonishment the north end of the needle was traversing a few degrees to the south of west. Mr. Burt called out, 'Boys, look around and see what you can find!' We all left the line, some going to the east, some going to the west, and all of us returned with specimens of iron ore, mostly gathered from outcrops. This was along the first mile from Teal Lake. We carried out all the specimens we could, conveniently."

Hon. J. N. Mellen, of Romeo, Michigan, has still in his possession one of the specimens found that day. This, it may safely be asserted, was the first discovery, by white men, of iron ore on Lake Superior. The line referred to, on the first mile of which these discoveries were made, is the east boundary of the section upon which the celebrated Jackson mine was afterwards found and opened. As, however, the Jackson ore is not magnetic, and does not outcrop on the line in question, it is more than probable it was not seen by the party, but that the specimens were taken from one or more of the flag or soft hematite ranges further east and south.

In the month of June, 1845, Dr. Houghton and Mr. Burt, while engaged in subdividing town 47 north, range 26 west, made a more particular examination with reference to iron ore, especially at the corner of sections 29, 30, 31 and 32, which sections were afterwards known as the Cascade (now Palmer) mines, and both ventured the assertion to Jacob

Houghton and other members of the party, that the deposits were very valuable, and would some day be made the basis of an active and profitable industry.

To the government surveyors, therefore, belongs the credit of having first given to the world information of the existence of iron in considerable quantities in the country bordering the south shore of Lake Superior. Such is the fact established not only by the published reports of those who had charge of the surveys, but one which is fully attested by living witnesses, who were themselves members of the party by whom the first discoveries were made. Such being incontestably the case, it is a little singular that Dr. Jackson, in his report of 1849, should have been in doubt as to the facts, or, as he appears to have done, assumed to give the credit to others. He says that in the summer of 1844, during his first visit to the Lake, he obtained from Peter B. Barbeau, then a trader at Sault Ste. Marie, a fine specimen of specular iron ore which had been given to Mr. B. by an Indian chief. He also learned at the same time that this chief knew of a mountain mass of ore, somewhere between the head of Keweenaw bay and the headwaters of the Menominee river, The next summer he informed Mr. Lyman Pray, of Charlestown, Mass., what he had heard, and suggested to him the propriety of looking up the mountain in question. Mr. Pray immediately proceeded to the Sault, where he employed the son of the Ojibway chief as a guide, and went with him to L'Anse; from thence, guided by the Indian, he traversed the then unbroken forest and found the mountain. On his return he informed Dr. Jackson that he had traveled four miles around the mountain and found only the same kind of ore, *and no rocks*. To Mr. Pray, therefore, he ascribes the honor of the first practical discovery of iron ore in the upper peninsula of Michigan, saying that "no linear surveys had then been made, and it is probable no white man had ever before explored that locality." It is barely possible that it may have been the Republic "mountain" which Mr. Pray found and explored; but if so, he must have been a novice, else he would have been able to find something more than specular iron ore, and, at least, a *few* rocks. It is noticeable, however, that Prof. Jackson does not once refer to the discoveries made by Mr. Burt and his party the year previous, although a catalogue of the specimens found by them fills three whole pages of the same volume of "Public Documents" in which his own report was originally published.

Mr. Barbeau himself (he still resides at the Sault Ste. Marie), informs us that the existence of iron ore in the upper peninsula was known to the white traders as early as 1830. He claims to have known of the iron deposits on the Jackson, Cleveland, and Lake Superior locations, fifteen years before the discoveries made by Mr. Burt, and says that the Indians not only knew at that time of the existence of iron ore, but that he had seen in their possession native lead sufficiently pure to be used in making rifle balls, and that they did so use it. But they never could be persuaded to tell where they found it, and up to this day have refused to give any information which would lead to its discovery. Mr. Barbeau was an old Indian trader, having entered the employ of the American Fur Company in 1827, and no man, perhaps, in the upper peninsula is more familiar with its early history. We can see no reason to doubt his statements; but it is more than probable that he had little appreciation of the extent or value of the iron deposits, of the existence of which he claims to have been aware as early as 1830. At all events it does not appear that he ever profited by his knowledge, but allowed others to step in, and by right of discovery, reap the harvest which he might have garnered. According to his further statement, Achille Cadotte, a French and Indian half-breed, was, in 1845, informed by an old Indian chief, then living at the mouth of Carp river, (now within the corporate limits of the city of Marquette,) that he knew where there was a mountain of iron ore, and went with the chief to see it. The name of this chief was "Man-je-ki-jik," (Moving Day.) Cadotte then communicated his discovery to Mr. John Westren, (?) who went with him to the mountain, and under his direction about a ton of the ore was carried down from what is now the Jackson mine to the mouth of the Carp, taken from there to the Sault in canoes, and thence to Detroit. That Mr. Barbeau is mistaken in at least one particular, is proved by the well substantiated fact that Mr. Westren did not visit Lake Superior until 1846.

In June, 1845, a company was organized at Jackson, Michigan, for the purpose of exploring the mineral regions on the south shore of Lake Superior. The company consisted of P. M. Everett, James Ganson, S. T. Carr, G. W. Carr, F. W. Carr, E. S. Rockwell, F. W. Kirtland, W. H. Munroe, A. W. Ernst, Fairchild Farrand, Abram V. Berry, John Westren, and S. A. Hastings. The articles of association were filed July 23d, 1845, and named Abram V. Berry as *President*, Frederick W. Kirtland as *Secretary*, Philo M. Everett as *Treasurer*, and George W. Carr and William A. Ernst *Trustees*.

The same day that the articles of association were executed, (July 23d.) a party of explorers, consisting of P. M. Everett, S. T. Carr, W. H. Munroe, and E. S. Rockwell, started for Lake Superior, and secured what is now the Jackson Mine. This party appears to have been under the leadership of Mr. Everett, who is now one of the oldest and most respected citizens of Marquette. While at Sault Ste. Marie, on their way up, Louis Nolan, a half-breed, told Everett and his party, of the existence of iron ore on Lake Superior, (Mr. Burt's discoveries of the year previous not being generally known,) and volunteered to go along and show them where it was. He accompanied the party to the mouth of the Carp, and all went as far as Teal Lake in search of the iron, but failed to find it. Returning to the mouth of the Carp, they proceeded on their way to Copper Harbor, the place for which they had originally set out. The enterprise was originally undertaken with a view to exploring for copper, and it is probable that the idea of finding iron was not seriously entertained until the exploring party reached the Sault and saw Nolan.

After leaving the mouth of the Carp, the party coasted up

the lake to Copper Harbor, where they fell in with the Indian Chief Man-je-ki-jik, who returned with them to the mouth of the Carp, and guided the party to the Jackson Mountain. That Mr. Everett was really the moving spirit in this, the first iron mining enterprise on the lake, would appear from the following letter written by him to Capt G. D. Johnson, late of the Lake Superior Mine. The letter, the original of which we have seen and read, is dated "Jackson, Mich., Nov. 10th, 1845," and is as follows:

"Since I have returned from Lake Superior, Charles tells me he promised to let you know all about my excursion, and wishes me to perform the task for him. In compliance with his request, I will therefore try and give you a brief description of my trip. I left here on the 23d of July last, and was gone till the 24th of October. I had some idea of going to Lake Superior last winter, but did not think seriously of going until a short time before I left. *I had considerable difficulty in getting any one to join me in the enterprise, but I at last succeeded in forming a company of thirteen.* I was appointed treasurer and agent, to explore and make locations, for which last purpose we had secured seven permits from the Secretary of War. I took four men with me from Jackson, and hired a guide at the Sault, where I bought a boat, and coasted up the lake to Copper Harbor, which is over 300 miles from the Sault Ste. Marie. There are no white men on Lake Superior except those who go there for mining purposes. We incurred many dangers and hardships. * * * * We made several locations—one of which we called Iron at the time. It is a mountain of solid iron ore, 150 feet high. The ore looks as bright as a bar of iron just broken. Since coming home we have had some of it smelted, and find that it produces iron and something resembling gold—some say it is gold and copper. Our location is one mile square, and we shall send a company of men up in the spring to begin operations. Our company is called the Jackson Mining Company. * * *
* * * * "Yours, etc.;
P. M. EVERETT."

The actual discovery of the Jackson Mountain was made by S. T. Carr and E. S. Rockwell, members of Mr. Everett's party. They were, as stated, guided to the locality by the Indian chief, but the superstition of the savage not allowing him to approach the spot, Carr and Rockwell continued the search alone, Mr. Everett having, for some reason, returned to the mouth of the Carp. The precise spot where this discovery was made, was until a year or two ago, and may be yet, distinguished by the remains of a huge pine stump, the upturned roots of which revealed to Carr and Rockwell the first knowledge of an iron range from which nearly ten million tons of ore have since been mined. The trunk of this tree, which at the time of their visit had been freshly uprooted, was afterwards sawn into lumber and carefully preserved to be afterwards manufactured into mementoes.

Eleven members of the Jackson Company, immediately after its organization, procured permits from the War Department to locate one square mile each of mineral land on the south shore of Lake Superior. The manner of locating lands with these permits, has already been described in this volume. The townships had not then been sub-divided, and the lands covered by permits could only be described by such permanent boundaries as would admit of their being entered on a map kept for that purpose in the office of the Mineral Land Agent. At the time of Mr. Everett's first visit, the country for twenty-five miles west of Presque Isle had been plastered over with these permits. The first one located was surveyed from a designated point or object near the mouth of Dead river, and being entered on the map, formed the eastern, southern or northern boundary of the next location. The "square mile" on which the Jackson is situated, had been located with permit No. 158, granted to D. Hamilton, of Watervliet, New York, who appears to have been wholly ignorant of its immense undeveloped wealth. Everett and his party, in their effort to secure their discovery, were unable to describe the land accurately, and made Teal Lake (not then marked on the agency map) its northern boundary. The mineral agent, not **knowing the exact** locality of the lake, entered the location so **that it** appeared **on the** map about twelve miles southeast **of where** it should **have been**. In a little book published by **Mr. Jacob** Houghton, in 1846, **we** find a reference **to** the Jackson location, in **which the** property is described as having been located by "**Permit No.** 593, somewhere in town 46 **north,** range 27 or 28 west," **the Hamilton** permit being marked on section 1 of town **47, range 27.** The locations made under these permits were entered **on the** map at the Mineral Land Office in pencil tracings, **so they** could be lifted and transferred at the option of the **owners.** When Everett **and his** party announced their discovery **of iron ore** and exhibited their specimens **the** owners of adjacent locations began to examine their **lands, and** failing to make **similar** discoveries, lifted their **permits and** transferred them **elsewhere.** As soon **as** Hamilton **abandoned his, the** Jackson **company** managed **to find** the **township lines, secured** a **transfer of** their permit, **and when the township was** subdivided, bought the land, section 1, **town 47 north, range** 27 **west,** at $2.50 per acre.

In the spring of 1846, another expedition was fitted out, consisting of A. **V.** Berry, F. W. Kirtland, E. **S.** Rockwell and **W. H. Munroe,** members of the Jackson Company, **and** several others. **The** object of this visit, as stated by Mr. Berry, **was to make further** explorations and **to use** the remaining permits on other **locations.** He **says:**

"**I found** our location much **beyond what I had** anticipated. After spending twelve days **in the woods, exploring** the surrounding country, including **what was afterwards known** as the Cleveland location, and building **what we called a** house, we returned to the mouth of **the Carp with 300** pounds of ore **on our** backs. We there **divided; one party was left** to keep possession **of** the **location, another** went farther up the lake to use the remaining **permits, while** I returned to the Sault with the ore. It was my intention at this time to use another permit on the Cleveland location, **but** on arriving at **the** Sault **I** met Dr. Cassels, **of Cleveland,** agent of a Cleveland

Company, and having arranged with him that his company should pay a portion of the expense of keeping possession, making roads, &c., I discovered to him the whereabouts of the Cleveland location. He took my canoe, visited the location, and secured it by a permit. On arriving at Jackson we endeavored on two occasions to smelt the ore which I had brought down, in our common cupola furnaces, but failed entirely. In August of the same year, Mr. Olds, of Cucush Prairie, who owned a forge (in which he was making iron from bog ore,) then undergoing repairs, succeeded in making fine bar of iron from our ore in a blacksmith's fire—*the first iron ever made from Lake Superior ore.* In the winter of 1846-'47, we began to get up at Jackson a bellows and other machinery for constructing a forge on the Carp; and in the summer of 1847 a company of men commenced building the same, and continued until March, 1848, when a freshet carried away the dam. * * * * The association was then, (1848) merged into an incorporated company, and by some means the pioneers in the enterprise are now all out."*

One end of this first bar of iron Mr. Everett had drawn out into a knife blade the better to exhibit the superior qualities of the metal.

The first comparatively thorough exploration of the Jackson location was made by Fairchild Farrand, in 1846, in the summer of which year some ore was mined. The old Jackson or Carp River forge, to which Mr. Berry alludes in his letter, was built under the supervision of William McNair, and was begun in 1847. It was located on the Carp River, about three miles east of Negaunee, and a short distance north of the old county road. It was finished early in 1848, the first iron being made on the 10th of February, 1848, by forgeman Ariel N. Barney, who now resides at Huron, Ohio. Mr. Barney, in additon to having been the pioneer iron maker on Lake Superior, established the first hotel at Marquette, was one of the first justices of the peace, an office which he held many years, and was afterwards Clerk and Register, as well

*Brooks' Geological Report, 1873.

as Judge of Probate. He was one of the hardiest among the early pioneers, and though upwards of sixty years of age, served as a private soldier in the war of the rebellion.

The Jackson forge was a primitive affair. The power was supplied by the Carp, across which a dam eighteen feet high was constructed. There were eight fires, from each of which a lump was taken every six hours, placed under the hammer, and forged into blooms four inches square and two feet long—the daily product being about three tons. It required two six-horse teams to draw this product to the mouth of the Carp, over ten miles of the most horrible road imaginable.

Soon after starting up, a freshet carried away the dam, and the forge remained idle until some time in the summer of 1848, when Mr. Everett came up as the agent of the company, had the dam repaired, and resumed the manufacture of blooms. The first blooms made at this forge—the first iron made on Lake Superior, and the first from Lake Superior ores, (except the small bar made by Mr. Olds,) was sold to the late E. B. Ward, and from it was made the walking-beam of the side-wheel steamer "Ocean." This forge was kept in operation till 1854, when it was finally abandoned, having proved anything but a profitable investment for the owners, or indeed any of the lessees by whom it was carried on the last four years of its existence. These lessees were first, B. F. Eaton, of Columbus, Ohio, who was ruined by it, financially, in less than six months. He was succeeded by the Clinton Iron Company, an association of forgemen from Clinton County, New York. The corporators of this Company were Azel Lathrop, H. Butler, Charles Parish and Daniel Brittell. Mr. Lathrop now resides at Centerville, on the Peninsula Division of the Chicago and Northwestern Railway, and Mr. Brittell is a resident of Marquette. These four gentlemen had previously been employed at the forge, and the company was formed for the special purpose of leasing and operating the works. The market price of blooms being at that time much below the cost of production, the company lost money, and after a brief period, suspended work. Hon. Peter White next tried his hand as lessee, with no better results; lastly, J. P. Pendill, Esq., took hold of the concern, but did not meet with the success his pluck and energy merited. Altogether, the forge made little iron and no money.

On the 6th of June, 1848, a meeting of the "Jackson Mining Company" was held, and an act of incorporation, passed by the legislature the preceding winter, was accepted, and the company re-incorporated under a special charter. The officers elected were—Fairchild Farrand, *President;* W. A. Ernst, *Secretary;* George Foot, *Treasurer;* F. W. Carr, F. W. Kirtland, Lewis Bascom, and John Westren, *Directors.* The capital stock of the company was fixed at $300,000, in shares of the par value of $100, the object of the company being the mining of copper, as well as iron. An amendment to the charter was obtained in 1849, by which the title of the corporation was changed to the "Jackson Iron Company," of which Ezra Jones was *President;* W. A. Ernst *Secretary;* John Watson, *Treasurer;* S. H. Kimball, James A. Dyer and James Day, *Directors.*

The first shipment of ore from the region was made in 1850, and consisted of about *five tons*, which was taken away by Mr. A. L. Crawford, of Newcastle, Pa. Mr. Crawford was then, as now, the proprietor of large iron works, and a part of this ore was made into blooms and rolled into merchant bars, to test its qualities. The iron was found to be most excellent, and served to attract the attention of Pennsylvania iron masters to this new field of supply for their furnaces and rolling mills. The same summer, Gen. Curtis, proprietor of large iron works at Sharon, Pa., came up to inspect the Jackson and Cleveland mines, his object being to obtain an interest in one or both, with a view of obtaining for his furnaces, a supply of ore of a better quality than he was then using. He succeeding in buying up enough of the Jackson stock to give him the control of its affairs, and for several years afterwards the location was generally known as "Sharon." In 1852, about seventy tons of Jackson ore was taken to Sharon and there made into pig iron in the "Old Clay" furnace.

Up to 1860 the history of the Jackson Company was simply a record of disappointments and financial embarrassment; there were frequent changes of management, until in 1861, the present board of directors, or a majority of them, were chosen. The breaking out of the war of the Rebellion occasioned a great demand for iron, and gave a new impetus to the development of the Lake Superior mines. In 1862 the Jackson Company declared its first dividend, and since then there has not been a time when its stock could be purchased for less than five times its par value. The managers are very reticent in regard to its affairs, and we are unable even to approximate its total net earnings since 1861, but feel safe in saying that they have been sufficiently large to be partitioned into handsome individual fortunes among the shareholders.

The first regular exportation of ore from the Jackson mine began in 1856, in which year about 5,000 tons were shipped to lower lake ports. Previous to that year, there had been mined about 25,000 tons, which had been converted into blooms at the Carp River and Marquette forges.

THE MARQUETTE IRON COMPANY.

In the summer of 1848, Edward Clark, of Worcester, Mass., came to Lake Superior in the interest of Boston parties, to explore for copper. While at Sault Ste. Marie he met Robert J. Graveraet, who persuaded him to stop at Carp River and examine the iron deposits. The Jackson company's forge was at work at the time, and Clark was so favorably impressed with what he saw that he returned home without visiting the copper region, taking with him one of the blooms, and specimens of ore from the Jackson location. The bloom being drawn into wire at a factory, proved the excellence of the iron, and Clark proceeded to form an association for the purpose of building a forge on Lake Superior, assisted by Graveraet. The latter went to Worcester that winter, (traveling to Saginaw from Mackinaw on snow shoes,) and together with Clark succeeded in enlisting a number of gentlemen in the enterprise, among them Amos R. Harlow, Esq., now one of the wealthiest and most respected citizens of Marquette. Against the capital of the others Clark and Graveraet were to put in leases of iron lands of which they claimed to be the owners, and accordingly Mr. Harlow, who was the owner of a small machine shop, constructed and purchased the necessary machinery for the projected works, and in the spring of 1849 shipped it to Lake Superior, following, with his family, a month or two later. Graveraet had preceded him, with a party of men, among whom was Hon. Peter White, then a mere lad, but who has since become one of the wealthiest and most honored citizens of the region. Where now stands the beautiful and flourishing city of Marquette, there was then no sign of a human habitation, save one or two Indian huts, and a small log warehouse, belonging to the Jackson Mining Company.

From a paper prepared and read by Mr. White, before a Marquette audience, in April, 1870, the following extracts are taken:*

"It was from this island, (Mackinaw,) twenty-one years ago this month that the little, (and, I might say almost worthless) steamer 'Tecumseh' took her departure for Sault Ste. Marie. It was a tempestuous April morning; the seas rolled mountain high, and before she had accomplished many miles a huge wave took off the yawl boat, swept through the steamer's gangways, washed overboard much of the freight from the decks, alarmed the passengers, and brought Captain Pratt to the conclusion that he had better turn his craft and run her for the haven of safety he had left only a few hours before. This steamer was not as fleet as the famous chief whose name she bore. He could probably have beaten her best speed, on foot and through a " thicket." Still, she did reach her starting point, and after a delay of twenty-four hours for repairs, she again started on her trip. There were many more passengers on board than the boat had either eating or

---

*The editor runs the risk of incurring Mr. White's displeasure in making these extracts, having qualifiedly promised not to make such use of his paper; but they are so important as a part of the early history of the region that he has concluded to publish it almost in full and brave the consequences.

sleeping accommodations for; but it was not intended that she should be more than twelve hours making the trip. * *

"On board were a party specially bound to settle and start the city of Marquette, and to claim and undertake to develop *all* the iron mountains that had then been, or should subsequently be discovered. The head and leader of this party was the lamented Robert J. Graveraet. At that time he was a fit leader for any great enterprise that required the exercise of pluck, energy and perseverance. He had an indomitable will, a commendable ambition and a splendid physical organization, capable of enduring an untold amount of fatigue, a disposition firm, yet gentle and generous to a fault, a figure that for grace, beauty, noble bearing and symmetrical proportions, I have never seen equaled. He had many virtues, but his end was sad indeed. Many a man without a tithe of the noble qualities he possessed, holds a place in history as a great hero.

"There were ten in our party, all but three of whom are now dead. The survivors are, Dr. E. C. Rogers, now a practicing physician of some note in Chicago, (a brother of Randolph Rogers, the sculptor,) James Chapman, for many years past a resident of Bayfield, Wisconsin, and myself. I have resided here continuously ever since.

"But I have digressed and got ahead of my story. The lively little steamer, (lively with bed bugs,) after threshing around several hours, finally got inside of the Detour, and there met with solid ice, two to three feet thick, and there were no indications of a speedy thaw. The boat was run about half her length into the ice, when some of the passengers debarked and ran up it in all directions. Some essayed the cutting of a canal with saws and axes, but soon gave it up as a slow job. The next day we backed out and tried another passage by way of the Bruce mines, and thus succeeded in hammering our way through to the Sault in just ten days from the time we left Mackinaw. In the meantime we had a bread riot, an insurrection, and once the boat sunk to her deck full of water. She would have remained there perhaps forever, but for the aid of an old fellow, we had named

"Old Saleratus," and at whom we had poked all manner of fun. He proved to be a ship carpenter, and after we had unloaded the boat and pumped her up, he found the leak, put in a new plank, and we proceeded on our way. * *

"We succeeded in crowding our large Mackinaw barge up the rapids or falls, at Sault Ste. Marie, and embarking ourselves and provisions, set sail on Lake Superior for the Carp River Iron Region. After eight days of rowing, towing, poling and sailing, we landed on the spot immediately in front of where Mr. George Craig's dwelling now stands. That was then called Indian town, and was the landing place of the Jackson Company. We put up that night at the "Cedar House," of Charley Bawgam. It is true his rooms were not many, but he gave us plenty to eat, clean and well cooked. I remember that he had fresh venison, wild ducks and geese, fresh fish, good bread and butter, coffee and tea, and splendid potatoes.

"The next morning we started for the much talked of iron hills; each one had a pack-strap and blanket, and was directed to exercise his own discretion in putting into a pack what he thought he could carry. I put up forty pounds and marched bravely up the hills with it for a distance of two miles, by which time I was about as good as used up. Graveraet came up, and taking my pack on top of his, a much heavier one, marched on with both, as if mine was only the addition of a feather, while I trudged on behind, and had hard work to keep up. Graveraet seeing how fatigued I was, invited me to get on top of his load, saying he would carry me too, and he could have done it, I believe; but I had too much pride to accept his offer. When we arrived at the little brook which runs by George Rublein's old brewery, we made some tea and lunched, after which I felt so much refreshed that I took my pack and carried it without much difficulty to what is now known as the Cleveland mine, then known as Moody's location. On our way we had stopped a few minutes at the Jackson forge, where we met Mr. Everett, Charles Johnson, Alexander McKerchie, A. N. Barney, N. E. Eddy, Nahum

Keyes, and some others. At the Cleveland, we found Capt. Sam. Moody and John H. Mann, who had spent the previous summer and winter there. I well remember how astonished I was the next morning, when Captain Moody asked me to go with him to dig some potatoes for breakfast. He took a hoe and an old tin pail, and we ascended the high hill now known as the Marquette Iron Co.'s Mountain, and on its pinacle, found half an acre partially cleared and planted to potatoes. He opened but one or two hills when his pail was filled with large and perfectly sound potatoes—and then said, 'I may as well pull a few parsnips and carrots for dinner to save coming up again'—and sure enough, he had them there in abundance. This was in the month of May.

"From this time till the 10th of July, we kept possession of all the iron mountains then known, west of the Jackson, employing our time fighting mosquitoes at night, and the black flies through the day; perhaps a small portion of it was given to denuding the iron hills of extraneous matter. preparing the way for the immense products that have since followed. On the 10th of July, we came away from the mountains, bag and baggage, arriving at the lake shore, as we then termed it, before noon. Mr. Harlow had arrived with quite a number of mechanics, some goods, lots of money, and what was better than all, we got a glimpse of some female faces. We were all much excited, and buoyant with the hope of a bright and dazzling future before us.

"At one o'clock of that day we commenced clearing the site of the present city of Marquette, though we called it Worcester in honor of Mr. Harlow's native city. We began by chopping off the trees and brush, at the point of rocks near the brick blacksmith shop, just south of the shore end of the Cleveland ore docks. We cut the trees close to the ground and then threw them bodily over the bank on to the lake shore; then, under the direction of Capt. Moody, we began the construction of a dock, which was to stand like the ancient pyramids, for future ages to wonder at and admire! We did this by carrying these whole trees into the water and piling them in tiers, crosswise, until the pile was even with the surface of the water. Then we wheeled sand and gravel upon it, and by the end of the second day we had completed a structure which we looked upon with no little pride. Its eastward, or outer end was *solid* rock, and all inside of that was solid dirt, brush and leaves. *We* could not see why it should not stand as firm and as long as the adjacent beach itself! A vessel was expected in a few days, with a large lot of machinery and supplies, and we rejoiced in the fact that we had a dock upon which they could be landed. On the third day we continued to improve it by corduroying the surface, and by night of that day it was, in our eyes, a thing of beauty to behold. Our chagrin may be imagined, when on rising the next morning we found that a gentle sea had come in during the night and wafted our dock to some unknown point. Not a trace of it remained; not even a poplar leaf was left to mark the spot. The sand of the beach was as clean and smooth as if it had never been disturbed by the hand of man. I wrote in the smooth sand, with a stick; 'this is the spot where Captain Moody built his dock.' The Captain trod upon the record, and said I would get my discharge at the end of the month, but he either forgot or forgave the affront. It was a long time before any one had the hardihood to attempt the building of another dock.

"The propellers would come to anchor, sometimes as far as two miles from the shore, and the freight and passengers had to be landed in small boats. Our large boilers, when they arrived, were plugged, thrown overboard, and floated ashore, and the other machinery was landed with our Mackinaw boat, or a scow which we had constructed. Cattle and horses were always pitched overboard and made to swim ashore.

"Under the lead of James Kelly, the boss carpenter, who was from Boston, we improved our time after six o'clock, each evening, in erecting a log house for sleeping quarters for our particular party. When finished we called it the Revere House, after the hotel of that name in Boston. This building stood on its original site as late as 1860. * * *

About this time we realized the necessity of procuring hay for our stock. A man called Jim Presque Isle informed Captain Moody that he knew of a large meadow a short distance above Presque Isle, covered with superb blue-joint grass; the only trouble was that it was flooded with water too deep to admit of mowing, but he thought we could, with shovels, in a few hours, cut a drain out to the lake which would carry the water off. So off we started in our boat, armed with shovels, axes, scythes, rakes and pitchforks. Capt. Moody nervously staked out the ground for the canal, and we dug each way from the centre for four or five hours, and at last opened both ends, simultaneously, when to our consternation the waters of the lake rushed in and raised that on the meadow three or four inches! We were not more than five minutes embarking all our tools and getting off. We tried to keep still about the matter, but it leaked out some way, and was the source of a great deal of sport.

"We continued clearing up the land south of Superior street, preparing the ground for a forge, machine shop, sawmill and coal house. Sometime in August, the schooner Fur Trader arrived, bringing a large number of Germans, some Irish, and a few French. Among this party were August Machts, George Rublein, Francis Dolf, and Patrick, James and Michael Atfield. All these have resided here continuously up to the present time, have been and are good citizens, and have become men of property. Graveraet and Clark had been to Milwaukee and hired and shipped them on a vessel. It was the great cholera year; Clark died at the Sault on his way back; several others had died on the vessel, and many were landed very sick. We were all frightened; but the Indians, who lived here to the number of about one hundred, had everything embarked in their boats and canoes within sixty minutes, and started over the waters to escape a disease to them more fearful than the small pox. Now, the medical talent of Dr. Rogers was called into requisition. He laid aside the hoe and axe he had learned to handle so dexterously, and took up the practice of his profession. It was found, on examination, that there were no real cases of cholera, but many of the new comers had the typhoid or ship fever, and that it was contagious was soon evident, for the doctor, and perhaps a dozen of our young men who had never known sickness before, were soon stricken down with it. Each one of my companions had, in succession, taken the position of nurse in the hospital, (a rude building called a hospital had been erected,) and had in regular order been taken down with the malignant fever. It was my turn, next; I looked upon it as a new promotion, abandoned my oxen, glad of a change, having no fear that I would catch the fever, and I did not. About the time I went in, Dr. Rogers was very low, indeed, unable to lisp a word, and to this fact I attribute the recovery of himself and associates; for, as I knew nothing of medicines, I discarded them altogether, and by advice of a Mr. Harding, Mr. Emmons and Mrs. Wheelock, I commenced rubbing and bathing them, and Mrs. W. furnishing suitable food, the result was that in two weeks they were all convalescent. Dr. Rogers often said afterward, 'if I could have told the fool what medicine to give, he would have killed us all.'

"At this time the first steam boiler ever set up in this county was ready to be filled with water, and it must be done the first time by hand. It was a locomotive boiler, and was afterwards put into the side-wheel steamer, "Fogy," which plied between Marquette and Chocolay so many years. A dollar and a half was offered for the job, and I took it; working three days and a night or two, I succeeded in filling it. Steam was got up, and then I was installed as engineer and fireman. * * * * *

"That summer there were but few boats of any kind on the lake. The propeller Independence was generally broken down, and the little propeller Napoleon, only came three or four times during the season. The reliable mail, freight and passenger craft was the schooner Fur Trader, commanded by the veteran Captain Calvin Ripley, from whom the picturesque rock in Marquette bay took its name. The *Fur Trader* was a small sail vessel, and usually made a trip in three or four weeks; but it was towards the last of October and neither she or any other craft had put in an appearance for nine or ten weeks. The stock of provisions was quite low; the butter and luxuries of all kind were wholly exhausted, only a few barrels of pork and flour remained, and the danger of being put on very short rations was imminent. Then Mr. Harding discovered, or pretended to discover, a conspiracy among the Germans to seize the warehouse and confiscate what provisions were left. He volunteered to command a guard to watch the warehouse, day and night. The provisions were doled out sparingly, the Germans became very much dissatisfied, and a short time after, (in November,) they "struck," and a large number of them started out of the country, intending to follow the lake shore to Grand Island, and go from there overland to Little Bay de Noquette. Only a few reached Grand Island; the weaker ones, foot sore, weary and hungry, lagged at different points along the beach, and probably many of them would have perished but for the return of those of the party who had reached Grand Island, and there learned that a propeller, loaded with provisions had arrived here the next day after they left. So they returned, and the cheering news revived the drooping spirits of their comrades, as they came up to them here and there along the beach, and they finally all got back wiser and better men. None of the Germans named as still residing here, went off with the party. * * * * * On the 27th of November our boat was started for Sault Ste. Marie, in charge of James Hilliard, (sometimes called Jim Presque Isle.) John H. Mann, Mr. Emmons and a German boy named Kellogg accompanied him; they were all drowned, the boat being afterwards found with two bodies in it, while the body of Mr. Emmons was not recovered till the following spring.

"As I have told two stories that militate against Capt. Moody's skill as an engineer, it is only fair that I should relate one which redounds to his credit as a navigator. We had by some means been apprized of the fact that the schooners *Swallow* and *Siskiwit* which had been loaded with grain and supplies for us at Sault Ste. Marie, had run by and laid up for the winter at L'Anse. The grain was absolutely necessary to keep the horses from starving. Capt. Moody promptly started for L'Anse, accompanied by James Broadbent, an old salt water sailor. On their arrival there, they found both the vessels stripped and laid up, and what was worse, frozen in the ice. But Moody had pluck enough to undertake any task, no matter how difficult or dangerous. He and his man went to work at once to refit one of the vessels—the *Siskiwit*—on the principle that might makes right. They paid no attention whatever to the urgent protests of her owner, Capt. James Bendry. They filled her with corn and oats from the *Swallow*, and employed a large number of Indians to cut a passage between two and three miles long, through the ice, so as to float the vessel out into the open water. They got her out on Christmas eve, and arrived here on Christmas day, the sails frozen stiff and immovable, and the ice a foot thick on her deck. They had not seen land from the time they left L'Anse until they reached Marquette bay, a heavy northwest gale and snow storm prevailing all the time. The vessel was unloaded and run into Chocolate River, where she lay until spring, when, in coming out, she ran on the beach and went to pieces.

"During that winter we had three or four mails only. Mr. Harlow was the first postmaster, and hired the Indian Jimmeca to go to L'Anse after the mail at a cost of $10 per trip. I believe the cost was made up by subscription.

"The Jackson Company had about suspended operations; their credit was at a low ebb; their agent had left in the fall, and was succeeded by "Czar" Jones, the president, but nearly all work was stopped, and the men talked seriously of hanging and quartering Mr. Jones, who soon after left the country. * * * In the spring, (1850) the Jackson Company "bust" all up, and all work at their mine and forge was suspended. By this time, the Marquette Iron Co.'s forge was nearly completed and ready for making blooms. Many dwellings, shops, &c., had been erected, together with a small dock at which steamers could land. This dock still forms the shore end of the Cleveland Company's merchandize pier.   *   *

"In the fall of 1850, B. F. Eaton, and his brother, Watt Eaton, arrived from Columbus, Ohio. They had leased the old Jackson forge and mine, and brought with them an immense number of men and horses, and a large quantity of supplies. They commenced operations with a grand flourish of trumpets and high sounding words that bid fair to eclipse and crush everybody else out of existence in short order. They burst all to pieces within a year, and never paid their men a dollar in money—those who took goods for pay were wise. Ben. Eaton was so disgusted with the country that he finally left the United States and went to Australia, and as far as I know has never returned.   *   *   *

"In the summer of 1851, we had pretty hard times, generally; no money, and not much of anything else. I think it was in September of that year, the county was organized. I was absent up the lake shore, fishing, at the time, and on my return was informed that I had been elected County Clerk and Register of Deeds. I told my informant (Amos Parish) that I was not of age; to which he replied, that the impression generally prevailed that I was over thirty, that no one would say anything if I did not, and that it was very desirable to have some one hold those offices who could write. I was flattered, and consented. Up to this time, we had been attached to Houghton county, the county seat being at Eagle River.

"On one occasion I was sent, in the dead of winter, on foot and alone, up to Eagle River to get the county clerk's certificate to a lot of legal documents. I went to L'Anse, thence across the ice to Portage entry, up the river, over Portage lake and across the Portage to Eagle River. I called on Mr. Kelsey, the county clerk, and attended to the business I had in hand. He inquired, 'When do you return?' 'Tomorrow.' 'Oh, no,' said he; 'we never allow a winter visitor to depart under two weeks, and as you are the first man who

MARQUETTE IN 1853.

has ever come from Marquette or Carp River up here, by land, we must give you a good time.' Mr. S. W. Hill and Henry Parke came in, and between the three they agreed that I should have a big party the next night. The thought occurred to me whether I had not better cut and run for home, but I concluded if I should, and they caught me, it would go hard with me; so I resolved to stay, and if necessary run the gauntlet, or fight for my liberty, if cornered. The next day Dr. L. W. Clarke, John Senter, Geo. Senter, William Morrison, William Webb, Joe Thatcher, and others called, paid their respects and tendered various civilities. I watched them all closely, but could not discover that my suspicions of a conspiracy against me were well founded. The gay party came off the next evening, and all my fears were dispelled. I was invited the next night to a party at Eagle River, and when I argued that my apparel was not suited for parties, I was forcibly taken into Senter's store, and there compelled to put on an elegant suit of clothes; and for the next eight or ten days I was put through such a round of pleasures and hospitable attentions never before nor since witnessed by me. I could not have been more civilly feasted and toasted had I been the Prince of Wales. Such was the hospitality of the early settlers of the copper region.

"At last, when I was about to leave, I was offered silver specimens, agates, or anything else they had. My wants were, however, few and simple, and I said, 'give me two cans of those elegant cove oysters, to take to my Carp River friends, and I will be delighted.' I worked my way back as far as Portage entry, and found the ice in L'Anse bay all broken up. Mr. Ransom Shelden then lived at the entry, buying fish and furs from the Indians. At that day, copper mining on Portage Lake had not been dreamt of. After my arrival at the Entry I was laid up for three days with '*Le mal de Racket*,' or snow shoe sickness. As soon as I could travel, I set out through the woods for the catholic mission. I knew nothing of the route except to keep in sight of the bay, and that I soon found was impracticable owing to the impenetrable nature of the underbrush—so I struck back for better walking. The distance I had to go to reach the mission was sixteen miles, and it seemed to me I had traveled thirty. I had no dinner; it was very cold—22 degrees below zero—the 18th of January—night was close at hand. I crossed a little valley, and as I mounted the hill, I looked back of me and caught the only glance of the sun I had that day. I knew that to reach the mission I ought to be going toward the setting sun! I turned my course in that direction, and in a short time came across a single snow shoe track, and was much pleased to think I was getting where some one else had so recently been; before long I crossed another track similar to the first, and soon a third. A little closer examination convinced me that they were all my own tracks, and that for hours I had been traveling on a circle, only enlarging it a little each time. It was now rapidly growing dark. Fortunately I had matches, but I had no axe, nor any provisions, except the two cans of cove oysters. I succeeded in starting a fire at the foot of a dead cedar that leaned over into the forks of a hemlock, and as fast as it burned to a coal it would slide down a little, and thus my fire was replenished all night. I was too much excited to be either hungry or tired that night. I slept some in an upright or sitting posture, before the fire; the snow was about five feet deep, and I had shaped an indentation of my own figure like a chair into the snow, and lined it with balsam boughs, so that it was quite comfortable. In the morning, after breaking all the blades of my congress knife in opening one of the cans of 'elegant cove oysters,' I boiled them in the can, and tried to eat them; but it was hard work; they wouldn't stay down. Through the kindness of the good Bishop Baraga, who knew that I was either hurt or lost, (he had left the Entry after I did) an Indian was sent out and found me about three o'clock, and before dark I was safely housed at the mission. After many more hardships, I succeeded in reaching home. * * * * * *

"I have in this paper merely touched upon some of the incidents of the first two or three years of the history of Marquette and the iron region. A few houses, a stumpy road winding along the lake shore; a forge which burnt up after impoverishing its first owners; a trail westward, just passable for wagons, leading to another forge, (still more unfortunate in that it did *not* burn up,) and to the undeveloped iron hills beyond; a few hundred people uncertain of the future, these were all there was of Marquette in 1851–'2.

"Little did we think that the region we came to settle would, in so short a time, be known and felt everywhere; that its mineral products would be borne by hundreds of vessels to the ports of all the great lakes. The Sault canal was then a project the consummation of which was devoutly wished, but not realized; and the boldest of us had not dreamed of a railroad from our little hamlet to the iron hills. We were 'building better than we knew.' We had fallen into the march of the century, not knowing whither it would lead us. We were like the fishermen of the Arabian Nights, who ignorantly opened a small sealed casket, which they had drawn out of the sea in their nets. It held an imprisoned genii, who emerged at first like a little vapor, which, while they wondered spread and ascended until it towered up like a vast column toward heaven."

The forge referred to in the foregoing paper, was completed and made the first bloom in just one year from the day Mr. Harlow landed with his men. It started with four fires, using ores from what are now the Cleveland and Lake Superior mines. It continued in operation, rather irregularly, until 1853, when the Marquette company was merged into the Cleveland, under the auspices of which latter company, the works were operated until destroyed by fire in the winter of 1853.

In 1852, John Downey, Samuel Barney and others, began the construction of a forge on the Little Carp, but after building a few houses, a wheel, etc., abandoned the enterprise.

The first opening at the

CLEVELAND MINE

was made in 1849 by the old Marquette Iron Company.

During the summer of that year, several log houses, a large log barn, and a log boarding house were built, but the actual quarrying of ore did not commence till fall. During the winter of 1849–'50, twenty or more double teams were kept employed hauling ore from the mine to the forge on the lake shore, which was then being built and expected to be completed the following summer. It was not necessary at that time to use powder in quarrying the ore, as thousands of tons had rolled down and lay in huge " stock piles " at the base and up the sides of the various iron hills in the district. The Marquette Company continued to work an opening on section 11, and one on section 10, during the years 1850–'51, and in the winter of 1851–'52, the ore being hauled to Marquette by teams during the winter seasons only. In the winter of 1852 this association sold out to the Cleveland Iron Company. The Marquette Iron Company was only an association of discordant elements, a mere partnership, in which each member denied that the others were partners. The Cleveland Iron Company was organized under a special charter, granted by the legislature previous to the adoption of the new constitution in 1850, which last prohibited the legislature from granting special charters to corporations. In the spring of 1853 the company abandoned its special charter and organized under the general mining law of the State, as the

CLEVELAND IRON MINING CO.

The articles of association, which were filed in April, 1853 were signed by John Outhwaite, Morgan L. Hewitt, Selah Chamberlain, Samuel L. Mather, Isaac L. Hewitt, Henry F. Brayton, and E. M. Clark,—capital stock, $500,000; shares 20,000. The title to, and possession of, the Cleveland, was, at an early day a " bone of contention" between various claimants. The first occupant was a Dr. J. L. Cassells, of Cleveland, who came up from the Sault, in 1846, and took possession of one square mile of territory for the " Dead River Silver and Copper Mining Company.", The Cleveland Company's mines were included within this territory. Cassells left the country the next year, and his claim was taken possession of by Capt. Samuel Moody, John H. Mann, and Edmund C. Rogers, the first two claiming what afterwards became the property of the Cleveland Company, and the last named "squatting" on the lands in sections 10 and 11, upon which the Lake Superior Company originally organized. Previously the Marquette Iron Company had been organized, and took a lease of these lands from Clark and Robert J. Graveraet, who claimed to have possession as the representatives of Moody, Mann, and Rogers, with power to sell or lease. A long and bitter controversy over the title followed; the Cleveland Company and Graveraet—the latter representing Mann and Moody —claimed priority. These conflicting claims were finally settled by a decision of the Interior department, which accorded the right of purchase to Lorenzo Dow Burnell, from whom the Cleveland Company purchased. The Company did not enter all the land in dispute, and what is now the Lake Superior mine proper was claimed by Graveraet, under the Rogers' pre-emption, in behalf of the Marquette Company. Rogers had lost his interest by failing to reach the land office at the Sault, in November 1850, to attend a Government sale of lands, being detained by a storm on the lake. The location was then purchased by one Isaiah Briggs, in the interest of John Burt, Esq., under an agreement to lease an undivided one-half interest to Graveraet for a term of ninety-nine years, which agreement was carried out. Graveraet assigned his lease to the Marquette Company, and that, together with the other assets of the Marquette Company, including 64 acres of land within the present limits of the city of Marquette, was purchased by the Cleveland Iron Mining Company in 1853. Subsequently, the Graveraet lease of an undivided one-half of what is now the Lake Superior mine was sold to the Lake Superior Iron Company. Out of these complications grows the present litigation between A. R. Harlow and the Lake Superior Iron Company, the former, one of the partners of the Marquette Company, now claiming that he never sold his interest, and bringing a suit to recover it, together with sufficient damages to cover what would have been his share of the profits since earned. This suit is now pending in the Marquette County Circuit Court.

The New England Mining Company was incorporated by special act of the Legislature, passed in 1848. The purpose for which the Company was formed was declared to be, the mining and smelting of ores and minerals in the state of Michigan, and the capital stock was placed at $300,000. The Company never accomplished anything in the way of mining, however, and in 1855 the charter passed into the hands of Capt. E. B. Ward, under whose auspices the New England mine was opened in the spring of 1864.

THE LAKE SUPERIOR IRON COMPANY.

One of the three oldest companies in the district, filed articles of association March 13th, 1853, capital stock $300,000, divided into 12,000 shares of $25 each. The incorporators were Heman B. Ely, Anson Gorton, Samuel P. Ely, George H. Ely, and Alvah Strong. The early history of this mine is given in connection with that of the Cleveland.

THE EUREKA IRON COMPANY

was organized in 1853, with a capital stock of $500,000, the corporators being E. B. Ward, Harmon DeGraffe, Silas M. Kendrick, M. T. Howe, P. Thurber, Thomas W. Lockwood, and Francis Choate. The company was formed for the purpose of mining Lake Superior ores, and manufacturing charcoal pig iron. A start was made to build a furnace near Marquette, but the location was changed to Wyandotte, where a furnace was completed and became the nucleus of the extensive iron works now in operation there. The company purchased of Mr. Harlow one hundred and sixty acres of land just west of Marquette, where they undertook to develop a mine. Considerable money was spent and a few hundred tons of ore mined, when the location was abandoned, the company becoming convinced that the ore did not exist in sufficient quantity to warrant further expenditure. The land was subsequently sold back to Mr. Harlow, who is still the owner A lease of the property was taken by some Marquette parties, a year or two since, and a feeble effort has been made to open a mine in or near the old Eureka Company's opening, but thus far without success. It is believed by many that a workable deposit of good ore will ultimately be found on the property.

THE COLLINS IRON COMPANY

was organized in 1853, and filed articles of association November 8th. The original members of the company were, Edward K. Collins, of steamship fame, New York, Solon Farnsworth, Edwin H. Thomson, Robert J. Graveraet and Charles A. Trowbridge; capital stock $500,000. This company built a forge in 1854, and began to make blooms in the fall of the following year. In 1858, Stephen R. Gay, under whose supervision the Pioneer furnace at Negaunee had been built the previous year, leased the forge, and put up a cupola, in which he made some pig iron. The company then erected a blast furnace, the work being done under Mr. Gay's supervision. It was completed and went into blast on the 13th of December, 1858. The Collins Company also purchased a tract of land near the New York and Cleveland mines, where a very considerable sum of money was expended in explorations, without, however, developing anything of value.

THE PENINSULAR IRON COMPNAY

filed articles of association August 28th, 1854, capital stock $500,000. The corporators were William A. Burt, Austin Burt, Wells Burt, John Burt, Heman B. Ely, Samuel P. Ely, and George H. Ely. The company acquired the title to 800 acres of land, wnich was subsequently sold to the Lake Superior Iron Company. A blast furnace was built by the Peninsular Company at Hamtramck, Detroit, in 1863, and in 1874 became the owners of the Carp River furnace, Marquette.

THE FOREST IRON COMPANY

filed articles of association September 22d, 1855, with a capital stock of $25,000. The corporators were Mathew McConnell, Wm. G. Butler, Wm. G. McComber, M. L. Hewitt and J. G. Butler. McComber, McConnell and Butler had built a forge on Dead River, where the Bancroft furnace now stands, and becoming embarrassed they sought relief through the organization of a company with sufficient capital to continue the works in operation. The company failed, however, after a brief career, and the property passed into the hands of Stephen R. Gay, who in 1860 erected a blast furnace on the site of the old forge.

THE PIONEER IRON COMPANY,

to the original projectors of which belongs the honor of having erected and put into operation the first blast furnace on Lake Superior, was the conception of Mr. Chas. T. Harvey, its first manager. Having induced some New York capitalists to embark in the enterprise of building a blast furnace on Lake Superior, work was commenced in June, 1857, though it is noticeable that the company's articles of association were not filed until the 20th of July following. The corporators were Moses A. Hoppock, Wm. Pearsoll and Charles T. Harvey. The builders were Stephen R. Gay and Lorenzo D. Harvey, the furnace being completed so as to make her first iron in February; 1858. It was a double stack furnace, and is still known as the Pioneer, although the property of another company. It is located in the city of Negaunee, convenient to the Jackson mine, from which its principal supply of ore is obtained, under the terms of a mining contract—the furnace owners mining their own ore, and paying to the Jackson Company a royalty of one dollar per ton of iron made. The furnace made no money in the first few years of its existence. In 1860 it was leased to I. B. B. Case for a term of four years, he agreeing to pay all the expenses, including royalty on the ore, and deliver the iron on board vessel at Marquette, for $17.50 per ton. This was less than the iron could be made for, and as a consequence, Mr. Case lost money, though the advance in prices occasioned by the war materially increased the revenues of the company. The furnace was destroyed by fire in August, 1864, but number two stack was immediately rebuilt. In 1856, the furnace passed into the hands of the Iron Cliff Company, by whom it is still owned and operated.

The foregoing are about all the companies that were organized previous to 1859, which are still at work, or which developed properties that have since passed into other hands.

RAILROADS.

When the first opening was made in the iron deposit on the Jackson location, there were, perhaps, not to exceed 50 white inhabitants within the present limits of Marquette county. There was then nothing but an Indian trail from the "Mouth of the Carp" to the "Iron Mountain." Upon the erection of the Jackson forge a wagon road was constructed from thence to the mine, and when, a few years afterward it was concluded that our iron deposits would pay for working, the road was completed from the lake to the mountain. Then a plank road was projected, commenced in 1853 or 1854, and completed in 1856. It was subsequently converted into a tram railway, on which mules were used as locomotives, and answered the purpose for which it was designed, until, in 1857, what is now the

MARQUETTE, HOUGHTON, AND ONTONAGON R. R.,

was completed between Marquette and the Lake Superior mine. The question of transportation of the rich ores of Marquette county to the furnaces of Ohio and Pennsylvania, was one which came to be seriously considered at an early day. A canal around the St. Mary's Falls was scarcely more to be desired, so far as the iron region was concerned, than was the construction of a railroad for the transportation of the ores to the lake side. Accordingly, in 1851, a year before the grant of lands for the construction of a canal around the Falls was made by the general government, Messrs. Heman B. Ely and John Burt began to agitate the question of a railroad, and the next year Mr. Ely caused a survey to be made. There being no general railroad law in the State at that time, Mr. Ely, assisted by his brothers, Samuel P. and Geo. H. Ely, undertook the work as an individual enterprise, having previously made a contract with the Jackson and

Cleveland Companies, and with Mr. John Burt as the representative of other companies, for the transportation of all their ores. This contract the two first-named iron companies subsequently attempted to break, and sought to defeat the railroad by constructing a plank-road in opposition to it, thus instituting a serious and embarrassing controversy, which continued until 1855, when all matters of dispute then pending between the Railroad Company, under charge of Mr. Ely, and the Plank-road Company, under charge of Mr. S. H. Kimball, were submitted to arbitration, and settled to the satisfaction of both parties—Messrs. C. T. Harvey and Austin Burt being arbitrators. Immediately after the passage of the General Railroad Law of this State, in 1855, the Messrs. Ely incorporated the railroad under the title of the Iron Mountain Railroad, and John Burt was first President. A year later the company was strengthened by the addition of Jos. S. Fay, Edwin Parsons, Lewis H. Morgan, and other capitalists; and in 1857, the road was completed and put in operation. Mr. H. B. Ely, to whose foresight and energy the origin and success of the enterprise was largely due, and to whom the interests of Lake Superior became otherwise greatly indebted, died in Marquette, in 1856, before the work upon which he had labored so intently was completed.

The death of his brother, and his own connection with the road, was the occasion of bringing to Marquette Mr. S. P. Ely, who has since been more largely identified with the business management of many of the leading enterprises in the Iron Region than any person resident on "Lake Superior." The Iron Mountain Railroad became, subsequently, a part of the Bay de Noquette and Marquette Railroad, this becoming afterwards, by consolidation, the Marquette and Ontonagon Road, and still later, by further consolidation, a part of the through line of the Marquette, Houghton, and Ontonagon Railroad. The plank-road, to which reference has been made, was built by the Jackson and Cleveland Companies jointly, but was never used as a plank-road; longitudinal sleepers were laid down, and covered with strap-rail, on which horse-cars were run. The road was used for two seasons, and cost $120,000, which amount was practically sunk.

C. & N. W. RAILWAY.

In the year 1857 a negotiation was completed between the Chicago, St. Paul & Fond du Lac Railroad Company, through the Hon. Wm. B. Ogden, its President, and the railroad and plank-road proprietors, by which that company became the owners of both roads (the Iron Mountain Railroad and the plank-road,) and of the charter of the Marquette & Wisconsin State Line Railroad, to which the grant of public lands had been made by Congress. In virtue of these transfers it was expected that a railroad line would be immediately built from Fond du Lac to a point on the Menominee river, in township 41 north, range 30 west, from whence it was to diverge in two branches—one to Marquette, and the other to Ontonagon. But the panic and financial crisis of that year prevented the negotiation of the proposed loans in Europe upon the basis of the land grants; the Chicago, St. Paul & Fond du Lac Company retained, however, the Marquette & State Line Railroad charter. In the course of time the Chicago & Northwestern Railway Company succeeded to the property and effects of its predecessor, including the Marquette & State Line land grant. It seemed impracticable then to build a line of railroad on the route first surveyed in 1857, and accordingly the Chicago & Northwestern Company obtained from Congress the privilege of a change in the line of the Marquette & State Line road to the Green Bay shore and the present line of the Peninsula division. This line was so nearly identical with that of the Bay de Noquette and Marquette grant, that the latter company determined not to continue the line to Bay de Noquette. The land grants, as to their interfering provisions, were adjusted by mutual consent between the Chicago & Northwestern and the Bay de Noquette Companies, and the latter company became merged in interest with the Marquette & Ontonagon Railroad.

The preliminary survey of the Peninsula Division line was made in 1865, it being then the intention of the company to run their road from the head of Little **Bay de N**oquette to Chocolay, four miles below Marquette. The next spring, however, the present line was selected, and work commenced on the 4th of July. In a little less than eighteen months, the track was laid into Negaunee, **and in less than two years** after ground was broken at Escanaba, **the** cars **were carrying ore** and passengers over the line. The main line **is 62½** miles in length, with about twenty miles of track branching off from Negaunee to the **mines.** The business of the road has more than answered the expectations of the company.

In 1872 connection was made **between** the Wisconsin **and** Peninsula Divisions **of the C. & N. W.** Railway by the completion of the company's main line from Fort Howard to Escanaba. In the same year the Marquette, Houghton & Ontonagon Railroad was opened to L'Anse, thus making complete railway communication from the head of Keweenaw, or **L'Anse** Bay to **Chicago, a distance of nearly 500 miles.**

The legislature **of** 1875 passed an act granting a most liberal subsidy of **State** lands to aid in the construction of a railroad from Marquette to the Straits of Mackinaw ; also, for the building of the Menominee Range Railroad from some point **on the Chicago &** Northwestern, below Escanaba, **to the new and promising** iron mines **on** the Menominee river. This last road **will be** completed **to** the Quinesaik **mine in town 40 north,** range 30 **west,** Menominee county, the present year. The line from Marquette to Mackinaw will, doubtless, **be** completed in the near **future, when** with **an extension of the M. H. & O. to** Ontonagon, **a** line from **L'Anse to** Houghton, and a branch from the Marquette & Mackinaw **to Sault** Ste. Marie, the railway system will be complete. It is confidently hoped and believed, however, **that when** the Northern Pacific **Company shall have completed its line between** the head of **Lake** Superior and **Puget's** Sound, it **will seek an eastern connection** along **the south shore** of **Lake Superior with the Cana**dian Pacific at Sault Ste. Marie, and thus constitute itself a grand trans-continental line between **the Atlantic and Pacific.**

ORE DOCKS.

In addition to complete and ample equipment for the transportation of ore over their lines, the M. H. and O. R. R. and N. W. Railway companies have extensive ore docks at Marquette, L'Anse and Escanaba. At the latter point there are two of these docks, one of which is 1,300 feet in length, 32 feet in height, and 37 feet wide, with a sufficient number of pockets to hold 20,000 tons. The other is nearly, if not quite, as extensive, the two costing something near half a million dollars.

The M. H. and O. R. R. Company's dock at Marquette has a total length of 1,222½ feet, is 38 feet high above the water, and 53 feet wide. It is supplied with four railway tracks upon which the ore cars are run over the pockets. There are 136 pockets, situated on both sides, of which 120 have a capacity of 55 tons each, and 16 (steamboat pockets,) of 100 tons each. Eight vessels can receive cargoes at the same time, and a vessel of average tonnage can be loaded in one hour and thirty minutes. It is estimated that the dock has a capacity for handling, with ease, 500,000 tons during a single season of navigation. A partial view of this dock may be seen in our illustration of Marquette in 1875.

The Cleveland Iron Mining Company's ore dock at Marquette is so exactly similar to the one last referred to, that it is not necessary to enter into a detailed statement of its size and capacity. Both are elaborate and costly structures, and together have a sufficient capacity to meet all the requirements of the ore trade for years to come.

The Railroad Company's dock at L'Anse, has a total length of 546 feet, is 36 feet wide and 38 feet high, and contains 80 vessel pockets, 40 on each side, with four steamboat pockets at the outer end. The pockets will hold about 75 tons each, and four vessels and one steamer can be loaded at the same time. It is not nearly so large as the other docks referred to, but can be extended whenever it may be necessary to provide for increased transportation facilities at that point.

Both railway companies have, in addition to their ore docks, extensive merchandise piers at their lake termini.

ST. MARY'S FALLS SHIP CANAL.

From the time of the first attempt to develop the mineral resources of Lake Superior, till the summer of 1857, a period of twelve years, the Falls of the St. Mary's river formed an insuperable barrier to communication between Superior and the lower lakes. These falls or rapids are nearly opposite the village of Sault Ste. Marie and about one mile in length, the fall being about seventeen feet. As has been stated, a number of steamers had been drawn over the portage between the years 1845-'50, but until the completion of the canal, in 1857, all articles of commerce, the products of the copper and iron mines, merchandise, etc., had to be transhipped at the Sault. To facilitate this transhipment, a flat bar railroad was constructed, and remained in use until the rapidly growing interests of the Lake Superior region demanded that the barrier should be wholly removed. The necessity for the improvement being brought to the attention of Congress, a grant of land amounting to 750,000 acres was secured to aid in the construction of a ship canal around the falls. These lands were given in trust to the State of Michigan, and on the 5th of February, 1853, the State, by act of the legislature, accepted the grant, and authorized the Governor to appoint commissioners to let a contract for the construction of the canal, and to select the lands.

These commissioners made a contract with Joseph P. Fairbanks, Erastus Corning and others, who agreed to build and complete the canal within two years, the consideration being the lands granted by the general government. This contract was soon after assigned to the St. Mary's Falls Ship Canal Company, which had been organized in New York on the 14th of May, 1853, under an Act of the Legislature of that State. Immediately after the passage of the act granting the lands, a survey for the canal was made by Mr. Charles T. Harvey, who, on the organization of the company was made general agent and superintendent of construction. This survey, in which Mr. Harvey was assisted by Mr. L. L. N. Davis, an experienced engineer from the Erie canal, was made late in the fall of 1852.

Early in the season of 1853, Mr. Harvey, with 400 men, proceeded to the Sault, and on the 4th of June broke ground for the canal. The remoteness of the locality, and many other unfavorable circumstances, rendered the construction of a work of such magnitude exceedingly difficult, and necessitated at every step of the operations unusual care and energy in the management as well as heavy pecuniary expenditures. Mr. Harvey remained in control of the construction for one year, when he was relieved and placed in charge of the finance, and also appointed agent for the State to select lands under the grant, in the Upper Peninsula. Mr. Harvey selected about 200,000 acres of land, 39,000 of which were taken in Marquette county, and were subsequently sold for $500,000 cash, to the Iron Cliff Company. Among the copper lands selected was the quarter section on which the Calumet and Hecla Company's mine is situated, and which was sold by the canal company for $60,000, now worth not less than $20,000,000. The 750,000 acres granted by the general government were entered by the company as follows: on the Upper Peninsula, 262,283 acres of iron, copper, and timber land, and 487,717 acres of pine land in the Lower Peninsula.

During the summer of 1854 the difficulties necessarily attendant upon building the canal were very much enhanced by disease among the workmen, some 200 of whom died of the cholera, and among them was Mr. Ward, who had charge of the construction. Mr. Harvey was then again placed in charge of the work, which, owing to the panic among the workmen, had become nearly suspended; but by the exercise of much skill and energy he succeeded in reorganizing the force, and pushing the work vigorously forward to final completion. On the 19th of April, 1855, the water was let into the canal, and in the following June the work was opened for public use, under the superintendence of Mr. John Burt.

The total cost of the original construction of the canal, which includes also the expense attendant upon the selection of lands, as contained in the report of the company under date of January 1st, 1858, was $999,802.46.

The Michigan Legislature, by joint resolution, adopted in 1869, ceded the canal to the General Government but it has never been formally accepted; nevertheless, under its system of internal improvement, the National Government has made the most liberal appropriations for its enlargement, and also for the construction of a new one, which last is designed, when completed, to be adequate to all the requirements of commerce. Considerably over one million dollars have been expended on the improvement of the canal, the total cost of which, it is expected, will exceed $2,000,000.

It is to be hoped that Congress may yet be prevailed upon to accept the ownership of this great improvement. It is a public work in which the people of the State of Michigan not only, but all the Lake States, if not the country at large, feel, or should feel, an interest. It was originally constructed, as has been seen, wholly at the expense of the General Government, and has never cost the State of Michigan one dollar that was not repaid in tolls imposed by the State Board of Control. The General Government, while leaving the canal to the ownership and control of the State, is expending large sums of money in its enlargement. It should assume the ownership and control as well, and then make it absolutely free, and no longer permit one State to manage, control, and impose a tax upon a great public work, which was built at the expense of *all* the States. What Lake Superior wants is free and unrestricted water communication with the other lakes—that will never be obtained until the canal passes into the hands and under the obsolute control of the General Government.

OF LAKE SUPERIOR.

The following table showing the amount of receipts for tolls, etc., taken from the annual report of Superintendent Gorton, indicates, to some extent, the rapid development of the Lake Superior mineral interests. It must be remembered that, since the opening of the canal, other means of transportation have been provided, and a very considerable part of the annual product of the mines and furnaces finds an outlet at Escanaba and through Lake Michigan:

STATEMENT SHOWING THE AMOUNT OF RECEIPTS FOR TOLLS, AMOUNT OF TONNAGE, AND NUMBER OF PASSAGES OF BOTH STEAM AND SAIL VESSELS, AND DATES OF OPENING AND CLOSING THE CANAL.

YEARS.	Gross Receipts.	Tonnage.	Number of Sail Vessels.	No. of Steamers.	Total Number of Passages.	Opened.	Closed.
1855	$ 4,374 66	106,295.00	....	..	....	June 18.	November 23.
1856	7,575 78	101,458.00	....	..	....	May 4.	November 28.
1857	9,406 74	180,820.00	....	..	....	May 9.	November 30.
1858	10,848 80	219,869.00	....	..	....	April 18.	November 20.
1859	16,941 84	252,632.20	....	..	....	May 3.	November 28.
1860	24,777 82	403,657.00	....	..	....	May 11.	November 26.
1861	16,672 16	276,639.00	....	..	....	May 3.	November 14.
1862	21,607 17	359,612.00	....	..	....	April 27.	November 27.
1863	30,574 44	507,434.00	....	..	....	April 28.	November 24.
1864	34,287 31	571,438.00	1,047	366	1,411	May 2.	December 4.
1865	22,339 64	409,062.00	602	395	997	May 1.	December 3.
1866	23,069 54	458,530.00	555	453	1,008	May 5.	December 2.
1867	33,515 54	556,898.76	839	466	1,305	May 4.	December 3.
1868	25,977 14	432,463.47	817	338	1,155	May 2.	December 3.
1869	31,579 96	524,884.72	939	399	1,338	May 4.	November 29.
1870	41,896 43	690,825 91	1,397	431	1,828	April 29.	December 1.
1871	33,865 45	752,100.54	1,064	573	1,637	May 8.	November 29.
1872	41,232 44	914,735.08	1,212	792	2,004	May 11.	November 26.
1873	44,943 18	1,304,445.25	1,549	968	2,517	May 5.	November 18.
1874	38,922 97	1,070,857.18	833	901	1,734	May 12.	....
1875	41,199 04	1,259,533.58	493	1,492	2,085	May 12.	....

* Includes steam barges and consorts.

From the same report we take the following tables, showing the amount of freight carried to and from Lake Superior ports, through the canal, between May 12 and September 30, 1875:

NATURE AND AMOUNT OF FREIGHT CARRIED TO LAKE SUPERIOR PORTS DURING THE SEASON OF 1875.

ARTICLES.	Name of Line.					
	Buffalo Boats.	Chicago Boats.	Canadian Boats.	Steam Barges and Consorts.	Sailing Vessels.	Total.
Pork, bbls................	1,585	4,835	2,482	......	......	8,902
Flour, bbls...............	7,245	9,074	6,881	......	......	23,200
Beef, bbls................	1,142	4,129	8,431	......	......	13,702
Bacon, lbs................	11,571	369,660	95,161	......	......	476,392
Lard, lbs.................	61,339	383,487	12,760	......	......	457,586
Butter, lbs...............	171,069	407,930	46,423	......	......	625,422
Cheese, lbs...............	73,143	126,395	23,530	......	......	223,068
Tallow, lbs...............	8,130	82,020	4,200	......	......	94,350
Candles, boxes............	70,635	6,912	4,670	......	......	82,217
Soap, boxes...............	8,179	10,244	1,240	......	......	19,663
Apples, bbls..............	17,282	1,029	637	......	......	18,948
Sugar, bbls...............	15,439	4,014	685	......	......	20,138
Tea, chests...............	2,365	382	908	......	......	3,655
Coffee, bags..............	4,452	435	134	......	......	5,021
Salt, bbls................	39,282	581	3,526	......	600	43,989
Vinegar, bbls.............	425	203	72	......	......	700
Tobacco, lbs..............	71,241	109,581	24,299	......	......	205,021
Nails, kegs...............	12,856	681	1,429	......	......	14,966
Dried fruit, lbs...........	29,573	5,620	4,870	......	......	40,063
Vegetables, bush..........	19,053	11,470	4,044	......	......	34,567
Lime, bbls................	12,431	839	426	850	1,799	16,345
Merchandise, tons.........	12,178	2,777	7,240	1,605	......	23,800
Coal, tons................	5,845	12	66	28,809	64,528	101,260
Lumber, M.................	93	8	210	707	......	1,078
Shingles, M...............	......	......	77	......	......	77
Lath, M...................	......	......	......	......	......	......
Window glass, boxes......	1,230	486	237	......	......	1,953
Hay, tons.................	809	809	619	......	118	2,355
Cattle, head..............	162	923	606	......	......	1,691
Horses and mules, head....	33	47	347	......	......	427
Sheep, head...............	147	1,421	603	......	......	2,171
Hogs, head................	4	526	338	......	......	868
Brick, M..................	1,029	11½	14	995	653	2,713½
Furniture, pieces.........	7,627	30,252	1,589	......	......	39,468
Machinery, tons...........	1,053	106	255	......	......	1,414
Engines...................	12	1	1	......	......	14
Boilers...................	42	34	2	......	......	77
Wagons....................	17	46	97	......	......	160
Liquors, bbls.............	2,184	1,515	819	......	......	4,518
Malt, lbs.................	265,633	591,600	6,000	......	......	863,233
Eggs, bbls................	422	1,101	56	......	......	1,579
Railroad iron, tons.......	256	190	8,703	2,170	498	11,817
Coarse grain, bush........	6,265	231,701	12,114	......	......	250,080
Ground feed, tons.........	20	1,823	232	......	......	2,075
Bar iron, tons............	1,258	50	43	......	......	1,350
Powder, tons..............	5	......	26	......	......	31
Kerosene oil, bbls........	3,031	122	124	......	......	3,277
Lard oil, bbls............	654	229	42	......	......	925
Moulding sand, tons.......	40	......	......	......	......	40
Cement, bbls..............	1,829	500	......	......	......	2,329
Stoves....................	6	......	......	......	......	6
Syrup, bbls...............	123	......	......	......	......	123
Empty bbls................	200	......	......	......	......	200
Beer, half-bbls...........	......	3,639	......	......	......	3,639
Crockery, bbls............	......	60	......	......	......	60
Telegraph wire............	......	......	45	......	......	45
Road scrapers.............	......	......	125	......	......	125
Wheelbarrows..............	......	......	150	......	......	150
Limestone, tons...........	......	......	......	1,525	11,970	13,495
Passengers................	3,669½	777	8,220	......	......	11,666½

NATURE AND AMOUNT OF FREIGHT CARRIED FROM LAKE SUPERIOR PORTS DURING THE SEASON OF 1875.

ARTICLES.	Buffalo Boats.	Chicago Boats.	Canadian Boats.	Steam Barges and Consorts.	Sailing Vessels.	Total.
Mass copper, tons	2,060		65			2,125
Ingot copper, tons	12,524	108				12,632
Stamp works, tons	3,648¾					3,648¾
Iron ore, tons	1,970	7,672		339,856	143,910	493,408
Pig iron, tons	17,351½	13,774		7,019	2,309	40,356½
Silver ore, tons	500	98	249			847
Hides	4,549	3,255	2,201			10,005
Furs and pelts, bundles	4,423	80				4,504
Tallow, lbs	6,700	22,600	5,881			41,181
Fish, half-bbls	4,131	4,907	4,849			13,887
Lumber, M	57	175		1,397	1,844	3,473
Shingles, M						
Wheat, bush	489,015		359,373	250,400	115,000	1,213,788
Flour, bbls	228,349	378	54,064	4,000		286,791
Feed, tons	573		1,059	40		1,672
Potash, casks	758					758
Oil cake, tons	299					299
Merchandise, tons	561	171½	37½			770
Fresh fish, cars	218					218
Rags, tons	54					54
Barley, tons	540					540
Horses	10	24	59			93
Wagons	5	3	20			28
Railroad iron, tons	500	65				565
Building stone, tons	69	629½		20	2,260	2,978½
Potatoes, bbls	123					123
Bones, tons	10	10				20
Scrap iron, tons	84					84
Slate, tons	85	713				798
Wool, tons	8					8
Empty beer kegs	2,978					2,978
Household goods, boxes	8					8
Whisky, bbls			25			25
Dogs			27			27
Lead ore, tons			75			75
Passengers	3,424½	586	4,008½			8,019

GEOLOGY OF THE LAKE SUPERIOR IRON REGION.

BY CHAS. E. WRIGHT, M. E.

The rock formations of our iron district are embraced under two grand divisions, the Archean and Silurian. The former is divided into two periods, the Laurentian and Huronian. These are usually tilted at high angles, their inclination or dip being more frequently greater than forty-five degrees (45°) than less. The Silurian age, the Upper and Lower groups, is represented on the Upper Peninsula of Michigan by the Potsdam, Calciferous, Trenton, Niagara, Onondaga and Helderberg periods. They are nearly all horizontally bedded or dipping only slightly to southward* The Silurian rocks, and the overlying drift, include, with the exception of a narrow neck of the Huronian, all the country of the Upper Peninsula of Michigan, south and east of Marquette. To the casual observer, the Archean rocks, in their broken and contorted beds, appear to have had no system in their formation—in texture and structure, frequently resembling the igneous rocks rather than the sedimentary, and even to-day are spoken of by some geologists, as being in a "fluid state,"† or are referred to a deep-seated Volcanic (Plutonic) origin. By other geologists their probable equivalents are considered‡ as highly metamorphosed sedimentary strata. The latter theory we have accepted as best explaining the numerous facts we have observed, not only in the field but those recently brought to light by the application of the microscope. Before beginning with the older period, the Lauren-

---
*See Michigan Geological Report, 1873, Part III.
†Michigan Geological Report, 1873, Part III.
‡Geology of Canada, 1863, Page 22.

tian, which underlies all of our other rocks, without it be, perhaps, an occasional primitive island arising above the former level of the Laurentian sea, we will review briefly the architecture of the rocks of this section, which may enable us to understand more clearly the ideas we wish to present. Let us imagine, if you please, the primitive earth's crust, composed chiefly of granitic rocks, which have formed and partially crystalized out of the amorphic magma, constituting the outer zones of the earth's shell. After their formation and even during its process, began the abrading forces of nature, no doubt largely assisted by the corroding influence of a dense and acid atmosphere, gradually wearing away the more prominent features of the earth's rocky face, depositing the loosened particles in the primitive and barren valleys of early time. When the sediment had attained considerable thickness, commenced the metamorphism of the strata, affording us the metamorphic granites and other crystaline rocks of the Laurentian period. Then followed a disturbance and tilting up of the strata, caused in a measure by the crystallization of the sediments and consequent enlargement of the mass, due to the fact that the crystallized material occupies more space than the amorphic, and by the contraction of the entire earth or globe, aided largely, no doubt, by the expansion of the outer shell, from the heat generated by this shrinking and consequent motion, and to many other causes, which even their simple enumeration would require more space than we can spare. Our Laurentian rocks are formed; and now follows another period, not of rest, however, for nature never ceases her labors, but coupled with time is constantly producing something new. She has already begun with her rude tools the gigantic task before her. The lofty mountain ranges and noble peaks of granite, slowly but surely disappear before her persistent energy, until nothing remains of their grandeur save the low, insignificant rounded knobs of the Laurentian. As nothing goes to waste, so do we find again the material of the Laurentian mainly re-deposited in the valleys of what is known as the Huronian sea. The question at once arises in our minds, how account for the different kinds of rocks? The simplest explanation we can offer for this is to advise our questioner to examine any exposure of coarsely crystalline rocks, where can be best observed the effects of weathering, and satisfy himself of the decomposition and dissolving out of some of the chemical elements of the minerals, of which the rock is composed, and then to consider that these chemical ingredients, combining with others are carried away and deposited directly, or by some intermediate agent, elsewhere. On the other hand, if he be of a mechanical turn of mind, let him watch closely a muddy stream made turbid by some local cause, and notice that the water gradually becomes clearer the farther it recedes from the disturbing force—the coarser particles are precipitated first, but many of the finer ones are held in the current until they reach the still waters where they slowly subside to the bottom of the lake or sea. The result of this chemical or mechanical action is, that the sedimentary strata they form are usually different in composition from the parent rock. Then again, thermal waters impregnated with solvent agencies may percolate the sedimentary beds and carry away in solution some of the ingredients, thereby changing the chemical nature of the material and affording a new mineral constituent. The many theories advanced to account for the formation of rocks, suggest an exhaustless subject; so for fear of exceeding our limits we will turn again to examine another era in that wonderful plan of creation. We will suppose the deposition of the Huronian period to have ceased, and the metamorphism and upheaval of the beds, wrought no doubt, by agencies similar to those of the Laurentian, to have ended. Nature again commences her work of levelling the mighty monuments she has constructed, as evidence of her great power, and as before she gathers up the ruins of the previous ages and reconstructs from them the lower beds of the Silurian. In this age, however, she has left behind unmistakable evidences of the presence of life. To the existence of this intermediate agent is largely due the formation of the Paleozic and more recent limestones. The Silurian sea, teeming at intervals with organic life, has supplied the carbonate of lime and magnesia it held in solution, to construct the shells and frames of the fauna, which thrived in that period, and their remains, when erratic, have settled to the bottom of the sea and formed immense calcareous beds, which subsequent metamorphism has changed into magnesian limestone. To consider these members in detail, or continue upwards through the succeeding ages to the present time, would oblige us to go outside of the Iron District we purpose to describe, and therefore would be foreign to our subject.

There now remains the comparatively recent Glacial period, which has had much to do with forming the present features of the country. Nearly everywhere in our iron district on the exposed surfaces of the granite and the quartzy ones of the Huronian may be seen groovings and striæ ploughed out or engraven by the glaciers. These markings have nearly a common trend, and from them we learn that the glaciers have traveled from northeast to southwest, scattering the boulders held within their icy embrace often hundreds of miles from their native ledge. As a singular instance may be cited an immense boulder of lean magnetic iron ore lying on the south bank of the Menominee river, just above the mouth of Pine river, Wisconsin. This boulder was originally partially exposed, but owing to the fact that it was left directly over a long line of magnetic attraction, and to its huge size, parties have completely undermined it, to satisfy themselves that it was not an outcrop of a solid ledge. These erratics of magnetic iron ore are strewn promiscuously through the drift south and southeast of the iron ranges, and frequently play strange freaks with the explorer's compass. Sometimes so strong is this local attraction that the north or south end of the needle will continue to point to one place when traveling around it, even when the circle is a hundred yards or more in diameter. Farther south, in northern Wisconsin, where the drift is often very deep, the boulders, apparently deposited in a moraine, have dammed the streams, "backing up" the water for miles above, while below these irregular dams are often dangerous rapids. With the Glacial period closes our hasty review of the architecture of the rocks of the iron district and those in the eastern portion of the upper peninsula of Michigan.

We will now examine, stratigraphically, the members of the periods we have been considering.

In the Laurentian fields are probably isolated islands of primitive rocks, but as yet, they have never been discovered, owing to the difficulty of distinguishing between igneous and metamorphic granites, and to the fact that the Laurentian on Lake Superior is comparatively an unexplored district. The Laurentian formation of our iron region is composed chiefly of granites and gneissoid rocks. The granites are medium to coarse grained. The essential minerals are generally plainly visible. The granites are usually massive and strongly jointed. The jointing planes are very prominent, and along the sides of cliffs present, sometimes, bold and very even faces, which frequently are mistaken by explorers for stratification. The bedding planes are ordinarily very obscure and difficult to distinguish, but with sufficient care, they may, in most cases, be made out.

Many of our granites would be valuable as building stone, and, no doubt, could be used for all purposes to which these rocks are applied. In all the thin, transparent sections of the Laurentian granites that we have examined under the microscope can be easily recognized the feldspar, quartz and mica, and as accessory minerals may be counted magnetite, hematite, amphibole, etc. The feldspars (monoclinic and triclinic) are generally slightly altered, and the mica sometimes wanting, (pegmatite) while the quartz is apparently unchanged. It is interesting to note the various stages of decomposition of the feldspar, commencing along the cleavage planes and producing at first only a slight fogginess, then a mossy like appearance, mottled with limpid spots, and finally, in the latter stages, a micro-granular mass, indistinctly outlined. In the quartz may be seen numerous very small liquid filled cavities, averaging say one four thousandth of an inch across, and which contain, an extremely minute vacuum or gas bubble. These tiny bubbles are usually in constant motion, dashing merrily about in their narrow confines. The presence of these fluid inclusions and the absence of any glass or stone filled cavities, so common to known igneous rocks, has had much to do in convincing us of the sedimentary origin of the Laurentian rocks. Under the microscope, in the polarized light, the sections present a very interesting field, and it is apparently evident from their structure and texture that these granites have crystallized "in situ." Passing from the Laurentian to the Huronian, we enter the home of our iron ores.

Beginning at the foot of the Huronian ladder, which we will suppose has nineteen steps, we venture upwards. These steps, we will assume, correspond to Major T. B. Brooks' division of the Huronian series. The first four steps are represented by mica schist, quartzite, magnesian schist, small quantities of specular ore, and locally large deposits of lean flag iron ores.* From the west end of Cascade mine has been taken considerable first-class ore. The other mines situated on this range are now idle. Leaving this unclassified field we arrive at No. V. In this member we find Massive Quartzites, which often graduate into Dolmitic Marbles.

An analysis of the Morgan furnace limestone from this formation, afforded:

Carb. of lime... 49.10
Carb. of magnesia.. 41.00
Oxide of iron.. .43
Silica... 8.00
Undetermined... 1.47

100.00

The novaculites, which have furnished excellent hones, belong to this formation; also some of the talcose schists. Taking another step, we reach No. VI., which is an Actinolo-

*See Brooks' report, 1873, page 147

magnetic Quartz Schist, banded with purplish, brownish and grayish slaty layers that are from one-sixteenth to two inches in thickness. On weathered surface it appears somewhat arenaceous. Under the microscope the actinolite (fibrous hornblende), quartz and magnetite are easily recognized. Ascending still higher to No. VII. we find a Hornblende Rock. It is usually medium grained, and dark greenish black in color, finely sprinkled with gray. Massive and jointed, rarely ever showing any signs of bedding, and were it not that these rocks are associated with other plainly stratified members, it would be quite impossible to define their original structure. Under the microscope a section of the rock is seen to consist chiefly of amphibole and quartz, with plain and striated fragments of feldspar, brownish scales of mica, and magnetite. These rocks are commonly known in the iron district as "greenstones," or "trap," and have been frequently mistaken by geologists for diorites.

No. VIII. of our series is a Banded Magnetic Quartz Schist, differing from VI. in containing less actinolite, while many of the layers on their polished edges present a graphic appearance, from small and dendritic fragments of brownish jasper. Formation No. IX. is a Hornblende Rock, similar to VII. It contains, however, more quartz and less mica and feldspar. No. X. Banded Magnetic Quartz Schist, very similar to the previous magnetic schist. It is much harder and jaspery, and there is less distinction in the texture and color of the stripes. Under the microscope the base of the rock appears composed of small angular quartz grains averaging about one six hundredth of an inch across. Scattered through this base are numerous still smaller particles of magnetite, also fragments of actinolite. This formation in some localities includes the so-called soft hematite ores. It is possible that these soft ore deposits are the result of the decomposition of the richer and less quartzy portions of this belt, caused, probably, from the dissolving out of the finely divided silica, by thermal alkaline waters. This appears all the more plausible, since in formation V. the marbles are traversed by irregular veins of quartz, which are evidently due to the infiltration of water holding silica in solution; and further, these dolomitic beds are often altered into silicious marbles or even quartzites apparently from the replacement of the carbonates by silica. Advancing another step up our imaginary ladder, we encounter a massive Hornblende Rock, No. XI., apparently identical with No. IX. Under the microscope may be seen in the thin sections large fragments of orthoclase feldspar, and fibrous ones of amphibole. The former often enclose the latter. No. XII. is a Specular Quartzose or jaspery Schist; it is often finely banded, and on the smooth surface across the bedding presents a very laminated structure. Where a bending in the formation has taken place, as at the Republic mine, may be seen some very interesting instances of folding and miniature faulting. Each stripe or group of them is so well characterized that they may be recognized at a glance, even where the throw has been several inches, or even feet, to the right or left. In this formation, as in X., are found valuable deposits of soft hematite ores.

One more step we climb, and the true iron belt is before us. In this member, No. XIII., are represented all the known varieties of the magnetic and red oxides of iron. The magnetic ores vary from a fine steely-grained to a coarse granular texture. The specular ores are sometimes granular to steely-grained, or are more or less micaceous. The magnetic ores are usually massive and jointed, while the specular ores are massive to slaty. The steely varieties are very hard to drill, and when massive and without joints require an endless amount of sledging to reduce them to the proper size for handling. On the other hand, some coarse granular magnetic ores and micaceous specular slate ores may be easily crumbled in the fingers. The first-class ores are very rich, and when carefully selected, average above 65 per cent. of metallic iron, though lumps weighing several tons can be had that are within one-half per cent. of absolute purity. The beds are from a few feet to one hundred or more in thickness. The deposit of ore often appears to be in lenticular shaped masses, one lense overlapping the other. The transition from the red to the black oxides is usually quite abrupt,* and small hand specimens may be obtained† where one side is nearly pure magnetite and the other portion composed of specular ore. Nearly all the specular ores have minute particles of magnetite disseminated through them. On the foot and hanging walls are often narrow beds of chlorite and talcose schists. Imbedded in some of these chloritic rocks overlying the magnetic ores are garnet crystals altered into chlorite, though some of them are partially unchanged.

Reluctantly we leave the ore formation to examine the next member of the Huronian series, No. XIV. It is a Gray Quartzite, of an even and somewhat arenaceous texture. Sometimes it is slightly micaceous; it differs from the Lower Quartzite in being less vitreous, and is apparently not so highly metamorphosed. The quartzite at some of the mines passes into a jaspery Quartz-Conglomerate or Breccia. Continuing our ascent, we find No. XV., usually represented by a Black Slate. It is frequently pyritiferous, and contains a small percentage of graphite; in some places it is quite plumbaginous.

We have not seen, as yet, in Marquette county any slate beds suitable for roofing purposes, though in the Huron Bay district are inexhaustible quantities of first-class roofing slates.

Next in order is a Limonitic Schist, No. XVI. It is possible that this is only a decomposition of the more pyritiferous lenses of the slate, or is derived in the same manner from the anthopyllitic schist—No. XVII.—immediately above. The so-called anthophyllitic schist is composed of anthophyllite and actinolite, with an admixture of oxide of manganese and of iron, also graphite. The anthophyllite is easily recognized by its radiated form. It is highly probable that portions of this belt are sufficiently rich in manganese to make them valuable for Bessemer iron ores. No. XVIII. is supposed to be

---
*Champion, Republic, and other mines.
†Edwards Mine.

a Quartzite. One more effort and we reach what we suppose to be the upper member of the lower Huronian, No. XIX. This is a Mica Schist, holding crystals of staurolite and andalusite; the staurolite is very prone to form crystals that are crossed either at right angles, or at a very oblique one. Having now very imperfectly considered the character of the different strata of the Huronian, we will sketch as briefly as may be, from our own observations, aided largely by the published results of others,‡ the outlines of the different periods of our Iron District. Beginning with the Lower Silurian, we find in the southeastern portion of the city limits of Marquette, isolated patches and bays of brown sandstone, nearly horizontally bedded, and resting unconformably on and against the Huronian. The Lower Silurian member has an irregular shore line as we proceed southward from this locality. The first six miles its course is southwesterly, the sandstone resting on the Huronian. We continue south about fifteen miles, along a very crooked shore composed of granite; when following this dividing line we travel westward some twelve miles further; then in a gentle curve we return to our southward course, and in town 42, range 27 west, we cross a neck of Huronian nearly six miles wide. Leaving this we skirt along the granite beach for fifteen miles more, when we meet again the Huronian, which forms the coast of the Potsdam for twenty miles or more, where it intersects the Menominee river and enters Wisconsin. Returning again to Marquette, we find the Potsdam sandstone skirting the south shore of Lake Superior nearly all the way to Keweenaw Bay, and from thence southwestward, there appears to have been an extensive Lower Silurian bay, having for its northwest shore, the Copper Range, or upper Huronian. The formation before us has furnished very excellent brown sandstone for building purposes, and many of the variegated varieties obtained from the Marquette quarries cannot be surpassed for beauty or durability. In the Huronian period it would be practically impossible to define the shore lines of the

‡ See Michigan Geological Report, 1873.

Huronian sea, owing, as we have seen, to the bending and upheaval of the strata, and the subsequent erosion. Our purpose, then, is not to describe original boundaries, but rather to trace out the upturned edges of the strata. Glancing over this section of the country we find the Huronian fields, limited by granite, or covered by the overlying silurian and drift. The general trend of the formation in the Marquette district is nearly east and west, and as we proceed westward from Marquette it gradually widens, until at Negaunee it appears to have attained its maximum width of about thirteen miles. The upper members of the Huronian are apparently wanting between Marquette and just east of Negaunee. The strata form a broad synclinal trough, resting on granite. The synclinal is corrugated in the direction of its axis with several minor folds. West and south of Negaunee and about Ishpeming, these minor corrugations are contorted and their upturned edges have a serpentine-like course. Nature here, apparently, in one of her uneasy moods, has, by disturbing the strata, brought to light her buried treasures, and rendered easy of development the several first-class specular iron ore mines about Negaunee and Ishpeming.

The Jackson mine at Negaunee, is the oldest iron mine of the district, and its products are largely sought for. At Ishpeming we have the Lake Superior, Barnum, Cleveland, New York, Lake Angeline, and other mines. Their ores are of the best quality and cannot be excelled.

About Negaunee are located a number of soft hematite mines. These ores are in good demand by Bessemer pig iron makers, owing to their low percentage of phosphoric acid. Southward of Ishpeming are the Saginaw, Winthrop, and other mines. The Saginaw ores are the first-class specular varieties, while those of the Winthrop are being used for the manufacture of Bessemer iron.

As we continue westward from Ishpeming the formation again becomes more regular, though here, as east of Negaunee, may be observed the inferior folds. On the south rim of our broad synclinal are located the Washington, Edwards,

Keystone and Champion mines. In the Washington and Edwards mines the ore—a fine quality of magnetic—occurs in pockets or irregular shaped lenses, while at the Keystone and Champion the ore belt is more uniform. At the Champion the vein or bed is nearly vertical, and on the lower level of the mine it is about one hundred feet wide. The ores, the magnetic and specular, are of a very superior quality, and in their present workings are very low in phosphorus and sulphur.

The Huronian, westward from Ishpeming, gradually narrows until it reaches Michigamme Lake, where it is only two miles wide. The northern edge of the trough maintains its course along the north shore of the lake, and includes within its iron belt the Michigamme and Spurr iron mines; also other and undeveloped mines. The ores of the Michigamme and Spurr mines are of the highest standard, and the former promises soon to lead the iron mines of Lake Superior in the amount of production.

After we leave the Spurr mine the course of the formation appears to be west-northwest, and when we arrive at a point about eight miles south of L'Anse the formation takes a short turn to the northeast, but before reaching Lake Superior it dips under the Potsdam sandstone, and we return about five miles further to the northwest, in nearly a parallel direction, on the northwest side of the Huron Mountains, along the Lower Silurian shore line to L'Anse. Coming back to the east end of Michigamme Lake, and tracing the southern rim of the synclinal, we find it makes a gradual southwesterly turn and in an easy curve comes round to a southeasterly direction, conforming in a measure to the east side of Michigamme Lake and its outlet. We continue on our course, passing the Kloman mine, and finally reach the Republic mine. The ores of these mines are mostly specular. In the Republic has been found a deposit of very pure magnetite. The specular ores are very rich in iron oxides and are favorably known to our iron men.

The formation has here made a horse shoe-like bend, twisting and contorting the strata, and returned in a northwestly direction along the southwest bank of the river. The strata are tilted at high angles, and in some instances are overturned. The dip, however, is usually away from the underlying granite, so that on each side of the river we find the strata inclining toward each other, thereby forming a narrow trough of less than one mile wide and six or seven miles long. On this range are located the Metropolis, Windsor, Canon, Erie and Magnetic mines. These mines are all on one of the lower iron belts. The Erie mine is reported to have mined out several hundred tones of magnetic ore. At the Magnetic mine has been done considerable work, and they are now exploring to find the upper iron belt. Immediately after we leave these mines the upturned edges of the Huronian begin to curve to the left, and in about one-half mile they have a direction of nearly due south, which continues for three or four miles, when it makes a little more easting, and finally we come to a point some eighteen miles south of the Republic mine; then we proceed southeasterly and easterly for about thirteen miles, when we meet the Potsdam formation mentioned above, in town 42, range 27 west. Following our previous trail southward for five or six miles, across this Huronian neck, we arrive on its southern edge. Proceeding now westward on the dividing line of the Huronian and Laurentian for thirteen or fourteen miles, we turn to the southwest, then to the east and north east for a short distance, and ultimately in a more uniform course to the southeast. We are now in the Menominee region. The formations are more regular and have a trend west by north. On the "Menominee range" are some first-class specular and hematite iron ore deposits, well adapted to the manufacture of "Bessemer pig iron," and the day cannot be far distant when their value for this purpose will be recognized. The following is an analysis of ore from the Quinnesaik mine:

Peroxide of iron	93.85
Alumina	.34
Lime	1.05

Magnesia	.15
Phosphoric acid	.11
Sulphur	Trace.
Silica	4.00
Water	.50
Total	100.00
Metallic iron	65.695
Phosphorus	.048

We have several analyses of ores from this region, and the average percentage of phosphorus is even less than the above, which cannot fail to be appreciated by those endeavoring to furnish pig iron suitable for the present demand in the steel trade.

Having in a superficial manner considered the region best known to us, and in which we are most interested, we will tarry a moment on the borders of the geologically unexplored Laurentian. In the Menominee region is a small Laurentian island, bounded on the north, west and south by the Huronian, and on the east by the Silurian. Immediately north of this and separated only by a narrow Huronian bay is a much larger granite island belonging to the same period, limited on the north by the Marquette iron district (Huronian) and on the west and south by Huronian, and to the east by Silurian. Still further north is another Laurentian island, even larger than the preceding. It is hemmed in on the north and east by Lake Superior and Potsdam Sandstone, to the west by the Huron Mountains, and on the south by the Marquette iron region. The first island has an area of about one hundred and fifty square miles. The second island of, say six hundred square miles, and the upper, or northern Laurentian island, probably numbers seven hundred square miles. With the Laurentian closes our very incomplete chapter on the geology of the Lake Superior iron region, and we hand our pen to the historian that he may finish the task we have only begun.

On the next two pages will be found a complete list of all the iron mines which have been opened in the district, together with their location, names of owners, general agents and their post office address, and character of ore

LIST OF LAKE SUPERIOR IRON MINES, WITH LOCATION, NAMES OF OWNERS, GENERAL AGENTS, POST OFFICE ADDRESS, ETC.

Name of Mine.	Location. S.	T.	R.	Owners.	General Agents.	P. O. Address.	Kinds of Ore.
Jackson	1, 2-3, 10-11	47	27	Jackson Iron Co	Fayette Brown	Cleveland, O	Specular and brown hematite.
Cleveland	9-10, 16-19, 20-21	47	27	Cleveland Iron Mining Co.	Jay C. Morse	Marquette, Mich	Specular hematite.
Superior		47	27	Lake Superior Iron Co	C. H. Hall	Ishpeming, Mich	Specular and brown hematite.
New York	8	47	27	New York Iron Mine	W. L. Wetmore	Marquette, Mich	Specular hematite.
Marquette	2	47	27	Marquette Iron Co	Jay C. Morse	" "	Specular hematite.
Lake Angeline	21-28	47	27	Pitts. & Lake Aug. I. Co.	A. Kidder	" "	Specular and brown hematite.
Iron Mountain	11	47	27	Iron Mountain Iron Co.	A. Kidder	" "	Flag and manganesious.
Republic	7	46	29	Republic Iron Co	P. Stackhouse	" "	Specular hematite and magnetic.
Champion	31	47	29	Champion Iron Co	A. Kidder	" "	Specular hematite and magnetic.
Barnum	9	47	27	Iron Cliffs Co	T. J. Houston	Negaunee, Mich	Specular hematite.
Michigamme	19-30	48	30	Michigamme Co	Jacob Houghton	Michigamme, "	Magnetic.
Spurr	24	48	31	Spur Mountain Iron Mining Company	Freeman Norvell	Detroit, "	Magnetic.
Kloman	1-6	46	29	Kloman Iron Co	Carnegie Bros	Pittsburgh, Pa	Specular hematite and magnetic.
Palmer*	19-30, 29-30	47	26	Palmer Iron Co	J. Kirkpatrick	Palmer P. O., Mich	Specular hematite and flag.
Washington	1-2, 11-12	47	28	Washington Iron Co			
Edwards	2	47	29	W. W. Wheaton	W. W. Wheaton	Marquette, Mich	Magnetite and specular hematite.
Keystone	32	47	28	Keystone Iron Co	C. M. Wheeler	Negaunee, Mich	Magnetic and specular hematite.
Foster	23	47	27	Iron Cliffs Co	T. J. Houston	Negaunee, Mich	Brown hematite.
Saginaw	19	47	27	Saginaw Mining Co	A. G. Stone	Cleveland, O	Brown hematite.
Salisbury	18	47	26			Negaunee, Mich	
Pitts. and L. Superior	30-32	47	26	Iron Cliffs Co	T. J. Houston		Flag.

*—Old Cascade, and includes what was formerly known as the Emma and Bagaley mines.

LIST OF LAKE SUPERIOR IRON MINES, WITH LOCATION, NAMES OF OWNERS, GENERAL AGENTS, POST OFFICE ADDRESS, ETC.—CONTINUED.

NAME OF MINE.	LOCATION.			OWNERS.	GENERAL AGENTS.	P. O. ADDRESS.	KINDS OF ORE.
	S.	T.	R.				
Michigan*	7	47	28	McComber Iron Co	Jay C. Morse	Marquette, Mich	Specular hematite.
McComber	6	47	26				Brown hematite.
Illinrosi	7	47	27	Winthrop Iron Co	H. J. Colwell	Negaunee, Mich	Brown hematite.
Winthrop	33	48	27	Shenango Iron Co	H. D. Smith	Appleton, Wis	Brown hematite.
Shenange	33	47	27	Carr Iron Co	M. H. Maynard	Marquette, Mich	Brown hematite.
Carr	33	47	26	Mitchell Bros	Owners	Marquette, Mich	Flag ore.
Green Bay	8	47	26	M. & P. Rolling Mill Co	W. W. Wheaton	Marquette, Mich	Brown hematite.
Rolling Mill	5-29	47	26	S. C. Smith Iron Co	Wallace Pierce	Sharpsville, Pa	Brown hematite.
Smith	18-29	45	26	M. T. Gaffney	M. T. Gaffney	Negaunee, Mich	Brown hematite.
Grand Central	6	47	26	Griphon Iron Co	W. C. McComber		Flag.
Gribbea	28	46	26	Allen Iron C.	M. H. Crocker		Brown hematite.
Allen	8	47	25	A. E. Goodrich	A. E. Goodrich		Specular hematite.
Goodrich	19	47	27				
Home	32	47	25	Home Iron Co	Henry Wick	Cleveland, O	Specular hematite.
Magnetic	30	47	29	Magnetic Iron Co	Samuel Peck	Marquette, Mich	Magnetic.
Hungerford	35	47	29		Samuel Peck		Specular hematite and magnetic
Negaunee	11	47	26	Loustorf & Mass	Loustorf & Mass	Negaunee, Mich	Brown hematite.
Stewart	7	48	28	Stewart Iron Co			Magnetic.
Cambria	25	48	31	Cambria Iron Co	J. H. McDonald	Negaunee, Mich	Specular and brown hematite.
Cannon	21	48	27	Cannon Iron Co	Samuel Peck	Marquette, Mich	Magnetic.
Breitung	10	39	29	E. Breitung	E. Breitung	Negaunee, Mich	Brown hematite.
Quinnesic	34	40	30	Milwaukee Iron Co	J. J. Hagerman	Milwaukee, Wis	Blue hematite.
Breen	22	39	28	Breen Iron Co	E. S. Ingalls	Menominee, Mich	Specular and brown hematite.
Spurr & Calhoun	7	47					Brown hematite.
Buckeye	26	48	33	Buckeye Iron Co	John Spaulding	Marquette, Mich	Specular hematite.
Bessemer	34	48	26	Bessemer Iron Co	W. C. McComber	Negaunee, Mich	Brown hematite.
Erie	28	47	30	Rawle, Noble and others	James F. Trowell	Republic, Mich	Magnetic and specular hematite.

* Formerly belonged to Michigan Iron Company, now bankrupt.

CLASSIFICATION OF ORES.

The Lake Superior mines yield five varieties of iron ore. The most valuable, so far as developed, is the specular hematite, which is a very pure anhydrous sesqui-oxide, giving a red powder, and yielding in the blast furnace from 60 to 68 per cent. of metallic iron, which is slightly red short. The ore occurs both slaty and granular, or massive. It is often banded or interlaminated with a bright red quartz or jasper, and is then called "mixed ore."

The next in order of importance is the magnetic, or black oxide, which, until recently, has only been found at a considerable distance west of the specular and soft hematite deposits, at the Washington, Edwards, Champion, Republic group, Keystone, Michigamme and Spurr, in which none of the other varieties have been found, except the specular hematite, commonly called "slate," into which the magnetic sometimes passes, the powder being from black to purple, then red. Recently a vein of very fine magnetic ore was struck at the New York mine, which, though not fully tested, promises to become a very important feature of the mine. It is not improbable that the specular and magnetic ores are varieties of the same ore, as they are much alike in richness, character of iron, and geological structure. This view is much strengthened by the fact that the specular ore is often found in octahedral crystals, which form is well known to belong exclusively to the magnetic oxide; hence it is probable that the specular deposits were once magnetic, and by some metamorphic action have been robbed of one-ninth their oxygen, which would make them chemically hematites.

Scarcely less important than the magnetic is the soft hematite of the district, which very much resembles the brown hematite (Limonite) of Pennsylvania and Connecticut. This ore is generally found associated with the harder ores, from which many suppose it is formed by partial decomposition or disintegration of the latter. It contains some water, chemically combined—is porous in structure—yields about 55 per cent. in the furnace, and is more easily reduced than any other ore of the district. It forms an excellent mixture with the speculars. There are, probably, several varieties of this ore which have not been well made out. That found at the Jackson and Lake Superior is associated with the specular, while the Foster bed is several miles removed from any known deposit of that ore, and has probably a different origin.

The flag ore is a slaty or schistose silicious hematite, containing rather less metallic iron, and of more difficult reduction than either of the varieties above named. It is often magnetic, and sometimes banded with a dull red or white quartz. The iron is cold short, which is one of the best qualities of this ore—the other ores of the district being red short. This ore varies much in richness, and comparatively little has been shipped. It is, however, probably the most abundant ore in the district.

A silicious ore, containing a variable amount of oxide of manganese, is found at several points, accompanying the flag ore, which will in time, unquestionably be found of great value as a mixture.

The iron ores of the district are generally found in hills, rising from one to five hundred feet above the level of the surrounding country. These hills (those given to exaggeration call them mountains) are simply immense deposits of iron ore, though partially or wholly covered by layers of earth and rock. It is true the ores are also found in the valleys, but where so found are usually covered with a deep drift, and consequently cannot be so easily mined.

That part of the Lake Superior Iron Region in which the most gratifying results have been obtained, is nearly all included within the limits of Marquette county, west of Negaunee, within a range of six miles wide, running in a northwesterly course from Lake Fairbanks, in town 47 north, of range 26 west, to Keweenaw Bay, in town 49 north, of range 33 west—a distance of nearly one hundred miles. The mines now opened and being worked are all situated on the east end of this range, the most remote being the Spurr Mountain, near the west end of Lake Michigamme.

Another extensive district or range is that known as the Menominee, extending so far as known, from town 39, north range 28 west, north to the south shore of Lake Michigamme. The deposits on the south end of this range, to which more extensive reference will be made later on, are not only quite numerous, but are believed to be very extensive and valuable, though as yet little has been done in the way of development. The celebrated Republic mine is situated on the northern end of this range.

The iron range again crops out some thirty miles south of Bayfield, where ore of a tolerably pure quality has been found. By reference to a geological map, it will be seen that the Marquette and Menominee iron ranges cross or form a junction with each other on the south side of Lake Michigamme, the one continuing to the west and northwest, and the other south and south-east.

We will now briefly review the mines in present operation, giving such facts and figures as will enable the reader to comprehend the progress which has been made, and form some estimate of the importance of the iron resources of the Lake Superior region. As we have stated, the first opening in the iron deposits was made at

THE JACKSON MINE

in 1846; but very little progress was made in the way of development until after the opening of the St. Mary's Falls' ship canal, ten years subsequent. The first shipments from the Jackson were made in 1856, all the ore mined previous to that time (about 25,000 tons) having been for the use of the Company's forge, of which full mention has already been made.

The Jackson Company's mines are situated within the corporate limits of the city of Negaunee, on section 1, of town 47, range 27, the whole of the section belonging to the company, and comprising the original entry made in 1845. The mines consist of a dozen or more cuts or openings, on as many different deposits of ore, though it is believed that some of them are continuous. The ore is a hematite, including both the hard and soft varieties—classified into specular, granular, slate and hematite—the latter referring solely to the soft ores. The beds are very irregular in their formation, but, generally, have a very perceptible dip to the north.

The production of the Jackson mine, for each year, is correctly given in the following table:

YEAR.	GROSS TONS.
1856, and previous	30,000
1857	14,000
1858	12,500
1859	10,500
1860	41,000
1861	13,000
1862	43,000
1863	61,000
1864	69,000
1865	55,000
1866	87,934
1867	126,390
1868	131,707
1869	128,245
1870	122,710
1871	132,297
1872	112,060
1873	116,336
1874	105,600
1875	90,568
Total	1,502,847

The following analyses of the Jackson ore is given to show its great purity, and freedom from all injurious substances:

NUMBER ONE—A MIXTURE OF THE GRANULAR PEROXYDE AND THE MAGNETIC OXYDE:

Oxygen	29.46
Iron	68.07
Insoluble	2.89
	100.42

No trace of manganese, phosphorus or sulphur, the insoluble portion consisting entirely of pure silicia.

NUMBER TWO—SLATE.

Oxygen	29.09
Iron	69.09
Insoluble	1.64
	99.82

We do not deem it necessary to enter into a detailed description of the Jackson. It is, perhaps, more generally known abroad than any other mine in the district, its ores always commanding the most favorable consideration of furnace-men. Mining operations are conducted in the most thoroughly systematic manner, and though economy is the rule, no necessary expense has been spared in the purchase of the best and most improved machinery and appliances. The mine affords employment to an average of about 250 men, and the pay roll will approximate $125,000 annually, though, of course, it was much larger previous to the panic.

The officers of the company are as follows: *President*, DAVID STEWART, New York: *Secretary and Treasurer*, G. P. LLOYD. New York; *General Agent*, FAYETTE BROWN, Cleveland; *Local Agent and Mining Supt.*, HENRY MERRY, Negaunee.

Captain Merry took charge of mining operations in 1858, and has held the position ever since. His long service with the company, and the constantly increasing product of the mine, attest his practical worth and ability.

THE CLEVELAND IRON MINING COMPANY

mined the first year (1852) 3,000 tons, which was made into blooms, at their forge, in Marquette, which continued in operation about two years after its purchase from the Marquette Company. This forge stood just south of the shore end of the Cleveland Company's ore pier, and was destroyed by fire December 15th, 1853. In 1855, the first shipments, 1,447 tons, were made to lower lake ports, and in 1856 the shipments amounted to 6,343 tons. The Jackson, though first wrought, did not make any shipments of ore till 1856, and the Cleveland, therefore, ranks as the pioneer in that respect. The following table shows the product of the mine from 1852 to 1875, inclusive, a period of twenty-four years:

YEAR	GROSS TONS
1852–4	3,000
1855	1,447
1856	6,343
1857	13,204
1858	7,909
1859	15,787
1860	40,091
1861	11,795
1862	37,009
1863	46,842
1864	45,927
1865	33,957
1866	42,125
1867	75,864
1868	102,213
1869	111,897
1870	132,984
1871	158,047
1872	151,585
1873	130,600
1874	108,580
1875	140,239
Total	1,417,445

The present operations at the mine are confined to pits No. 2 and 3—originally separate openings, but now one—Nos. 1, 4 and 5, the "Incline" and the School-house mines, the exact condition of each of which we shall describe as accurately as possible. In No. 2 and 3, which is, in the main, a large open cut, the 90 foot level has been reached, with the hoisting shaft sunk to a considerable depth below it. To the west of this open cut there are openings through to the New York, where the vein has been worked out to below the 60 foot level, pillars of ore being left to support the hanging wall. At this point the vein, which was only about eight feet thick at the outcrop, widened out to 150 feet, at the 60 foot level, but at some distance below, tapers down to about 90 feet. The dip of the deposit is, at this point, to the south, the foot wall being nearly perpendicular. The New York vein, which is identical with this deposit, has been worked down to the Cleveland line for a distance of 230 feet west, thus insuring, without further exploration, a run of over 400 feet of ore at this point. There is here a vast body of pure ore which cannot be exhausted for many years. The ore is raised through a shaft supplied with a double skip road, operated by the engine and drums in the main engine house, situated between No. 2 and 3 and the Incline mine. The same engine was formerly used for hoisting from the Incline mine, but is now employed exclusively in raising the ore and water from No. 2 and 3.

No. 4 is situated about 400 feet east of the last mentioned opening. The vein, which was about 14 feet thick at the start, dips to the west at about the same angle as the deposit in 2 and 3, and at a depth of 125 feet attains, in some places, a thickness of 45 feet. Here it has been ascertained that what was considered the foot wall is only a thin strata of rock, under which there is another bed of ore, the extent of which has not yet been determined; the same feature characterizes the hanging, above which there is another vein of ore ten feet thick. These veins evidently run under the east slope of No. 2 and 3, and cut out what was supposed to be a right angle or curve in the foot wall. This is an underground opening, and connected by a drift with the Incline mine. The ore is hoisted out by engine and drums, stationed on the hill at the east of the mine, which also do the hoisting for Nos. 1 and 5.

No. 5 is an open cut in which the vein has been opened about 150 feet lengthwise, the vein holding a uniform thickness of about 20 feet, 120 feet below the surface, to which depth the ore has been worked out.

No. 1 is where the first opening was made in 1854, and presents a vein of ore about 14 feet thick, dipping to the south-west, and which has been worked down to a uniform depth of 30 feet. This vein has been traced to the New York line, a distance of over 400 feet, and lies immediately under the deposit in No. 2 and 3, with about ten feet of diorite between them.

By far the largest body of ore to be seen in any one opening in the district, is at the so-called "Incline mine." This is a large open cut, 100 feet deep, and embracing a superficial area 200x400 feet. The length indicates the extent of vein

or deposit which has been opened, though it varies in width
or thickness from 13 feet at the east end to 162 feet near
the middle, tapering down again to about 30 feet at the
west end. This deposit presents some peculiarities which
are puzzling to the geologist. Originally, an inclined tram-
road was put down, from the engine-house, at the northwest end of the opening, under the impression that the ore
dipped to the south and east. Afterwards it was found that
the ore dipped under the supposed foot wall on the north side
of the pit; the incline was taken up, and three skip roads on
the south wall substituted for hoisting purposes. The south
wall is nearly perpendicular, and when the ore was found
to be dipping to the north, it was but natural to suppose that
a correct understanding of the formation had been reached.
Later, however, it was found that the ore, 75 feet below
the surface, extends under this supposed foot wall on the
south side, and excavations for blacksmith shop and boiler
room have been made, 20 feet south, in ore, without encoun-
tering anything which looks like a foot or hanging wall.
Certain it is that the ore in the bottom dips under the op-
posing bodies of rock, and, as yet, neither foot nor hanging
wall has been reached. Above this huge ore deposit there
is a vein fourteen feet thick, dipping at an angle of 45
degrees to the north, which has been worked to some extent
by driving in "breasts," leaving arches to support the over
hanging rock. This vein, however, has not been found very
reliable, in some places narrowing down to less than three
feet. Some idea of the extent of the "Incline mine" may
be gathered from the fact that nearly 70,000 tons of ore have
been mined from it alone in a single year, and that it can
be made to yield a larger product if necessary. An open
cut, thirty feet deep, is now being made across the bottom
at the widest part, by which two underhand stopes with faces
30x160 feet will be obtained, on each side. From these stopes
not less than 100,000 tons of ore can be mined. The ore is
raised by means of four skip roads, three on the south side
of the cut and one at the northwest side, all operated by the

new machinery furnished last year by the Iron Bay foundry, and which is located at the southwest end of the cut.

The School-house mine is west and south of the other openings, and has been opened on a vein which has a north and south course, with dip to the west. About 350 feet of vein, which carries an average thickness of fourteen feet, has been opened to a depth of 130 feet. It is an underground mine, with four incline shafts, which are supplied with skips for hoisting. These skips are operated by machinery of the most approved pattern, and which, owing to its distance from other openings, is not applied to any other purpose. This mine contributes about 30,000 tons of ore annually to the company's product.

The average number of men employed at the Cleveland is 350. The ore generally, is a very hard, compact red specular, and for that reason the cost of mining is, perhaps, greater than at any other mine in the district. In No. 2 and 3 pit there is ground so exceedingly hard that frequently from five to six hundred freshly sharpened drills are required to drill an inch and a half hole one foot deep. The ore, however, is of the best quality, a fact which is attested by the eagerness with which it is sought after by furnacemen all over the country. More than this, the deposits are not likely to show any signs of exhaustion for years to come—certainly not within the remaining years of any of the present stockholders.

The officers of the company are: *President and Treasurer*, SAMUEL L. MATHER; *Secretary*, FRED. A. MORSE; *General Agent*, JAY C. MORSE; *Superintendent*, F. P. MILLS.

Mr. Mills has had local charge during the past sixteen years—a fact which tells the whole story of his ability as a practical miner.

THE LAKE SUPERIOR MINE.

The Lake Superior Iron company filed its articles of association in March 1853, the capital stock being $300,000, represented by 12,000 shares of the par value of $25 each. Mining operations were not commenced, however, until sometime in the summer of 1857, and the first shipments (4,658 tons) were made the following year. The estate originally purchased consisted of 120 acres in sections 9 and 10, town 47, range 27. Subsequent purchases enlarged the company's estate to something over 2,000 acres, and it now has mines opened and in operation in sections 16, 19, 20 and 21, in addition to those opened on the tract originally purchased. With the purchase of additional lands the capital stock was increased to $500,000, all of which was returned to the stockholders in dividends previous to the panic of 1873, up to the close of which year the company had mined and sold 1,433,097 tons of ore, of the aggregate value of about ten millions of dollars.

We shall not attempt any description of the geological formation at the Lake Superior openings in sections 9 and 10, the peculiarities of which are a puzzle to those who have made the geology of the district a study. Major Brooks, who made a most thorough and careful examination of the mine while engaged in the state geological survey of 1869, referring to the eastern portion of the mine, says in his report "I confess myself unable to give any intelligent hypothesis of its structure." Were he to visit the mine now, we very much fear that he would find it a harder conundrum to solve than it was at the time he made his survey. The formation is unlike anything else in the district. Instead of a comparatively narrow vein or belt of ore, enclosed by nearly vertical walls, we find here a huge basin or trough, the rims of which form a foot wall on either side, from 400 to 500 feet apart at the upper edges. There are, in fact, two foot walls of talcose schist, one dipping to the north at an angle of 69 deg., and the other sloping at the same angle to the south, while there is no such thing as a hanging wall to be seen. Along the sloping walls of this basin there is a vein or stratification of pure ore—that lying next to the south wall varying from twenty to ninety feet in width, and gradually widening out as depth is attained. Along the north wall, in No. 2 cut, a vein of pure ore ten or twelve feet thick was mined out down to the first level, one hundred feet from the surface, at which point there appears to have been a break in the formation, by which the ore belt was shoved over to the south a few feet, as is evidenced by the fact that though the miners lost track of the ore at the bottom of the level as stated, it has again been found in a lower drift, and running parallel with the vein which was supposed to have been exhausted. The same break occurs at the Barnum, a short distance west, where the vein was lost and found again in the same way, and has been worked out to a considerable depth below the break. Between these foot walls and the overlying veins or stratifications of pure ore, the basin appears to have been filled in with a jumbled mass of rock and ore—a chloritic schist with stratifications of pure specular ore, which appear to have no connection with the main deposits on either side. There is but one acceptable theory in regard to this formation, and that is that the vein or deposit lying against the north and south foot walls are identical and connect underground—though some affect the belief that the formation will be found different at a greater depth, and that the ore overlying the north and south walls are but branches of or feeders to the main deposit, which will be found confined within regular foot and hanging walls below, the smaller lenticular masses in the chloritic schist, with which the bowl of the trough or basin is filled, having the same structural connection. There is little doubt, at all events, but that the ore will be found to connect beneath the mass of rock lying between the upturned edges of the basin, cutting it out altogether. This rock will, therefore, necessarily have to be taken down and removed; and it is more than probable that it will be found to contain enough pure ore to pay the cost of its removal.

The principal work being done at present is in Nos. 1 and 2. No. 1 is a large open cut which has been worked out to a depth of 105 feet, the floor constituting what is known as the first level. This cut is about 400 feet in length, on the south side of the basin, the ore widening out from about twenty feet at the east end to ninety feet near the middle, from which point it again gradually narrows down to forty feet at the west end. This refers to the body of ore which constitutes the floor of the first level, the deposit at the west end being only one foot thick at the outcrop, and though not fully informed we infer that the same general features characterize the whole of the deposit so far as opened. It would appear that the belt of the ore lying along the southern foot wall does not maintain the same proportions, but dips under the mass of rock with which the basin is filled, so that at a depth of 100 feet from the surface it has attained a thickness nearly, if not quite, three times as great as the measurement of the outcrop. This fact strengthens the belief that the ore will ultimately be found to underlie the whole of the mixed ore and rock between the upturned edges, and should the same general features be found in the ore belt which lines the slope of the north wall in No. 2, it will not be many years before the peculiarities of the formation, which have puzzled the wits of the ablest geologists, will be satisfactorily determined.

The ore from No. 1 cut is raised through a main shaft, which is down to the second level all the way in rock, and 125 feet distant from the ore deposit. From the bottom of this shaft there are two drifts into the cut on the second level, in which there are four stopes with faces of sixty feet each. A shaft has been sunk to the third level, at the east end of the cut, around which the ore has been taken out so as to give an open under-hand stope of forty-eight feet. A new skip road is being constructed to this third level, the ore from which has hitherto been raised in buckets to the second level, and thence out through the main shaft. This new skip road will be operated by one of the drums in No. 1 engine house, it being the intention to abandon the old shaft as soon as all the ore above the second level has been taken out. The distance from surface to the third level is 232 feet. The new shaft referred to, together with the skip road, will be continued down to a fourth level, sixty feet below the third, which will give a sufficient number of stopes to enable the management to fill any demand that is likely to be made upon the mine.

On the south side of No. 1 cut there are two skip roads to the second level, which are operated by the engine and drums on the hill. These will likewise be carried down to the third and fourth levels, and the ore taken out in that direction will pass down a tram-road to a dock near the hematite mine, where it will be transferred into the railway cars.

In No. 2 cut, which is along the north slope of the basin north and west of No. 1, there are three skip roads down to the first level, all operated by the engine and drums in No. 1 engine house. One of these skips will be transferred to No. 1, and the others continued down to the third and fourth levels.

In the west end of No. 1 a drift has been made fifteen feet into the vein, about thirty feet below the surface, from the end of which a winze is being sunk to the second level, leaving the whole body of ore between the winze and open cut to support the walls. At the bottom of this winze a drift will connect with the open cut, through which the ore will be trammed to the skip road on the south side. West of this some 500 feet is another opening not now being worked, where the vein is found to be ten feet in width, and still further west, 500 feet, a shaft has been sunk twenty-two feet, all the way in ore. The shaft, which follows the foot wall, is 10x12, but as yet no hanging wall has been found, and consequently the width of the vein at this point is undetermined.

Our observations thus far have been confined to the hard ore deposits on sections 9 and 10—now we come to the hematite mine, which is situated a short distance southeast of No. 1 cut, an opening known as the "Trebilcock pit" lying between. The latter is a large open cut fifty feet square, worked out to a depth of 100 feet or more. The walls are of mixed hard ore, and almost perpendicular. Were it not for a vein some eighteen or twenty feet in width which extends easterly from this cut and appears to be a part of the same deposit, there would be strong reason to regard this as merely a pocket of hematite ore, having no connection with other

BARNUM HOUSE, ISHPEMING.

parts of the mine; it is probable, however, that it is a part of and connected with the main hematite deposit which lies to the south and east. The hematite mine is almost, if not quite, as great a puzzle as the formation in Nos. 1 and 2. There is here a very large body of the best soft hematite, into which a shaft has been sunk 230 feet to the second level. There is, perhaps, nothing in the formation which cannot easily be understood; but how to successfully work so large a deposit is a more perplexing conundrum than the geological peculiarities in Nos. 1 and 2. Some idea of the extent of this deposit may be gathered from the fact that 36,000 tons were raised last year. The great breadth of ore between the walls —from eighty to one hundred feet—renders underground work on the plan or system usually employed in hard ore mines next to impossible. For this reason but a small proportion of the deposit has thus far been mined, and the as yet unsolved problem, is how to obtain with safety the greatest amount of ore at the least cost. So far, operations have been confined to the sinking of a main shaft, as before stated, to a depth of 230 feet, from the bottom of which, on each level, drifts have been run in various directions, and several large chambers excavated in different parts of the deposit, generally on the side next to the foot wall. One of these drifts extends from the bottom of the shaft on the first level, southeasterly to the foot wall, and from thence northerly to a point 50 feet below the present level of the Trebilcock pit. The first half of this drift has been partially filled up by a fall of rock, and another is now being driven from the main shaft in a westerly direction, and will intersect it at a point about half way between the foot wall and its northern terminus. The intention is to then sink a shaft in the Trebilcock pit to connect with this drift, and thus open a new outlet for the ore mined in that cut, and also facilitate mining operations by opening an underhand stope with a face of fifty feet. The two cuts will thus be connected and thereafter constitute one mine. There are similar drifts and lofty chambers, from which last the ore has been worked out as far as it could be done with safety, on the lower level. The shaft, which was supposed to be on the hanging wall side of the deposit, (and is, should there be such a thing as a hanging wall), is down to within a few feet of the foot wall, and cannot be carried down to another level in ore. Sooner or later a new shaft, one or two hundred feet in the rear of the present one, will have to be sunk through the rock so as to strike the ore at a lower level. This will be necessary to the carrying out of the only feasible plan upon which the mine can be worked—which is to sink to the lowest level ever intended to be reached, and then excavate chambers of a certain width, leaving alternate bodies of ore to support the roof and walls, and as fast as these chambers are mined out filling them up with rock and waste material. In this way it is believed at least nine-tenths of the ore can be taken out; and such is the plan which must ultimately be adopted. There is in this hematite mine an immense body of ore, and it will be many years before it will be exhausted by the most thorough and practical system of mining which can be brought into practice. Although drifts have been made across the formation eighty feet from the foot wall towards the hanging, the latter has not yet been encountered, and the real extent of this most remarkable deposit is, therefore, not yet fully determined.

Capt. John Oliver, one of the most experienced miners in the district, is foreman in the hematite mine, which position he has held for the past seven years.

The company's mine on section 16, known as the "Parsons," has not been worked the past two or three years, though a deposit of good ore has been developed. On section 21, the company has a hematite mine, which, however, has never been worked extensively, though the ore is of good quality, and the mine one that could be made very productive. Near by is the old New England mine, now the property of the Lake Superior company, and from which over 100,000 tons of ore have been mined. These two openings are divided only by the section line between 20 and 21, and when operations are resumed will doubtless constitute one mine. In the hill just north a shaft is now going down in a narrow vein of very fine slate ore. This is doubtless a part of the Saginaw range, which has been traced across the whole of sections 19, 20 and 21.

On section 19 the company has another mining location, upon which considerable work has been done, and which is familiarly known at Ishpeming as the "New Burt." The location adjoins the Saginaw, which lies to the west of it, and is a continuation of the same range. Here is found a belt of hard granular and slate ore, in which several openings have been made, but only three of which are at present being worked. These cuts are numbered respectively 1, 2 and 3, commencing at the Saginaw line. No. 1, is a large open cut, worked out to a depth of 100 feet, the width being, perhaps, seventy feet. It is supplied with a skip road operated by steam power. There appears to be a body of pure ore about 55 feet in thickness at the bottom, and lying next to the hanging wall. The formation is somewhat peculiar, there being no well defined foot wall; lying under the belt of pure ore is a body of mixed ore, 25 feet thick, and under that an extensive deposit of soft hematite of inferior quality. This peculiar formation is noticeable wherever the ore belt has been opened on the section. Nos. 2 and 3, have also been worked out to a depth of 100 feet; these two pits will be connected by the sinking of a winze in No. 3, and a drift from thence to the hoisting shaft in No. 2. In No. 1, the shaft will be carried down fifty feet during the winter, and connected with a winze in the west end. A winze will also be put down in No. 2, and connected with the main shaft. These winzes will give several underhand stopes, and greatly facilitate the taking out of the ore. The ore is raised from Nos. 1 and 2, on skip roads operated by engine and drums manufactured by S. F. Hodge, of Detroit. Two steam drills, of the Wood and Waring patents, are to be employed, and it is believed they will not only facilitate operations but very materially curtail the cost of mining.

East of No. 3, several openings have been made in about the same quality of ore, one of which is very promising. They are not now being worked, but can at any time be made to add largely to the product of the mine.

There was mined and shipped at the "New Burt," in 1875, about 12,000 tons of first-class ore, and if necessary, the product can be doubled this year. Capt. P. T. Tracy, one of the pioneer miners of the copper district, and who has likewise had much experience in iron mining, is the local superintendent.

We append herewith a statement of the total product of the Lake Superior mine during the eighteen years past:

YEAR.	GROSS TONS.
1858	4,658
1859	24,668
1860	33,015
1861	25,195
1862	37,709
1863	78,976
1864	86,773
1865	50,201
1866	68,002
1867	119,935
1868	105,745
1869	131,343
1870	166,582
1871	158,047
1872	185,070
1873	158,078
1874	114,074
1875	129,339
Total	1,677,410

The company gives employment to about 300 men.

The following are the officers of the company:

President, JOSEPH S. FAY; *Treasurer*, RICHARD S. FAY; *Secretary*, A. C. TENNEY.

Hon. S. P. Ely, who had filled the position of general agent from the inception of the company, resigned in 1874, and was succeeded by Chas. H. Hall, Esq., the present efficient general manager. Mr. Hall is ably assisted by Jeff. D. Day, Esq., who has been in the employ of the company for a number of years. Capt. G. D. Johnson, whose name was at one time inseparable from that of the Lake Superior mine, resigned last fall, after eighteen years of continuous service as superintendent. He is now engaged in silver mining, in the Tintic district, Utah.

THE NEW YORK MINE

is located in Section 3, Town 47, Range 27—a leasehold of forty acres, adjoining the Cleveland on the north. The fee is owned by A. R. Harlow, Esq., of Marquette, from whom it was leased for a term of years by a corporation styled the New York Iron Mining Company, organized in 1865, with Samuel J. Tilden, J. P. Sinnett and J. Rankin, of New York, as corporators. This company is a consolidation of the New York and Boston Iron Mining Company, and the New York Iron Mine, incorporated March 31st, 1865. The stock is now all held by S. J. Tilden and W. L. Wetmore.

Mining operations were commenced in 1864, in which year 8,000 tons were mined and sold to other companies.

At one time there appeared to be two well defined veins crossing the tract diagonally, lying one above the other, and separated from each other by a thin wall of rock. More recent developments, however, show that these veins run together at a lower depth, or else that the lower one pinches out altogether. This lower vein has been worked to some extent on the east half of the tract, but at one or two points has been exhausted, and the cuts made in taking out the ore have been partially filled up with waste rock from the upper vein. There is still, however, a good face of ore in the east end of this lower vein, and it is being worked to good advantage.

The upper vein referred to above, is the one from which the bulk of the product for the past ten years has been mined. This has been opened an entire length of about 800 feet. The dip of the vein is to the south at an angle of about 38° from the perpendicular, and it has been worked out for most of the distance to an average depth of about 200 feet on the incline. The ore belt averages about 18 feet of pure red specular—an ore that has acquired great popularity among furnacemen. This vein was originally worked as an open cut, with an incline tram-way from the west end of the opening down to the bottom, the deposit then appearing to be a pocket rather than a well defined vein. When it was found that the ore dipped under the overlying mass of rock, a new system was inaugurated. The tram-road in the west end was taken up, skip roads properly located on the floor of the incline were substituted, as much of the overhanging rock as was considered dangerous or liable to fall was taken down, and the vein was then attacked by cutting out chambers ten or fifteen feet deep, leaving strong pillars of ore to support the hanging wall. This plan has been followed since 1872, and works most successfully. A row of these pillars extend along the whole open front of the mine, and as mining progresses others are left here and there, so that it would be impossible for any considerable portion of the wall to cave in. At the east of the mine about 250 feet of this vein has been worked down to the Cleveland line, but what has been lost at this point has been regained by the extension of the vein farther west. At a point some distance west of the open cuts referred to, a shaft was sunk 140 feet striking a body of very fine magnetic ore. From the bottom of this shaft a drift has been made, apparently across the formation, 12 feet south, and another a few feet north, showing 20 feet of pure clean ore, though neither the foot nor hanging wall has been reached. At this point the ore belt appears to swing around to the north, and the developments show that this magnetic deposit lies immediately under the red specular. From the bottom of this shaft a drift has been made through into the main mine, which is supplied with a tram-road to connect with No. 1 skip, and can if necessary be continued to others, so that there will be no difficulty in hoisting out all the ore that can be mined from the new deposit, which appears to be of great extent. The strange feature of this new discovery is that the ore is a very pure magnetic—the first ore of the kind yet found in the district east of the Washington and Edwards mines.

The machinery in use consists of three engines—one of

which operates two drums for hoisting from the incline referred to, and which engine and drums are made to do all the work of no less than seven skip roads. This is accomplished by changing the ropes as required. When No. 1 skip is filled, and the signal is given, the rope on one of the drums is unhooked, and that belonging to No. 1 skip is attached in its stead, and so on, among the whole seven. The men in the engine house find very little time to indulge in dime novels, as they might, were each skip supplied with a separate drum. Another engine is, or was, used for hoisting from No. 5, a cut near the Northwestern railway track, where there is a twenty foot vein of good ore. This opening is not now being worked, as is also the case with the cut west of the store on the north side of the creek. There are eleven skip roads in all, and it requires no less than eleven steam pumps, including one 8 inch plunger, to drain the mine of surplus water.

About 150 men are employed—all miners, except thirty or forty teamsters, landers and laborers. Nearly all work in and about the mine is done by contract. The men get a certain price per ton for mining the ore, and others a certain price for filling and landing, etc.; only a few general utility men being employed by the month or day. A general and most rigid system of economy prevails, and is noticeable in every department. Capt. W. E. Dickenson, who is an old copper miner, has been superintendent for the past six years, and is likely to continue as long as he will consent to serve in that position.

The following is a statement of the product of the New York mine each year since the commencement of mining operations:

YEAR.	GROSS TONS.
1864	8,000
1865	12,214
1866	33,761
1867	43,302
1868	45,665
1869	67,698
1870	94,809

1871	76,381
1872	68,950
1873	70,882
1874	77,010
1875	70,754
Total	669,426

On another page will be found an engraving showing a section of this mine, as it appears at a depth of **200 feet from the surface.**

THE REPUBLIC MINE.

In our review of the iron district, published in 1871, under the sub-title of "undeveloped iron lands" we referred to what was then known as Smith mountain, as being, perhaps, "the most extensive body of iron ore yet discovered on Lake Superior." At that time, aside from the owners of the property, but few persons had ever visited what is now the site of one of the most active and prosperous mining industries in the region. In the summer of 1870, the writer, together with several of the owners, visited the location, going from the east end of Lake Michigamme and down the river, in a small boat, with the celebrated woodsman, Jack Armstrong, for a pilot over and around the rapids. That was then the most feasible route, unless the visitor preferred to ride a horse through swamps and over the most abominable trail it was ever our fortune to traverse. We found at the foot of the "mountain" a little log hut, the only habitation, which was occupied at the time by Maj. Brooks, who was then engaged on the state geological survey. The extract above quoted was based upon the observations made at that time, and it is interesting to note how nearly the prediction that the mine could be "made to yield a hundred thousand tons the first year after the commencement of operations," has been verified. We find now a "location" with a population of at least a thousand people, all of whom are dependent upon the business of the company for subsistence. The little old log cabin has given way to an array of sixty-seven neat and substantial frame tenement and boarding houses, office, store, warehouse, saw mill, blacksmith and carpenter shops, slaughter house, glycerine and powder magazines, engine and boiler houses, stables, ore docks, and pockets, etc., all the property of the company, and erected at a cost of not much, if any, less than $200,000. There is also a commodious school building, hotel and railway depot, aside from the new town of Iron City, where there are a number of stores, boarding houses, etc. To a person who visited "Smith mountain" in 1870, or even a year later, the change appears almost miraculous.

The articles of association of the Republic Iron company were executed April 15th, 1870, Samuel P. Ely, Edward Breitung, Jonathan Warner, Edwin Parsons and John C. McKenzie being the original incorporators. The company being organized, the first important step was to secure the construction of a branch railway from some point on the Marquette, Houghton & Ontonagon railroad, to the mine. An arrangement was effected with the Marquette, Houghton & Ontonagon railroad company, and work on the branch road was commenced late in 1871, and completed the following autumn, the first train of loaded ore cars leaving the mine on the second of October, 1872. The mine was opened in that year, the work being commenced before the completion of the branch, the shipments from the second of October to the close of navigation being 11,025 gross tons. The product of the mine since it was first opened is given as follows:

YEAR.	GROSS TONS.
1872	11,025
1873	105,453
1874	126,956
1875	119,768
Total	363,202

The Republic is situated in section 7, township 46, N., range 29, W., on the easterly shore of Smith's bay, a widening of the Michigamme river, about thirty-six miles from Marquette, by rail. The ore, thus far, has all found an outlet through this port, the Marquette, Houghton & Ontonagon railroad having no competitor in the transportation of the product of the mine to the lake side. An attempt to describe the mine without the aid of an engraving would be futile. The vein is very irregular, and has so many crooks and turns that a well engraved sketch is actually necessary in order to give the reader anything like an intelligent idea of the formation. The ore deposit lies under or behind a belt of quartzite, which last seems to form the bed of the bay. The quartzite forms the margin and apparently the basin of the bay, around the south end of which it curves in the form of a crescent. Behind and beneath this quartzite lies the ore vein, and underneath the ore a ferruginous jasper, backed by diorite (greenstone). The vein, as we have said, is very irregular in its course, and at one or two points narrows down to only a few feet in width, while at others it is so wide as to have the appearance of an immense bed deposit rather than that of a vein or mere stratification. The outcrop of the ore belt is from one to two hundred feet above the level of the bay, and from four to eight hundred feet from the water's edge, the intervening ground being occupied by the company's buildings, docks, pockets, railway tracks, etc., these being near the foot of the hill or bluff. The vein of pure ore, thus far developed, has been opened for a distance of about 3,500 feet, of which 2,000 feet is continuous and without a break. The average width of the vein is from 20 to 50 feet, though in No. 4 pit there is a body of ore fully 120 feet in width. The vein is nearly perpendicular, and thirteen openings have been made upon it. These are known as Nos. 1, 2, 3, 4, 5, 6, 7, 8, 9, 10, 11, and the "Gibson" and "Ely" pits. Nos. 3, 8, 10, 11 and Gibson are not now being worked. At many places where the vein has been opened the ore is found projecting itself into the foot wall in the shape of a letter V. From some of these spurs and projections thousands of tons of pure ore have been taken, and the great apparent width of the vein in No. 4 is partially the result of one of them, and in one of the cuts—No. 2, we believe,—the vein itself assumes a letter V shape around a projection of the foot wall. In fact, the formation presents many peculiarities difficult, if not wholly impossible, to describe—and we shall not at present attempt further details in that direction.

The work now in progress, together with the new engine-house and machinery, now in operation, contemplates a marked improvement in the future working of the mine. The vein, for a length of nearly 2.000 feet, has been mined out from a depth of from 50 to 75 feet below the outcrop, in open cuts. It is the intention now to adopt a thorough system of underground mining, and with this view shafts have been sunk from the floors of No. 5, 2 and 7, from which the ore will be hoisted by the new machinery.

The shaft in No. 5, is down 100 feet, and is designed for a double or alternate lift,—that is to say that it will be supplied with two cages, one of which rises to the top as the other descends to the bottom. This shaft, as also the other two, incline from the perpendicular so as to conform to the dip of the vein, and will be protected by solid arches or pillars, in the rear of which winzes have been sunk to a level with the bottom of the shaft, and from which stopes of 50 feet, the whole width of the vein, are thus secured. No. 5 shaft is a most perfect piece of mine work, being substantially timbered and having two separate compartments, leaving, on the side next to the engine-house, sufficient room for the pump, and also space for hoisting whenever it shall be found necessary to sink the shaft to a lower level—when it can be done without interrupting the operation of the cages. The shafts in two and seven are for single cages, which will also be operated by drums in the engine-house. These three shafts will furnish the outlet for all the ore raised from 1,200 feet of the vein. The cages, as will more clearly appear from a description of the machinery given below, receive the loaded cars at the bottom of the shafts, which, when hoisted to the top, are run off upon the tramroads and thence to the pockets. The lift in No. 5 shaft will be 100 feet, and in Nos. 2 and 7, 50 feet. The ore from Nos. 5, and 2, shafts will be raised to the surface proper, and from thence pass down the incline tram-roads to the railway; that taken out through the shaft in No. 7, will be hoisted to the floor of the present open cut and pass out through the tunnel which was completed a year or two ago, and is supplied with a tram-road.

The new hoisting machinery, which is of the most massive and powerful kind, was manufactured at the Iron Bay foundry, Marquette, and is something new in this region. The plan or system is similar to that in vogue in the anthracite coal regions of Pennsylvania, though differing from it somewhat in construction and minor details. Instead of the skip now in general use at our mines, cages are substituted, each large enough to accommodate a car holding three tons of ore. In the principal shaft, nearest the engine house, (No. 5 pit) there are two of these cages, which when empty or when containing an empty car each, suspended by means of a wire rope three by one-half inches in size, and wound upon a cylinder or winze, counterbalance each other in such a manner that when one rises to the top of the shaft the other descends to the bottom. Immediately that a loaded car appears at the surface it is run off upon a dump track, and an empty one rolled into its place in the cage. This change, at the same time, takes place at the bottom of the shaft, with the difference that the car rolled out is empty and the one supplying its place is filled with ore. Signals are interchanged, and the engine makes the necessary revolutions for the ascending and descending cages. As the cages and cars thus suspended exactly neutralize, by counterpoise, the weight of each other, the only resistance to be overcome is that of the ore itself. At the top of the shaft the loaded cars are run off upon a track, dumped, and returned by a switch to a position directly in the *rear* of the cage, all ready to be pushed into the place of the one coming from the shaft. At the bottom, the empty cars are run directly to the face of the wall and filled by the miners immediately from the stope, thence returned and take a similar position to the cage as at the top of the shaft. The shafts in Nos. 2 and 7 are supplied with single cages, operated by two single winding drums, each five feet in diameter, and capable of holding 600 feet of one and a half inch round wire rope. The alternating cages in the main shaft are operated from a double drum, friction gear, and eight feet in diameter, with a capacity for 750 feet of flat wire rope. This double drum operates in such a manner as to unwind the rope of one cage while the other is being taken up, so that though both cages are in motion at once, much time is saved by reason of the fact that while one is discharging its load the other is receiving it.

The new engine house is a substantial brick structure, 40x72 feet, with a boiler room 20x45, and machine shop 25x40. The boilers are two in number, each 48 inches in diameter, and 25 feet one inch long. Two engines, 18x24, connected, supply the power for the drums and pump. The foundation for the engines and drums is of the most substantial kind, being a net work of heavy timbers filled in with solid masonry, being additionally secured by no less than 70 inch and a half round iron bolts. There were forty-five sticks of timber, 18 inches square and from 24 to 38 feet in length, used in the foundation. Some idea of the machinery referred to may be gathered from the fact that its weight is upwards of sixty tons.

In addition to the length of vein above referred to, a new opening is now being made southwesterly from the Ely pit, on the curve of the formation, where a vein of pure slate ore, from two to seven feet wide on the surface, can be traced a distance of 600 feet.

One important feature about this extraordinary mine is the fact that between the walls very little rock or impure ore is found—the rock where found at all, away from the walls, being in the shape of small islands, or, as the miners call them, "horses," which need not necessarily be removed, and in underground mining may possibly be utilized as pillars to support the roof of the mine. However, there are but few of these, and aside from them, the vein is all pure ore—how pure the following analyses, which have been furnished us, tell most conclusively:

An abstract of fourteen analyses taken by various parties in the interest of the manufacturers. A part being only for specific properties

Number	BY WHOM PROCURED.	Metallic Iron.	Phosphorus.	Silica.	Lime.	Magnesia.
1	Cambria Iron Works, surface specimens in 1871	65.11	t'ce			
2	do do do	67.75	.05			
3	do do do	68.01	t'ce			
4	do do Magnetic	69.88	.018			
5	Brown, Bonnell & Co., for iron and silica	69.24		1.08		
6	do do Magnetic	71.82		.84		
7	E. R. Taylor, chemist	68.40	.080	.86	.82	.33
8	Lucy Furnace Company	68.24	.150	3.53		
9	do do	65.86	.073	4.63		
10	do do	69.89	.060	2.02		
11	do do	67.55	.045	2.56		
12	Cambria Iron Company, in 1872	68.40	.050			
13	do do in 1874	68.40				
14	do do in 1875	70.60		1.10		
	Average M. Iron 14 anal. Phos. 10 anal.: Silica. 8 anal	68.48	.083	2.07		

The mine gives employment to about 230 men, and commenced shipments this spring from stock piles aggregating at least 50,000 tons.

Capt. Peter Pascoe, who has been the superintendent in charge ever since the first blow was struck, is justly proud of his mine, and the work he has accomplished gives conclusive proof of his rare ability as a miner.

The following are the present officers of the company:

President, DAVID MORGAN, Irondale, Ohio; *Vice-President*, EDWARD BREITUNG, Negaunee, Mich.; *Secretary*, T. DWIGHT EELLS, *Cleveland, Ohio; *Treasurer*, JOSEPH PERKINS, Cleveland, Ohio; *General Agent*, POWELL STACKHOUSE, Marquette, Mich.

THE MICHIGAMME MINE.

On the north shore of Lake Michigamme, in town 48, range 30, is situated the Michigamme mine, owned and wrought by a company of the same name. It is in what is generally denominated the Michigamme range, which apparently begins at a point near the head, or east end of the

*Since deceased, leaving a vacancy.

lake, and extends west a distance of eight miles or more, and embraces the Empire, Hoskins, Michigamme, Spurr Mountain, Stewart, Iron King and Harney locations, of which, however, only the Michigamme and Spurr Mountain have attained prominence as successful mines. The Michigamme company own, including the 200 acres embraced in the town site, an estate of 1,400 acres, lying in a compact body. Upon this property the vein has been opened in seven places, the openings being numbered from east to west, successively. At present, operations are confined to that portion of the vein lying between No. 3, and a point about 200 feet west of No. 7, a run of about 1,600 feet. From the west end of this run the line of ore deposit has been traced by needle attractions, outcrop and test pits, a distance of 3,500 feet. East from No. 3, through Nos. 2 and 1, the line of deposit continues on the company's property half a mile, and for still another half mile under Lake Michigamme, of which last the company owns the mining right. The total length of vein owned by the company, is about two miles. Work was originally commenced by running an adit level along the vein, a few feet above drainage, tapping the ore at the most convenient points, by open cuts through the drift and hanging wall on the south. This system was continued until the ore above the adit level, between Nos. 3 and 7, was nearly worked out, and the employment of machinery was found to be necessary. It was found that the line of deposit between Nos. 3 and 7 was of sufficient extent to constitute in itself a mine of good proportions, and a thorough examination and study of the vein, as far as developed, led the board of directors, acting upon the advice and suggestions of Mr. Houghton, the general agent, to determine upon a system of underground mining, exclusively. Work was therefore abandoned in Nos. 1 and 2, from which about 10,000 tons had been mined. This portion of the deposit lies in alternate layers of ore and rock, while that west of No. 3, to and beyond No. 7, is nearly all pure ore; the width or thickness of the vein averaging not less than twenty feet. It is thought, however, that in the east portion of the vein the ore cuts the rock out, or *vice versa;* and that the most economical way of determining the question would be by a gradual extension of underground work, east from No. 3, at some time hereafter. The same policy will be adopted in future operations on the vein west of No. 7. The plan is a most conservative one, inasmuch as it simply comprehends the opening of an underground mine on the most prolific part of the vein, (as far as developments show) and the gradual and economical extension of underground work east and west, until the whole of the workable deposit is developed and made productive.

With this end in view, shafts have been, or are being, sunk in Nos. 4, 5, 6, and 7, to a depth of 100 feet below the adit level. Twenty-five feet below the adit level, a drift is being made on the vein, the whole length of the proposed underground mine, leaving twenty-five feet of solid ore as a roof. This roof is cut only by the four shafts, 8x14 feet each. These shafts are in the ore next to the hanging wall, the whole body of ore in the rear being left intact; at each side of these shafts winzes will be sunk from the drift above, leaving a sufficient body of ore to protect the shaft and support the walls. At the bottom these winzes will be connected with the shafts by drifts through the intervening walls or screens, and thus will be obtained stopes of from 60 to 75 feet on both sides of each shaft. The ground will then be broken from the top with an underhand stope, and the ore falling to the bottom will be hoisted out in skips through the shafts. As we have said, this plan contemplates the opening of an underground mine, embracing 1,600 feet of vein, and the sinking of the shafts and winzes referred to, will open enough ground for two years' steady work. It will be readily perceived that the plan thus outlined differs materially from the common system of underground mining, in that the cost of tunneling on each separate level is saved; there will be no drifting or tunneling on any of the levels except to connect the shafts and winzes at the bottom by a drift through a few feet of ore, if we exclude all mention of

UNDERGROUND SECTION NEW YORK IRON MINE.

ever, that in the east portion of the vein the ore cuts th[e] rock out, or *vice versa;* and that the most economical way [of] determining the question would be by a gradual extension o[f] underground work, east from No. 3, at some time hereaft[er.] The same policy will be adopted in future operations on [the] vein west of No. 7. The plan is a most conservative on[e,] inasmuch as it simply comprehends the opening of an unde[r-] ground mine on the most prolific part of the vein, (as far [as] developments show) and the gradual and economical [ex-] tension of underground work east and west, until the who[le] of the workable deposit is developed and made productive.

With this end in view, shafts have been, or are being, su[nk] in Nos. 4, 5, 6, and 7, to a depth of 100 feet below the [adit] level. Twenty-five feet below the adit level, a drift is be[ing] made on the vein, the whole length of the proposed und[er]ground mine, leaving twenty-five feet of solid ore as a r[oof.] This roof is cut only by the four shafts, 8x14 feet e[ach.] These shafts are in the ore next to the hanging wall, [the] whole body of ore in the rear being left intact; at ea[ch] side of these shafts winzes will be sunk from the drift abo[ve,] leaving a sufficient body of ore to protect the shaft and su[p]port the walls. At the bottom these winzes will be co[n]nected with the shafts by drifts through the intervenin[g] walls or screens, and thus will be obtained stopes of from 6[0] to 75 feet on both sides of each shaft. The ground will then be broken from the top with an underhand stope, and the ore falling to the bottom will be hoisted out in skips throug[h] the shafts. As we have said, this plan contemplates t[he] opening of an underground mine, embracing 1,600 feet [of] vein, and the sinking of the shafts and winzes referred [to,] will open enough ground for two years' steady work. It w[ill] be readily perceived that the plan thus outlined differs [ma]terially from the common system of underground minin[g,] that the cost of tunneling on each separate level is sa[ved;] there will be no drifting or tunneling on any of the l[evels] except to connect the shafts and winzes at the bottom [by a] drift through a few feet of ore, if we exclude all menti[on]

UNDERGROUND SECTION NEW YORK IRON MINE

the drift immediately under the roof, without which, it would have been impossible to carry the underground plan into execution. The shafts and winzes down and connected, the stoping parties will work both ways until the whole body of ore down to the first level is worked out; in the meantime the shafts and winzes have been sunk to the second level without in any way interfering with or retarding operations in the level above, and thus a uniform product for each and every month in the year is secured. We regard this plan one of the best that could possibly be devised, as being calculated to secure the largest product at the least expense.

As might naturally be inferred, the most powerful and elaborate machinery is necessary to the successful working of a mine on the plan adopted by the Michigamme company. The water from the mine will be raised by a steam pump placed in each shaft, instead of from one main pumping shaft, as is the case in most of the mines in the district. By this means the necessity of drifts or tunnels on each and every level to drain the mine, is obviated. But the machinery for hoisting the ore must necessarily be of the most powerful kind, and the new engine and hoisting drums at the Michigamme answer fully to that description. The engine is 28x36, and the drums, of which there are four—one for each shaft—are eight feet in diameter, with six feet face, each capable of holding enough $1\frac{1}{2}$-inch wire rope to hoist the skip from a depth of 1,300 feet. They are worked by V friction gear, with steam brakes; there are four steam brake cylinders, 12x12, one to each drum. The machinery is all placed on a solid foundation of stone masonry, in the bottom of which are iron bed plates, to which are secured the numerous heavy iron bolts, by means of which the timbers upon which the engine and drums rest are held firmly and securely in their places. This machinery was constructed at the Michigan Iron Works, S. F. Hodge, Detroit, and is first class in every particular. The building in which this machinery is placed is a most substantially built stone structure, 50x70 feet in size, with a wing 28x38 feet, in which are the boilers.

The building is situated on the summit of the hill, between shafts Nos. 5 and 6, about midway of the line of deposit embraced within the limits of the underground system described above. The machinery is capable of raising, with moderate ease, from 800 to 1,200 tons of **ore per** day, a daily production which it is possible, even probable, **the** mine may attain, should the demand for ore ever again **warrant a vigorous** prosecution of work.

The **product of** the mine, since it was first opened **in 1872,** has been as follows:

YEAR.	GROSS TONS.
1872	141
1873	29,107
1874	45,294
1875	44,763
Total	119,305

The following named gentlemen constitute the Board of directors: Hon. W. H. Barnum, Lime Rock, Conn.; Ralph Crooker, Boston, Mass.; Charles J. Canda, New York City; Charles B. Hebbard, Detroit, and Jacob Houghton, Michigamme, Mich.

The officers are:

President, Hon. W. H. BARNUM; *Secretary and Treasurer,* JAMES ROOD, Chicago; *Superintendent,* JACOB HOUGHTON.

The business office of the company is at No. 9, Metropolitan block, Chicago.

SPURR MOUNTAIN MINE.

This property embraces the north half of the southwest quarter and south half of the northwest quarter of section 24, township 48, range 31, Baraga county. Work at this mine was commenced on the 23d day of September, 1872; but little was done that year. Railway communication had not been completed, **and active** operations were not commenced until late in the season, just as winter set in, when provisions had to be packed in from Champion, a distance of ten miles, on the backs of the **pioneers,** through as rough swamps as can be found anywhere in the district. During the winter, however, the Marquette, Houghton and Ontonagon railway was completed to L'Anse, a switch laid down to the mine, a station house, and several boarding and dwelling houses erected, and in the spring the company was ready to commence shipments from a very considerable stock-pile, the mine having been sufficiently opened to afford a yield of about 2,500 tons in February and March, 1873. In the month following, the product reached 3,200 tons, and in May 6,100 tons were mined. In June a conflagration occurred from fire communicated by the railway engines to the dry wood on both sides of the track, which swept the location of all its buildings, except the station house and the company's office, and operations at the mine were suspended for two weeks.

The mine now embraces about 900 feet of the vein, about the center of the company's tract on an east and west line, leaving over five hundred feet on either side to be opened at such time or times as the demand for an increased product may warrant enlarged operations. The vein lies against the bluff, which seems to form the foot wall the whole length of the range, and dips at an angle of about twenty degrees south. The average width of the vein is about twenty feet, almost pinching out at one or two points, and at others swelling to a thickness of nearly forty feet. There are four shafts or openings—Nos. 1, 2, 3 and 4. Nos. 1 and 2 are skip shafts, through which the ore is raised by steam power from a depth of 150 feet. From Nos. 3 and 4 the ore is raised by horse power, but it is the intention to discard the whim and derrick at no distant day, and put in skip roads and cars, to be operated by drums the same as Nos. 1 and 2. The mine is at present drained by two steam pumps, one in each of the main shafts. The plan of mining is similar in some respects to that adopted at the Michigamme. There will be no sinking farther than is necessary to accommodate the skip roads, and provide the proper underhand stopes, of which there will be eight in all. During the winter the skip shafts, so-called, were sunk sixty feet below the present working level, so as to open enough ground to insure a large product during the present season. There is very little if any dead work to be done, the ore raised from the skip shafts being sufficient to pay the expense of sinking. A sufficient number of arches are left to support the walls, and though at the time of our visit the mine presented anything rather than its most favorable aspect, we could readily perceive that operations were being skillfully conducted, and that the plan adopted was, perhaps, the only one that could be employed to secure the largest product at the smallest cost.

The machinery employed in hoisting from Nos. 1 and 2 consists of a powerful engine and two drums, the latter four feet diameter and four feet face, large enough to hold sufficient wire rope to hoist from a depth of 800 feet. These drums will be duplicated in the spring, and the new set applied to the operation of Nos. 3 and 4. The machinery was manufactured at the Iron Bay foundry, in this city, and works most satisfactorily.

No explorations of the vein west of the mine proper have yet been made, but there seems to be no good reason why the line of deposit may not be found to continue unbroken to the western line of the company's tract. Immediately west, at the Stewart mine, a good show of ore has been found, and the magnetic needle indicates almost conclusively that the deposit extends all the way through the north half of section 23, west of the Stewart. To the east of that part of the vein which has been opened, there appears to be a break or depression caused by a small creek which flows through the tract, but east of this stream an opening has been made, and from it about 3,000 tons of ore have been mined. Near the surface, however, the ore is considerably mixed, and great care is necessary in its selection.

The mine gives regular employment to about 125 men. Since the commencement of operations the shipments of ore have been as follows:

YEAR.	GROSS TONS.
1873	31,933
1874	42,068
1875	23,094
Total	97,095

Colonel Freeman Norvell, one of the early pioneers of the copper district, is the general manager, and Captain William Morrison, an experienced miner, mining captain.

THE SAGINAW MINE

is in section 19, town 47, range 27, about two miles southwest of the city of Ishpeming. The mine was originally opened by Messrs. Maas, Lonstorf & Mitchell, in the winter of 1871-'72, under the terms of a fifteen years' lease. In 1872 these gentlemen sold their lease to a party of Cleveland gentlemen, connected with the Cleveland Rolling Mill company, who afterwards organized the Saginaw Mining company. The lessors of the property reside in East Saginaw—hence the name of the mine and company. The mine produced the first year after being opened 18,503 gross tons, a product which has increased with each succeeding year, as will be shown by the table below.

Mining was originally prosecuted in open cuts, or quarries, by removing the overlying rock and lean ore. It was soon found, however, that the underground system was the only plan upon which the mine could be successfully worked, and in the summer of 1872, a shaft was sunk in the soft hematite, which underlies the hard ore, its direction corresponding with the dip of the vein. Other shafts were subsequently sunk to the sixty foot level, at such convenient distances apart as to provide for the successful prosecution of work along the whole length of the vein on the company's property. These shafts are numbered respectively, 1, 2, 3 and 4, from west to east. The leasehold consists of a tract of five-forties, four of them being the center of the section, and the fifth being the northwest quarter of the northeast quarter. The vein or belt of ore crosses this last mentioned tract from east to west, being continuous with the ore belt of the Superior on the east, and the Albion and Goodrich on the west. The same general geological features described in our article on the "New Burt," are noticeable at the Saginaw, and the character of the ore is about the same. There are two varieties of hard ore—slate, and an exceedingly rich granular, the latter containing an unusually large percentage of magnesia.

About 900 feet of the vein has been opened. Shafts 2, 3 and 4 are down to the second level, 160 feet, and are now sinking to the third, sixty feet below the second. At several places the vein is cut by cross-courses of rock, through which drifts have been made on the first and second levels, allowing the main bodies to stand as supports to the hanging wall. From No. 4 shaft there is a run of 70 feet of ore to the Superior line, where one of these rock crossings is encountered, dipping into the Saginaw. West of this shaft there is a continuous run of pure ore for a distance of 180 feet to another rock crossing, through which a drift leads into No. 3. It will be seen, therefore, that in No. 4 the ore belt has a length of 250 feet—the width of the vein being on the average about 25 feet. The ore in No. 4, is of the variety known as "slate." West of the crossing between Nos. 3 and 4, there is another run of pure ore 100 feet, to a heave in the formation, which throws the vein to the north about twenty-five feet, west of which the vein continues unbroken another 100 feet to another of the rock crossings referred to, which makes a break of twenty-five feet in the ore. West of this break the vein holds a width or thickness of from twenty to thirty feet to No. 2 shaft. From the crossing between Nos. 2 and 3 to the shaft, the ore is a very rich granular, wholly unlike the deposit in No. 4. West of No. 2 shaft, the vein has been opened 120 feet, at which point another wall of rock has been encountered, but beyond which ore has been found in No. 1 shaft. No. 1 shaft is down 75 feet in "slate and steel" ore, but, owing to the great flow of water, had to be abandoned until such time as the water could be drained into No. 2, the main pumping shaft. Indeed, much trouble is experienced from the great flow of water, in all the openings, three pumps being required to prevent the mine from being flooded. These pumps are kept in constant operation, day and night, and the expense of maintaining them is a very prominent item in the cost of mining.

The general dip of the vein east of No. 2 shaft, is about fifty degrees north; west of No. 2 the strike is only about fifteen degrees in the same direction. The width or thickness of the ore deposit, is given as it appears on the second level; it is proper, however, to add that the width gradually increases as greater depth is attained, the general average at the outcrop having been but little more than ten feet.

The hoisting machinery employed at present consists of three drums, operated by one of Merritt's 18x24 engines, the boilers for which also furnish the steam for all the pumps. The power is hardly equal to the requirements of the mine, and another engine for hoisting and pumping has been purchased, and is now on the ground, and will probably be set up and put in operation early in the summer. This engine and machinery, which is of the most approved pattern, was manufactured for the company at Cleveland, and when put in motion will furnish all the facilities for hoisting and pumping that are likely to be required in many years to come.

The following table exhibits the product of this mine each year since it was first opened:

YEAR.	GROSS TONS.
1872	18,503
1873	37,138
1874	45,486
1875	55,318
Total	156,445

The mine gives employment to about 175 men. Capt. Sam. Mitchell, an active, intelligent, practical miner, is the superintendent. Everything about the mine gives prominent indication that he is thoroughly competent for the position he holds. He has taken all necessary precautions, from the beginning, to secure the mine with timbers and the necessary arches and pillars of ore, and an accident involving the loss of life, at the Saginaw, is scarcely possible, except it be the result of carelessness on the part of the employes. One noticeable feature, is the fact that but very little rock is removed from the mine—only that which is taken from the drifts through the rock crossings referred to, being taken out. It is safe to estimate that not to exceed 1,000 tons of rock have been raised during the past year, and were it not for the unusual flow of water, the cost sheet would, we think, exhibit a less amount of cost per ton of ore mined, than that of any other hard ore mine in the district.

The officers of the company are: *President*, A. B. STONE, Cleveland, O.; *Vice President*, H. CHISHOLM, Cleveland, O.; *Secretary and Treasurer*, A. G. STONE, Cleveland, O.

The entire product of this mine is shipped over the Northwestern line to Escanaba, though it possesses the facilities of a branch connecting with the M., H. & O. R. R. These tracks run immediately under the docks connected with the various shaft houses, and in the season of navigation the ore is transferred directly from the skips to the railway cars, thus avoiding the cost of re-handling. But few horses are employed, and there is no carting of ore as at many other mines in the district. Altogether, the Saginaw is in the best possible condition for future production, and it is safe to say that the annual product can be very largely increased, whenever the demand for ore shall warrant the prosecution of mining operations on a larger scale than has been the order at all the mines during the past two years.

THE MARQUETTE MINE

is contiguous to the Cleveland, and is owned by the stockholders of the latter company, though under a separate organization. The following is a list of the officers:

President, JOHN OUTHWAITE; *Secretary*, FRED. A. MORSE; *Treasurer*, SAMUEL L. MATHER; *Agent*, JAY C. MORSE; *Superintendent*, F. P. MILLS.

The first shipments were made in 1864, though it appears that work was commenced much earlier. We append a statement of the product of the mine for the past twelve years:

YEARS.	GROSS TONS.
1864	3,922
1865	6,652
1866	7,907
1867	7,862
1868	7,977
1869	2,798
1870	3,702
1871	—
1872	11,924
1873	2,148
1874	—
1875	3,088
Total	57,980

THE EDWARDS MINE

is situated in section 2, town 47 north, range 29 west—the workings being confined to the southwest quarter of the southeast quarter. The first opening was made in the fall of 1865, but nothing more was done that year than to sink a few test pits by way of exploration. Active operations were commenced the following spring, by the Pittsburgh & Lake Angeline company, under a lease from J. W. Edwards, the owner of the land. The company continued operations till the fall or winter of 1873, when owing to the depressed state of the ore market, operations were wholly suspended. In the spring of 1875, the company sold its mining equipment to Mr. Edwards and surrendered the lease. Mr. Edwards at once made arrangements for a renewal of operations, but had scarcely got fairly to work, when a fire destroyed his engine house and pumping and hoisting machinery, occasioning a partial suspension of work of several weeks' duration. The machinery was replaced by that formerly employed at the Kloman, a new engine and boiler house was erected, and operations resumed within six weeks after the suspension caused by the fire. Soon after, Mr. Edwards sold the forty acre tract upon which the mine is situated, together with 400 acres adjoining, to W. W. Wheaton, Esq., who at once took possession and assumed the general management. The mine adjoins the Washington, is about 28 miles distant from Marquette, on the Republic branch of the M., H. & O. railroad near its junction with the main line. The bluff or hill in which the Edwards is located crosses the tract from northeast to southwest, the ledge being generally covered with sand, gravel and iron boulders. On the north side of the ore the rocks are quartz, either compact, fibrous or slaty, the latter form externally resembling talcose slate. On the south is a range of green stone. The vein, to which operations have been principally confined, is about forty-five feet in width, widening out at some places to fifty. The ore is of two kinds —one of a dark bluish black color, highly crystalline, very heavy, and when free of quartz, almost a pure magnetic or black oxyde, yielding by analysis 71.87 of metallic iron. The other is a red oxyde, very heavy, and of the quality designated as "slate" ore.

It must not be inferred from what we have said that the deposit is confined to a single vein; on the contrary, there are no less than four regular veins, separated by walls of talcose slate varying from 16 to 40 feet in thickness. These veins all cross the tract from northeast to southwest, as shown in the following diagram:

NORTH.

Vein—Magnetic Ore.
Talcose Slate.
Magnetic Ore, 20 feet.
Slate Ore, 22 feet.
Talcose Slate, 16 feet.
Magnetic Ore.
Talcose Slate, 40 feet.
Magnetic Ore, 50 feet.

SOUTH.

At present operations are confined to the two middle veins, from which it will be very easy to reach the others by drifts through the intervening walls of rock. The north vein is fifty feet in width, and the ore is believed to be equally as rich as those now being worked.

The work in the Edwards is all underground, the ore being raised through two main shafts, which are now down to the fifth level, 300 feet from the surface. These shafts are 380 feet apart, and are now being carried down to the sixth level, through ore. They are both on the incline of the foot wall, and are supplied with four skips—two for hoisting the ore to the surface, and two that are employed in hoisting to the pockets at the lower end of the skip roads, underground, the latter not being completed down to the lower levels. The vein in No. 3 pit is 50 feet thick, and has been opened out 340 feet lengthwise. In No. 2, the vein is smaller, though large enough for all practical purposes. A large deposit has been found west of No. 3, on the fourth level, and is being mined and brought out to No. 3 shaft.

The mine is now in excellent condition, and there is no reason why, with careful management, it may not be made to yield a handsome profit to the owner. The product for 1876 is estimated at about 40,000 tons—30,000 tons magnetic and the balance first-class specular, or "slate." The Edwards ore has always maintained a good reputation, and furnacemen are fully acquainted with its merits. Since the mine came into the hands of Mr. Wheaton he has been using the ore as a mixture with his Rolling Mill hematite, and red speclar ores, with the most satisfactory results, making the best grade of Bessemer pig.

About 80 underground miners are employed at present, but enough ground has been broken to afford room for double that number, should the demand for the ore warrant increased production. The ore can be mined and placed on the cars as cheaply as at any other hard ore mine in the district.

The product of the Edwards since since the commencement of operations has been as follows:

YEARS.	TONS.
1866	2,843
1867	4,928
1868	17,360
1869	19,151
1870	24,232
1871	26,437
1872	28,380
1873	38,968
1874	2,849
1875	12,800
Total	177,048

Jas. Bale, an experienced miner, is superintendent, assisted by Gordon Murray, mining captain.

THE NEGAUNEE HEMATITE RANGE.

In 1872 there seemed to be the best of reasons for the belief that the then newly developed hematite mines, near Negaunee, would assume majestic proportions, and become a distinct and most important feature of the Lake Superior iron trade. All the properties on this range were in demand. Whilst being owned and controlled by proprietors in the neighborhood, who could have given their neighbors all the advantages which might come of favorable bargains, the inquiries from abroad and the numerous attempts which were made to buy interests in these properties, by foreign as well as by local operators, caused the owners to put their "forties" and "eighties" at enormous values. One "forty," for instance, where a mine was partially developed, was held at $200,000,—a price which no one, unless demented, would think of paying for a hematite mine, especially with the royalties added. The panic came, and the lease of the same "forty" has been forfeited, as have also the leases of a number of other properties, then considered valuable and held at a high valuation.

The characteristics of this range are brown and red hematites, varying in quality from forty-five to sixty per cent. in Metallic iron, in the blast. The brown ore exists in the largest quantity, and some of it is sufficiently hard and compact to compare favorably with the specular ores. It lies in small pockets, and in large masses or deposits, the smaller deposits being usually mixed with more or less jasper.

The most important and prolific of the mines opened on this range is the

ROLLING MILL MINE,

which is situated in section 7, town 47 north, range 26 west, where the company owns a forty acre tract—the southwest quarter of the northeast quarter of the section—and also an undivided half of the forty acres adjoining it on the east; Mr. A. L. Crawford, of Newcastle, Pa., owning the other undivided half, which, however, he has leased for a term of years to the company. The first opening was made in the fall of 1871, in which year only 236 tons were taken out and shipped to the furnace in Marquette. The ore was found to be most excellent as a mixture with the specular and magnetic ores, and preparations were at once made for permanent work; since then operations have been continued uninterruptedly, and with the most gratifying results. The mine is justly regarded as the best soft hematite mine in the district, the bed or deposit being of unusual extent, and the ore carrying not only a high percentage of metallic iron, but being possessed likewise of peculiar properties which render it easy of reduction, and very desirable for Bessemer pig.

Four pits have been opened—Nos. 1, 2, 3 and 4. Work is at present confined to Nos. 2 and 3, which are virtually one, showing a solid bed of ore 400 feet in length, and believed to be not less than 200 feet wide. These pits have been opened out to a width of over 100 feet from the foot wall, and a careful examination encourages the belief that there is a breast of ore nearly as wide lying between the open pit and the hanging wall, which last has not yet been reached by drift or otherwise. The ore in this pit has been worked out to a depth of 70 feet, and the floor appears to be a body of solid ore. A main hoisting shaft is being put down from the foot of No. 2 skip, which will give an open stope from which it is estimated that at least 30,000 tons of ore can be mined. The estimated production of the mine for 1876, is from 40,000 to 80,000 tons, the amount depending to a great extent on the state of the market.

The location of the mine is especially favorable, being situated only one mile from the city of Negaunee, at which place it is connected by a side track with both railways, and is thus afforded the advantage of competing routes for the transportation of its product. Thus far, by much the larger bulk of its product has been shipped to Marquette, a part being used at the company's furnace, and the balance shipped to lower lake ports.

The improvements at the mine consist of a large engine, agent's dwelling, a sufficient number of comfortable houses for employes, carpenter shops, barn, etc. The ore is raised from the mine in skips operated by a reversible 12x18 engine and four drums. Two of these drums are five feet in diameter, and the others three feet, all V friction gear, and of sufficient capacity to do all the work required of them with ease and facility. They were made at the Iron Bay foundry, Marquette; the engine is from the Detroit Bridge works.

The mine gives employment to an average force of 100 men. The shipments the past five years have been as follows:

YEAR.	GROSS TONS.
1871	236
1872	6,772
1873	11,319
1874	16,643
1875	37,806
Total	72,776

W. W. Wheaton, Esq., is the general manager, and the increased production of the mine since he assumed control of the company's affairs, is the best possible evidence of the energy and ability which characterizes his management. Captain James Bale is superintendent.

THE M'COMBER MINE

Which is also on this range, was opened by Wm. C. McComber in 1870. In 1872 the leasehold was sold to the McComber Iron Company, of which S. L. Mather, Cleveland, Ohio, is president and treasurer, and Fred A. Morse, of the same city, secretary. Jay C. Morse, of Marquette, is the general agent. This mine is situated on the hill just south of Negaunee, on lands owned by James P. Pendill, Esq., who receives a royalty of fifty cents per ton on all the ore mined. The land was once the property of the Detroit Iron Mining Company, which filed its articles of association in 1857. This company having made some unsuccessful explorations, sold the land to Mr. Pendill, by whom further unsatisfactory explorations were made. Mr. McComber having secured a lease, went diligently to work, and in the first year developed a mine which has since added very materially to the production of the district.

The improvements at the mine consist of a number of substantial buildings for the accommodation of employes, engine and hoisting machinery, etc. There are four hoisting shafts, and one central pumping shaft, the necessary pockets, side tracks, etc., to facilitate shipments, and altogether the mine may be considered one of the best hematite properties in the district.

The production of the McComber has been as follows:

YEAR.	GROSS TONS.
1870	4,866
1871	15,942
1872	24,153
1873	38,969
1874	2,641
1875	10,407
Total	96,978

THE GRAND CENTRAL MINE

was opened in 1870, by S. S. Burt and I. S. Waterman. It is a leasehold, paying a royalty of 75 cents per ton, under the terms of a sub-lease from Hon. E. Breitung. It was worked till the close of 1873, with fair results, when, owing to the panic, work was suspended, and the sub-lease forfeited. In 1875, Mr. M. T. Gaffney, of Negaunee, obtained the lease, and re-opened the mine, working a small force a part of the summer. The mine has produced ore as follows:

YEAR.	GROSS TONS.
1870	1,809
1871	2,921
1872	9,925

1873	6,629
1874	....
1875	987
Total	22,271

The other mines opened on this range are: The **Green Bay**, the Negaunee, the **Allen**, the Ada, Himrod, Hematite, and Spurr & Calhoun. Some other leases were given, but these are the only mines that have been wholly or even partially developed.

The Green **Bay** mine was opened by a company of that name in 1871, and mined and shipped up to the close of the year 8,582 tons, when work was suspended. Last summer the lease passed into the hands of the Mitchell Bros., practical miners, who have renewed operations, and propose to work the mine for all it is worth. The Negaunee mine is the leasehold property of Maas & Lonstorf, and has mined and shipped 11,684 tons. The mine has not been wrought since 1873. The Allen was opened by Messrs. Allen, Crocker and Shelden, who mined and shipped 9,347 tons in 1872-'73, since which the mine has been dormant. The Himrod mined and shipped 2,074 tons, and then suspended. The other so-called mines on the range never made any shipments.

THE CASCADE DISTRICT.

There are embraced in this range or district the mines of the Palmer **Iron** company, (formerly Cascade Iron Co.,) Pittsburgh and Lake Superior, Gribben, Carr and Home.

THE PALMER IRON COMPANY

has an estate of 3,120 acres, located on sections 19, 20, 29, 30, 26 and 27, in ranges 26 and 27, towns 46 and 47. The ore is of the granular, **slate and hematite** orders, or the micaceous specular and **magnetic oxides, ranging** from 60 to 66⅔ per cent, in **richness, some of it yielding as** high as 68 per cent. The deposit of granular ores, as shown by the openings already made, and the test-pits which have been put down on the property, lies in crescent shape from west to east, with the center of the curve lying south. For the most part the elevations and outcrops are from fifty to two hun-

NORTHWESTERN HOTEL, MARQUETTE.

dred feet above the base of mining and shipping levels, giving working faces in some instances two hundred feet in height, while the depressions show no variation in quantity or quality of the ore. At one point in the course of the crescent, a depression occurs where a branch of the Escanaba river falls some forty feet over an iron ledge, showing that the depth of the iron in the bluffs on either side of the stream is in all probability not less than two hundred and fifty feet, including the elevation, and possibly considerably more. To the south of the ridge of this crescent another bluff of iron is located, like a bulwark in front of the main wall of a line of military fortifications.

The openings on the Palmer property consists of Nos. 1, 2, 3, 4, 5, 6, and the West End mine. The first opening was made at No. 4, on the east, in the summer of 1864, but not until a branch road was brought in, a distance of six miles, from the Chicago & Northwestern Railroad, in 1871, was there any effort made to take out ore. In September of that year operations were commenced at No. 4 for shipment, and some 4,100 tons were taken out and sent to market before the close of the season. In addition to the openings referred to, may be mentioned the Emma and Bagaley mines, which had been leased to other parties, and the leases of which have been forfeited.

The product of the Palmer mine, including the Emma and Bagaley has been as follows:

YEAR.	GROSS TONS.
1871	4,171
1872	39,495
1873	28,920
1874	18,198
1875	4,071
	94,855

It is proper to add that operations were suspended at this mine from the fall of 1874 till some time in the following summer, the old Cascade Company having met with financial reverses by which it was forced into bankruptcy. The new company commenced operations last summer, its business affairs being under the general management of Joseph Kirkpatrick, Esq.

THE PITTSBURGH AND LAKE SUPERIOR

adjoins the Palmer, and was energetically worked in 1872, and during a part of 1873, the shipments having been as follows:

YEAR.	GROSS TONS.
1872	1,160
1873	21,498
1874	1,362
Total	24,020

The mine is now idle, and the quality of the ore is such that a renewal of operations at any time in the future is questionable.

THE GRIBBEN MINE

was opened by the Gribben Iron Company in the summer of 1872. The ore is a red specular, though scarcely up to the standard of first class shipping ores. The only shipments (4,517 tons,) were made in 1873. Is now idle.

THE CARR MINE

was opened in the summer of 1872, and after mining 2,603 tons, suspended operations.

THE HOME

is also a new mine, not now being wrought. Its product in 1873-'4 was 3,229 tons.

Of this Cascade range, aside from the West End, of the Palmer, very little can be said of a commendatory character. The deposits are, it is true, very extensive, but with the exception named, the ore cannot be considered first class. There is, notwithstanding, a large amount of good ore to be found at all the mines on the range; but it is generally so closely associated and intermixed with the leaner ores as to render separation well nigh impossible. Until the demand for the ores of the district is such as to call for those of a second or inferior quality, it is not probable that operations at these mines will be resumed.

THE SMITH MINE.

The property of this company is located on sections 18 and 20, range 25, town 45, consisting of 412 acres, in the former section, and 386 in the latter, all being located west of the west branch of the Escanaba river. The company was organized on the 1st of November, 1871, through the purchase of an interest in the property by the late Gen. James Pierce, of Sharpsville, Pa., and Henry Fassett, of Ashtabula, Ohio. The original tract was the property of Silas C. Smith, and consisted also of section 28, in the same range; but this section still remains the property of Mr. Smith. The first opening was made on section 20 some two years previous to the organization of the present company, and sufficient ore taken out to render satisfaction regarding its character and quality. Subsequently the south-east quarter of section 18, was found to present better advantages for mining, and this was adopted by the new company as the principal point for working.

The ore is mainly a hard brown and red oxyde, with strong indications, as the deposit is worked, of running into a hard specular ore. The mine is supplied with shipping facilities by a branch railroad, five miles in length, connecting with the main line of the Chicago & Northwestern railway, about eighteen miles below Negaunee. Operations at the mine were entirely suspended in the summer of 1873, owing to the general blow out among the Shenango Valley furnaces, and particularly those at Sharpsville, of which Gen. Pierce was the principal owner. It is more than probable that operations will be resumed the present season. Shipments have been as follows:

YEAR.	GROSS TONS.
1872	13,445
1873	9,328
Total	22,773

WINTHROP AND SAGINAW RANGE.

This range is opened at intervals for a distance of two miles, from the Shenango mine, about two miles south-west of Ishpeming, in a westerly direction, to what is known as the Goodrich mine.

While the formation at either opening does not correspond entirely with that of the others, and while the ores are specular, slate and brown hematite, sometimes in separate pockets and sometimes juxtaposed, there is good reason for believing that the deposit is continuous, dipping north and west, with the hematite on the foot wall, the slate under the hanging wall, and the specular between.

THE GOODRICH MINE.

This mine is the most westerly one opened on the range. It is the property of Capt. Goodrich, Chicago, and was opened in 1873. It had been explored a few years ago, by the St. Clairs, of the Washington, but after a tunnel was driven into an elevation for some distance, without satisfactory results, the work was abandoned. Subsequently, some Negaunee and Green Bay parties came into possession of the lease, the largest interest of which afterwards went into the hands of Capt. Goodrich.

The geological formation here is very irregular. The alluvial, mineral and rock, are thrown together in the utmost confusion. The work is located on an upheaval, three sides of which are accessible for cut and breast mining. Each of these sides yield ore, and enough has been taken out to satisfy the owners that they have a good mine. The ores are banded hard hematite, of but little value, bird's eye in large quantities, maganeseous slate, and a granulated specular ore. It has a branch connection with the Chicago & Northwestern, and the Marquette, Houghton & Ontonagon railroads. The product of the mine thus far is reported as follows:

YEAR.	GROSS TONS.
1873	3,258
1874	3,100
1875	1,780
Total	8,138

The Goodrich will ultimately develop into a first class mine. That the Saginaw vein extends through the property, there is little room to doubt, and the existence of a deposit of fine slate ore on the property is known to those who explored the land before it came into the possession of the present owners. All that is required to bring the Goodrich into prominence is a reasonable expenditure through the medium of an intelligent, competent management.

THE ALBION MINE

was opened in 1872. It is situated between the Saginaw and Goodrich; was worked for nearly two years, but did not re-imburse the owners for the money expended. It is, perhaps, a good property, but its successful development will require more capital than was anticipated. It was consequently abandoned, the lessees forfeiting their lease. The total shipments were 2,228 tons.

THE NEW ENGLAND

formerly owned by Capt. E. B. Ward, is now the property of the Lake Superior Company, and has been fully described in connection with the other mines of that company. The mine was opened in 1866, and up to the time it passed into the hands of the present owners, the shipments were:

YEAR.	GROSS TONS.
1866	3,150
1867	9,075
1868	8,257
1869	12,632
1870	24,871
1871	33,359
1872	17,465
1873	181
Total	108,990

The Saginaw forms the subject of a sub-division elsewhere in this work, and the "New Burt" is fully described in connection with the Lake Superior company's mines.

THE WINTHROP

adjoins the old New England on the east, and is the property of the Winthrop Iron company, though now under lease to Messrs. A. B. Meeker and H. J. Colwell. Work was commenced in the summer of 1870, since which time the shipments have been as follows:

YEAR.	GROSS TONS.
1870	3,469
1871	11,088
1872	14,239
1873	33,456
1874	7,549
1875	7,502
Total	77,303

The ore is an excellent brown hematite, quite popular with furnacemen, and yields by analysis from sixty to sixty-five per cent.

The workings at the mine embrace an excavation some three or four hundred feet in length, with an average width of perhaps fifty feet, worked down to a depth of about sixty feet at the deepest point. The deposit from which the bulk of the product is taken is about forty feet wide, but the length has not yet been determined—being continuous with the Shenango on the east, and extending west, it is believed, across the entire tract. This deposit was, until lately, supposed to be all there was of the mine, but recently what was believed to be the footwall of the mine was ascertained to be nothing but a thin layer or stratification of soapstone, behind which lies another large deposit of clean ore, the extent of which has not, however, been fully determined. It is found also that another deposit lies back of the present hanging wall, and it looks to us as if it might eventually be found to cut out both walls, and that what now appears to be three separate deposits are really one, the foot and hanging walls of which have not yet been reached. Let this be as it may, there is certainly a large body of fine ore in sight from which it will not be difficult to mine 50,000 tons the coming year, should that amount be called for.

The ore is hoisted by means of an incline from the railway pockets to the bottom of the mine, the cars upon which are operated by a wire rope so arranged that an empty car descends the incline whenever a loaded one is drawn up. The hoisting machinery was made by Crane Bros., Chicago, and is of sufficient capacity to meet all the requirements of the mine at present, and, by adding additional drums, for years to come.

THE SHENANGO MINE.

This mine lies immediately east of the Winthrop—in short, the two are working in the same opening—the Shenango being only on a lower level—and are practically the same body of ore.

Shipments have been as follows:

YEAR.	GROSS TONS.
1872	197
1873	8,658
1874	7,549
Total	16,404

The mine has not been worked the past year, but mining will probably be resumed the present season. The officers of the company are: *President,* C. DONKERSLEY, Marquette; *Vice President,* GEO. C. REIS, New Castle, Pa.; *Secretary and Treasurer,* HENRY D. SMITH, Appleton, Wis.

THE HOWELL HOPPOCK

is a partially developed mine, located about half a mile south of the Winthrop. The ore is lean and silicious, for which it is not probable a market can ever be found. After mining 2,205 tons, the company abandoned the mine.

MICHIGAN MINE.

About one mile south of Clarksburgh Station, a mine was opened in 1872, with fair promise of success, by the Michigan Iron Company. Some 3,000 tons were mined and used at the company's furnace, but the mine was finally abandoned, owing to the financial embarrassment of the company. A separate joint stock company was afterwards organized for the purpose of working the property, but have never done anything. The vein carries an average width of about ten feet, the ore being a rich granular.

THE EMPIRE MINE

is situated on the line of the M. H. & O. R. R., between Champion and Michigamme, on the south-west quarter of section 22, town 48, range 30, but has never been sufficiently worked to prove that it has any particular merit.

THE IRON KING AND HARNEY

are new undeveloped properties lying between the Michigamme and Spurr, upon which considerable money has been expended, but without developing anything of particular value.

THE STEWART MINE

is in section 23, west of the Spurr. A fair deposit of ore has been found, but very little work has been done since the beginning of the panic. The mine is the property of the Stewart Mining Company, and the prospects are fair for the development of a first class mine, whenever work is resumed and continued.

In the Republic group, properly speaking, are situated the Kloman, Cannon, Metropolis, Erie, Berea, Chippewa and Magnetic mines.

THE KLOMAN MINE

is situated on the Michigamme River, opposite the Republic. It is owned by Pittsburgh parties, and was opened in the interest of the Lucy furnace. Work was commenced in the fall of 1872 and continued till the spring of 1875, when the mine was abandoned and allowed to fill with water. The vein was opened along a distance of 1,000 feet, to a depth of 30 feet below drainage, and the abandonment of the mine by the owners was a matter of astonishment to the people of the district. The shipments were as follows:

YEAR.	GROSS TONS.
1873	21,065
1874	35,088
1875	8,059
Total	64,212

The machinery was sold to W. W. Wheaton, by whom it is now employed at the Edwards mine. It is hardly to be expected that a mine which yielded so well in the early stages of development, will be permanently abandoned; we look for a renewal of operations at the Kloman, either by the present owners, or by others, whenever a revival of the iron trade shall seem to warrant increased production by the district at large.

THE METROPOLIS

was, a year or two ago, heralded abroad as a new property of great value, and one which would ultimately rival the Republic in the quantity and quality of its product. A company was formed in Pittsburgh, to whom the stock was sold at fancy figures, and work was commenced with a grand flourish of trumpets. After the expenditure of a very considerable sum in opening the newly discovered deposit, the property was abandoned as worthless, very little if any shipping ore being found.

THE ERIE

is a new mine, belonging to Rawle, Noble & Co., together with some Chicago parties, and promises to develop into a valuable property. In the work of exploration, some 3,000 tons of first class ore has been taken out and hauled a distance of six miles to the railway. Capt. James F. Trowell is Superintendent.

THE CANNON MINE

is the property of the Cannon Iron Company. Considerable exploration work has been done, with a fair prospect for the developement of a good mine, as soon as railway communication is secured. Samuel Peck is the General agent.

THE MAGNETIC

is another promising new mine, though remote from railway communication. A shaft has been sunk in what appears to be a large deposit of good ore, and further explorations are in progress with a view to determining its extent. Mr. Peck is also agent for the Magnetic.

THE CHIPPEWA AND BEREA

are new properties, upon which large deposits of lean ore have been found, but so far very little, if any, first class ore has been uncovered.

THE IRON CLIFFS COMPANY,

owns the Foster, Barnum, Salisbury, Excelsior and Rowland mines, and also work the Pioneer mine under a lease from the Jackson Iron Company.

THE FOSTER MINE.

The old Foster openings at the Cliffs location were largely extended during 1873, and two new openings made on the highest elevation of the property, which have yielded large quantities of good ore. The ore at all the openings varies considerably in quality, some of it being strongly manganeseous, some red oxide, and some hard brown.

Near the mine is the new Cliffs furnace, of which more will be said further along. Another opening, known as the Salisbury, is on the south side of Lake Angeline ridge, adjoining the Pittsburg and Lake Angeline Company's property. A large area of dark hematite has been worked out here. In short, the bed is regarded as among the best in the region, extending across the boundaries of the Cliffs and the Pittsburg and Lake Angeline Company.

The product of the Foster has been as follows:

YEAR.	GROSS TONS.
1866-'7-'8	6 0.80
1869	14.000
1870	23,458
1871	13,203
1872	18,139
1873	27,372
1874	3,318
1875	667
Total	106,157

THE BARNUM MINE

is on section 9, town 47, range 27, and but a short distance from the Lake Superior Company's principal openings. It was first opened in the summer of 1867, but shipments did not commence till some time in June, 1868, in which year 14,380 gross tons were mined and shipped. The ore is a very fine specular, fully up to the shipping standard.

A branch of the C. & N. W. R'y was laid to the mine in

June, 1868, and all the shipments have been made over that road, though the opening is within a stone's throw of the side tracks of the M. & O. R. R., at the Lake Superior mine.

The mine is supplied with pumping and hoisting machinery, of the most substantial kind, capable of raising 500 tons every 24 hours.

The following table of shipments will give an adequate idea of the value and capacity of the mine.

YEAR.	GROSS TONS.
1868	14,380
1869	33,484
1870	44,793
1871	45,939
1872	38,381
1873	48,076
1874	41,403
1875	43,209
Total	309,665

Wm. Sedgwick, an experienced miner, who served his apprenticeship with Capt. Merry, at the Jackson, is superintendent.

The shipments from the other mines owned by the Iron Cliffs Company have been as follows:

EXCELSIOR.

YEAR.	GROSS TONS.
1872	756
1874	1,065
1875	2,860
Total	4,681

SALISBURY.

YEAR.	GROSS TONS.
1872	545
1874	7,480
1875	4,330
Total	12,355

There has been shipped from the Rowland mine 2,288 gross tons, making a total product for all the Iron Cliffs Co's mines, of 432,858 gross tons, not including the Pioneer, which has been placed to the credit of the Jackson.

THE IRON MOUNTAIN MINE

is on the south half of section 14, Town 47, Range 27, the estate comprising 320 acres. The mine was opened in the fall of 1864, and the first shipments made in 1865, in which year the C. & N. W. R'y Company supplied the mine with a branch railroad. The following table exhibits the product of the mine since being opened:

YEAR.	GROSS TONS.
1865	898
1866	6,860
1867	5,000
1868	3,836
1873	112
1875	1,635
Total	18,341

The Iron Mountain ore is of the specular or sesqui-oxyde variety, the deposit being an immense well-stratified bed, at such an elevation above drainage as to give a face of from 40 to 100 feet for over a quarter of a mile. The layers are of such thickness as to break readily by blasting into slabs of convenient size for shipment. A trap uplift, running from north-west to south-east, divides the ore bed, and inclines the same about 30 degrees. The first opening was made on the south-west shore of Foster Lake, in the ore bluff on the north slope of the trap uplift—the deposit being nearly a quarter of a mile in length, and from 900 to 1,500 feet in width. A working face of 30 feet was obtained in driving an open cut of 150 feet through the ore, which gradually improved in quality, till what is thought to be the best ore on the location, in any considerable quantity, at least, was reached. From this cut has been taken all the ore shipped from the mine. The ore makes iron of an excellent quality, being perfectly free from anything of an injurious nature, but it is rather lean for the present market, yielding only from 50 to 55 per cent. in the furnace, against 67 per cent. of other Lake Superior ores. The ore was found, however, to possess one quality which encouraged the company to persevere in their efforts to introduce it to the favorable consideration of iron makers, and that is, its decidedly cold-short properties. The Lake Superior ores produce, invariably, red-short iron, if we except the magnetic ores which are sometimes neutral. The Iron Mountain ore neutralizes the red-shortness of the other Lake Superior hematites, and when mixed with them, makes a quality of iron which is highly prized and the most useful.

As will be noticed, the mine has been wrought very irregularly, and at present it is dormant.

THE WASHINGTON MINE

comprises a valuable estate of 1,000 acres in town 47, range 29. The company was organized in 1864, and commenced mining the same year, the first shipments being made in 1865. The following is a statement of the product:

YEAR.	GROSS TONS.
1865	4,782
1866	15,150
1867	25,440
1868	35,757
1869	58,462
1870	79,762
1871	48,725
1872	38,381
1873	38,014
1874	28,390
1875	9,641
Total	382,504

The company, becoming embarrassed financially, suspended operations in the spring of 1875, since which time the mine has not been worked. A large amount of money was expended in improvements, the driving of a tunnel into and through the main deposits, and the mine was just in good shape for a large and economic production, when the panic occurred, and the company found it impossible to continue mining operations. The mine, which we regard as one of the best in the district, is for sale or lease, on favorable terms.

THE BESSEMER MINE

is in section 35, Town 48, Range 27, on the south shore of Teal Lake, and but a short distance from the City of Negaunee. The land upon which the mine is situated is owned by the Teal Lake Iron Company, by whom it was leased to the Bessemer Iron Company. Work was commenced in the fall of 1875, on a large body of soft hematite, similar in appearance to the Jackson hematite. About 3000 tons have been mined, and will be shipped the present season. The principal stockholders are Wm. C. McComber, Alex. Bengley and Delon E. Patterson.

THE CAMBRIA MINE

adjoins the Bessemer on the east, and is also a part of the estate of the Teal Lake Iron Company. It was leased last spring by the Cambria Iron Company, in which J. H. McDonald and R. P. Harriman are the principal shareholders, the property having been previously partially developed by Mr. Harriman. The indications are most favorable to the development of a good mine, the ore being, apparently of excellent quality, and comprising both the hard and soft hematites. There was mined and sold in 1874, 2,610 tons, and the new company has now several thousand tons ready for shipment.

THE LAKE ANGELINE MINE

is situated on the south side of Lake Angeline, on the line of the Marquette, Houghton & Ontonagon railroad, about seventeen miles west of Marquette. It is the property of the Pittsburgh & Lake Angeline Iron company, which was incorporated in 1865. The company owns 1,376 acres of land, (originally purchased by George E. Hall, who opened the mine,) and formerly worked the Edwards mine under lease.

The Lake Angeline mine has been opened on a stretch of the deposit 1,700 feet in length, in which four openings are being worked. From near the water's edge, along which the railway track extends, the hill running parallel with the shore rises rapidly to the base of a vertical bluff of crystalline trap, 200 feet in height. Along the base of this bluff is the ore deposit. Along the front of the deposit, near the surface, there was a strip of mixed ore and jasper, but this was worked out, giving place to a much better and more uniform quality of ore.

The working pits are four in number, and though not designated on the company's maps by numbers, for the sake of convenience we will refer to them as 1, 2, 3 and 4, commencing at the west end. No. 1 pit, is an open cut one hundred feet in length, and varying from thirty to fifty feet in width. The present work is being done on a level thirty feet below the surface of the lake; the ore is a soft red hematite, of a good quality. The extent of the deposit is not known, as it has not been deemed safe to approach the hanging wall for fear of seams which would admit the water from the lake and flood the mine. It is believed, however, that in sinking deeper this danger will be overcome, and the hanging wall safely reached on a lower level.

Between Nos. 1 and 2, is the pump shaft, from the bottom of which drifts for drainage extend into both openings. No. 2 pit is six hundred feet long, the main level being about forty feet below the lake. Another level forty feet deeper gives a working face of forty feet. The ore is raised by derricks, operated by steam power.

East of No. 2, three hundred feet, is another open cut working on the main level, with stopes of thirty feet. The ore is raised from this cut on a skip-road, operated by steam. Still further east is No. 4, also an open cut, with a working face of thirty feet. The ore in all these pits is of the red specular variety, and of good quality.

On the south side of the bluff is the brown hematite mine, which is an opening 40x150 feet, and which yields as fine a quality of hematite as can be found in the region. The pit is supplied with pumping and hoisting machinery, and is most favorably situated for profitable mining.

The product of the Lake Angeline has been as follows:

YEAR.	GROSS TONS.
1864	19,500
1865	20,151
1866	24,073
1867	46,607

1868	27,651
1869	35,432
1870	58,467
1871	33,645
1872	35,221
1873	43,933
1874	31,526
1875	26,370
Total	307,976

The company employs regularly about sixty men. The officers are: *President*, JOHN OUTHWAITE; *Secretary and Treasurer*, L. E. HOLDEN; *General Agent*, A. KIDDER; *Superintendent*, HARVEY DIMOND.

THE CHAMPION MINE

is in the south half of section 31, town 48, range 29. The mine was opened on a deposit of magnetic and slate ore of remarkable extent and uniform purity, and though little was done previous to 1868, it has developed into one of the standard mines of the district. The first opening was made in 1867, though very little was done except in the way of exploration until the following spring, when just as the first shipments began, the destruction of the docks at Marquette caused a suspension of operations till October. In that month the first shipments were made, the season closing with a total of 6,255 tons. Since then the shipments have been as follows:

YEAR.	GROSS TONS.
1868	6,255
1869	19,458
1870	73,161
1871	67,588
1872	68,405
1873	72,782
1874	46,769
1875	57,979
Total	412,397

At the inception the property belonged to the Marquette & Ontonagon Railroad company, the land upon which the mine is located being a part of its government subsidy; but in 1869, the Champion Iron company was organized and purchased the mine.

There are two main deposits of ore, one known as the

north and the other as the south deposit. These deposits are lens-shaped, lapping each other so that the hanging wall of the south deposit runs into and helps to form the foot wall of the other. There are three working shafts, numbered respectively 1, 2 and 3. No. 1 shaft is in the north deposit; No. 2 is 212 feet west on the same deposit, and No. 3 is in the south deposit 250 feet west of No. 2. These deposits lap each other about midway between shafts Nos. 2 and 3, the north deposit here making a bend and forming a junction with the other near No. 3 shaft. Nos. 2 and 3 shafts are down to the fifth level, 300 feet from the surface, and No. 1 to the fourth level—240 feet. The mining system is similar to that adopted at the Michigamme; winzes are sunk on either side of each shaft, leaving pillars to protect the shafts and support the walls. The winzes and shafts are then connected by a drift, and the ore mined from underhand stopes of 60 feet. There is, consequently, no drifting except the few feet necessary to connect the shafts and winzes.

It was determined in the beginning to adopt the underground system of mining, but after a few years, for some reason, the roof was removed from a part of the workings. Now it has been determined to secure the mine by leaving twenty feet of the floor of the third level, properly arched, for a new roof. This is accordingly being done, the ore on the length of deposit opened having all been mined out down to that level. The north deposit has been opened over a length of 644 feet. East and west of No. 1 shaft there are considerable bodies of ore remaining above the fourth level, as also east and west of No. 3. In No. 2, there is very little ore remaining above the fourth level, and the principal mining work is being done on the fifth. In the north belt the deposit carries a width of from twenty to thirty-five feet on the fourth level; in the south deposit, which has been opened over a length of 370 feet, the breadth of ore is from forty-five to sixty feet, except at the junction of the two deposits, where there is a body of pure ore fully one hundred feet wide. About 170 feet west of No. 3 shaft, the south deposit pinches out entirely, but a drift through a narrow wall of rock struck another body of ore which has been worked into fifty feet, and found to be thirty-four feet wide on the fourth level.

About one thousand feet west of No. 3 shaft, explorations have brought to light a vein or deposit of very pure red specular ore, wholly unlike anything found in the other deposits. This deposit, which was only four feet on the surface, widened out to thirteen and a half feet in going down twelve feet, and it is believed will prove a very material addition to the hitherto known value of the mine.

The mine affords employment to about two hundred men, mostly practical miners. The ore is all hoisted in skips operated by drums, the engine and machinery being of sufficient capacity to raise 1,000 tons per day from the lowest level.

The officers of the company are:

President, JOSEPH S. FAY, Boston; *Treasurer*, W. P. FAY, Boston; *Secretary*, WM. E. STONE, Boston; *General Agent*, A. KIDDER, Marquette; *Superintendent*, JAS. PASCOE.

THE KEYSTONE MINE

is in section 32, town 48, range 29, just east of the Champion, and is owned by a company of the same name, which filed its articles of association late in the fall of 1872. Work was commenced in November, 1872, and the first shipment of ore made on the 4th of June following. The developments since made show a deposit of ore 600 feet in length, the width of which is, as yet, undetermined. It is probably one among the best of the small hard ore mines in the district, the ore being substantially of the same character as that of the Champion—magnetic and slate.

The company met with a good many discouragements in the beginning, it being found necessary to erect a considerable number of buildings for the accommodation of the miners, involving a large expenditure in addition to the actual cost of opening the mine. When the financial crash came, the bottom dropped out of the ore market, and a sus pension of operations followed. Work was resumed, however, late in the summer of 1875, and a small force has been kept at work ever since, with the best of indications for a large yield whenever the state of the ore market shall warrant active mining work.

The product of the mine has been as follows:

YEAR.	GROSS TONS.
1873	10,426
1874	5,227
1875	3,346
Total	18,999

The officers of the company are:

President, GEO. C. REIS, Newcastle, Pa.; *Secretary and Treasurer*, ROBERT McCURDY, Youngstown, Ohio; *General Agent*, C. M. WHEELER, Negaunee, Mich.

THE BUCKEYE

Iron Company was organized in 1873, with a view to operations on the south half of section 36, town 48, range 30, which adjoins the Champion half section, on the west. Best judges of the geology of the situation decide that the Buckeye Company have good reason to believe that they will sooner or later develop a good mine, but as yet their labor has not been crowned with success, present or prospective. That they are on the Champion range, there is not a doubt, but to strike the range at exactly the right point is what the Buckeye people tried to do during the summer of 1873. A little more patience, and a little more expenditure of money will, more than likely, place them just where they want to be placed—ON THE RANGE—for the doubt about a good deposit of ore on this property is greatly preponderated by the facts in geology, which makes faith. No work has been done on the property since the fall of 1873, though the developments made by the Champion Company near the line, would appear to render the discovery of the same belt an easy task.

BLAST-FURNACES.

As might readily be inferred, the most important manufacturing interest on Lake Superior is the smelting of iron ore in the blast furnace. The attempt to establish iron manufactures on Lake Superior was made under many disadvantages, and at a time when, if successful, those engaged in the enterprise could not hope for large returns on the amount of capital and labor invested. It was made, in fact, before anything had been done toward the developqment of the mines, and when it would have been next to impossible to get the iron to market, except at an immense expense for transportation. And, in fact, the first effort at iron making on these shores succeeded only in so far that it served to show the sterling qualities of the ores, and the readiness with which they could be converted into blooms or pig metal.

In the summer or fall of 1846, one year after the discovery of the Jackson Mountain by Mr. Everett and his party, the Jackson Company undertook the erection of a forge on the Carp river, about three miles east of Negaunee. The building of the forge was intrusted to Wm. McNair, who was sent here as agent for the company. He had never seen a forge, and did not succeed in accomplishing anything toward its erection till the following year. In July 1847, Ariel N. Barney and his brother-in-law, Aaron K. Olds, arrived at the mouth of the Carp, having been sent up by the company. They were both practical iron makers, and expected to find the forge nearly ready for work. In this they were disappointed, as nothing had been done save that a few timbers had been hauled upon the ground; they soon discovered that McNair knew absolutely nothing about the business he had undertaken, and it was not long until Mr. Barney was empowered to go on and build the forge, and to him really belongs the credit of having built and put into operation the first iron manufacturing establishment on Lake Superior.

The first bloom was made on the 10th day of February, 1848, by Mr. Olds, and was hammered into bar iron by Mr. Barney. This is the correct date of the first manufacture of iron on Lake Superior.

In May, of the same year, Messrs. Barney, Olds, and one or two others, started in a small boat for the Sault, taking with them about 300 ℔s. of bar iron, among it the first bar made at the forge. This iron was taken to Jackson, and there exhibited as a specimen of what could be done on Lake Superior.

The forge continued in operation till sometime in 1852, when it was abandoned. It never paid the interest on the money invested, but, having served the purpose of a thorough test of the Jackson ore, the company very wisely concluded to abandon it, and devote the whole of their capital and energy to the development of their mines.

Another forge was built at Marquette, just south of the shore end of the Cleveland dock, by a Worcester (Mass.) company, in 1849, under the direction and superintendence of A. R. Harlow, Esq. It was destroyed by fire in 1853, and was never rebuilt. Two other forges were subsequently built at Forestville and Collinsville.

The first pig iron from Lake Superior ore was made by S. R. Gay, at the Collins forge. It was made as an experiment, in the forge chimney, which had been converted into a temporary stack. The result confirmed Mr. Gay in his determination to build a blast furnace, which he afterwards did.

There are now in the district twenty-one blast furnaces, and one rolling mill. On another page will be found a table, exhibiting the name and condition of these furnaces, together with their location, name of general agents, and their post-office address.

LIST OF BLAST FURNACES IN THE UPPER PENINSULA OF MICHIGAN, TOGETHER WITH THEIR LOCATION, NAMES OF OWNERS, GENERAL AGENTS AND POST-OFFICE ADDRESS.

NAME.	LOCATION.	OWNERS.	GENERAL AGENTS.	P. O. ADDRESS.	REMARKS.
Pioneer	Negaunee	Iron Cliffs Co	T. J. Houston	Negaunee	Two stacks—both in blast.
Collins	Marquette	Collins Iron Co			Abandoned.
Bancroft	Marquette	Bancroft Iron Co	J. C. Morse	Marquette	One stack—in blast.
Northern	Chocolay	Northern Iron Co	L. D. Harvey	Harvey P. O.	One stack—not in blast.
Morgan	Morgan	Morgan Iron Co	C. Donkersley	Morgan P. O.	One stack—in blast.
Greenwood	Greenwood	Michigan Iron Co*	H. J. Colwell	Negaunee	One stack—not in blast.
Michigan	Clarksburgh	Michigan Iron Co.*	H. J. Colwell	Negaunee	One stack—not in blast.
Jackson	Fayette	Jackson Iron Co	Fayette Brown	Cleveland, O.	Two stacks—one in blast.
Champion	Champion	Morgan Iron Co	C. Donkersley	Morgan	Destroyed by fire in 1874 and not rebuilt.
Cliffs	Tilden	Iron Cliffs Co	T. J. Houston	Negaunee	One stack—not in blast.
Marquette & Pacific	Marquette	M. & P. Rolling Mill Co	W. W. Wheaton	Marquette	One stack—bituminous—in blast.
Escanaba	Escanaba	Escanaba Furnace Co			One stack—not in blast.
Grace	Marquette	Lake Superior Iron Co.	C. H. Hall	Ishpeming	One stack—anthracite—not in blast.
Munising	Munising	Munising Iron Co	E. P. Williams	Marquette	One stack—not in blast.
Bay	Onota	Bay Furnace Co	H. S. Pickands	Onota	Two stacks—one in blast.
Deer Lake	Ishpeming	Deer Lake Iron Co	E. N. Hall	Ishpeming	Two stacks—not in blast.
Peat Furnace	Ishpeming	Lake Superior Iron Co.	C. H. Hall	Ishpeming	One stack—not in blast.
Menominee	Menominee	Menominee Iron Co	M. R. Hunt	Depere, Wis	One stack—in blast.

*In Bankruptcy—J. M. Wilkinson, Marquette, Assignee.

These are all charcoal furnaces, except the Grace (anthracite) and Marquette & Pacific (bituminous). They are all hot blast and propelled by steam, except the Collins, Bancroft and Deer Lake, which have water power. The last named, together with the Morgan, Greenwood and Champion, have banks level with the furnace mouth—the others hoist their stock. The blast is heated in ovens, containing from 18 to 30 ox bow pipes, to from 450° to 650°, averaging above the melting of lead. The air at this temperature is forced into the furnace through two three or four inch tuyeres, under pressure of from $1\frac{1}{2}$ to $2\frac{1}{2}$ lbs. per square inch. The furnace linings are 40 feet high, $9\frac{1}{2}$ feet at bosh, or greatest diameter which is about 13 feet bottom. The hearth is about one-third the greatest diameter, and the mouth about one-half. The boshes are very steep, being one run to from three to four rise. All these dimensions vary at different furnaces.

The prevailing charcoal wood, and that which furnishes four-fifths of the fuel of this district, is the hard maple—next, yellow birch. At present one-third of the furnaces are using considerable hemlock, pine, and other soft woods, which are far less valuable for coal. The coal consumed per ton of iron varies widely, depending on the nature of the fuel and ore; it may be set down at 110 bushels for best stock and work, and 140 bushels for inferior stock. This at 10 cents per bushel, which may be called the average for 1875, gives an average of $12.00 for fuel, or one-half the cost of the iron. The ore would average one-fourth the cost, or $6.50. The largest item of the remaining fourth would be furnace labor and superintendence—producing a total of about $24 as the cost of iron at the furnace. The freight, commission, and interest account will increase the cost of the iron to, perhaps, not less than $30, sold.

THE PIONEER,

as its name implies, was the first furnace built in the district. Both stacks were built under contract, by S. R. Gay, for the Pioneer Iron Company, by whom it was owned and operated until the spring of 1866, when it was leased to the Iron Cliffs

Company. The property thus leased consisted of the two furnace stacks, about 4,000 acres of land, including a part of the village plat of Negaunee, and an ore lease from the Jackson Company. Subsequently, the whole property was purchased by the Iron Cliffs Company.

The furnace has two stacks—Nos. 1 and 2. No. 1 was first started in April, 1858, and made, in three blasts, 6,688, tons of iron, blowing out on January 20th, 1860. No. 2 was blown in May 20, 1859, and continued in successful operation until destroyed by fire in August, 1864. It was immediately re-built, and again put in operation January 15th, 1865, blowing out on the 2d of June of the same year, after having made 13,574 tons, in thirteen blasts.

The total amount of iron made by the Pioneer since first blown in is stated as follows:

YEAR.	GROSS TONS.*
1870 and previous	49,419
1871	8,193
1872	6,985
1873	7,098
1874	11,080
1875	17,606
Total	100,381

THE CLIFFS FURNACE

is also the property of the Iron Cliffs Company. It is located in Tilden township, about six miles from Negaunee, and was completed and put in blast in the early part of 1874. Since then it has turned out 6,830 tons, having been in blast only a part of the time during the past two years.

THE NORTHERN IRON COMPANY'S

furnace at Harvey, three miles below Marquette, on the lake shore, was completed in 1860. The following table exhibits the product each year since the furnace went into blast:

YEAR.	GROSS TONS.
1860	600
1861	400
1862	2,060
1863	1,897
1864	3,006

*2,268 pounds; 2,240 pounds constitute one gross ton of iron ore.

1865.. 3,046
1866.. 2,687
1867.. 1,363

Total.. 15,059

This furnace has not been in blast since 1867. In 1873 the furnace was remodeled, and changed into a bituminous stack, a large amount of fuel was secured, but for some reason, best known to the owners, was not blown in.

THE COLLINS FURNACE

was built originally by S. R. Gay, Esq., in 1858, and made her first iron on the 13th day of December, in that year. Charles Lovelace, Esq., now superintendent of the Fox River furnaces, at Depere, Wis., was the iron maker until 1863, when he was succeeded by Patrick Dundon, now with Mr. L. at Depere. During the first four or five years the yield of pig iron was about eight tons a day, and an old paper before us notes, as a marked improvement, the fact that on the 17th of June, 1863, the furnace "turned out 10 tons of handsome metal." The following table shows the product of the Collins for the fifteen years she has been in operation:

YEAR.	GROSS TONS.
1859	2,575
1860	1,950
1861	2,060
1862	2,207
1863	1,141
1864	800
1865	1,709
1866	4,114
1867	4,052
1868	4,268
1869	3,416
1870	4,100
1871	4,174
1872	3,431
1873	2,000
Total	41,997

The furnace was blown out and abandoned in the fall of 1873, having exhausted her fuel supply.

THE MICHIGAN FURNACE,

located at Clarksburgh, on the line of the M., H. & O. R. R., twenty-six miles west of Marquette, was built by the Michigan Iron Company, in 1866, and went into blast February 10th, 1867. She has made iron as follows:

YEAR.	GROSS TONS.
1867	3,930
1868	4,383
1869	5,713
1870	4,858
1871	4,460
1872	4,001
1873	4,467
1874	6,621
1875	3,098
Total	41,531

THE GREENWOOD FURNACE

was erected by the M. & O. R. R. Company, and made her first iron in June, 1865. She had a most successful run till near the close of 1867, when, after a very large years' work, the stack was found to be defective, and had to be taken down and re-built. This was accomplished the next summer, but before again going into blast the owners sold the property to the Michigan Iron Company, who took formal possession about the middle of August, 1868.

The product of the Greenwood for each year is quoted as follows:

YEAR.	GROSS TONS.
1865	1,948
1866	3,505
1867	4,959
1868	1,806
1869	4,480
1870	3,992
1871	4,450
1872	4,212
1873	4,416
1874	4,839
1875	1,595
Total	40,202

The Company being unable to meet its liabilities was, in 1875, thrown into bankruptcy, and both its furnaces, together with its real and personal estate, passed into the hands of an assignee.

THE MORGAN FURNACE,

built and owned by the Morgan Iron Company, went into blast November 27th, 1863, making in the first year 337 tons of iron. The Morgan has been, perhaps, the most successful enterprise of the kind in the district, having made, in the first ten months, a clear net profit of 220 per cent, thus enabling the company to pay back all the original outlay for land and machinery, leaving a dividend of 100 per cent. to be divided among the stockholders. The Morgan is situated on the line of the M., H. & O. R. R., eight miles west of Marquette. It was built under the immediate supervision of C. Donkersly, Esq., one of our most practical and efficient iron masters, who now operates the furnace under a lease from the company.

The product of the Morgan has been as follows:

YEAR.	GROSS TONS.
1863	337
1864	4,023
1865	3,489
1866	3,749
1867	5,057
1868	4,203
1870	5,952
1871	4,792
1872	4,356
1873	6,324
1874	5,973
1875	5,377
Total	53,632

In 1868-'9 the fuel immediately adjacent to the furnace was exhausted, and a tram-road was built a distance of nine miles to lands owned by the company, new kilns were built and a steady supply of fuel secured.

THE BANCROFT FURNACE,

now owned by the Bancroft Iron Company, is situated on Dead River, about four miles from Marquette, and was built in 1860 by S. R. Gay, Esq. The first account we have of it is in 1861, in which year the shipments were reported at 2,430 tons. We are able to give a statement of the product of the furnace for every year except 1864-'5, of which the records were destroyed in the fire of 1868. The following is the table estimating the years referred to:

YEAR.	GROSS TONS.
1861	2,430
1862	2,802
1863	2,626
1864 (estimated)	3,000
1865 (estimated)	2,700
1866	2,451
1867	3,245
1868	3,800
1869	3,407
1870	3,710
1871	3,850
1872	4,250
1873	4,100
1874	3,688
1875	5,277
Total	51,336

THE CHAMPION FURNACE,

now one of the things of the past, was located near the east end of Lake Michigamme, and was built by the Morgan Iron Company in 1867. She made in her first run of ten months 4,282 tons. The product of this furnace is given as follows:

YEAR.	GROSS TONS.
1868	4,282
1869	5,560
1870	5,576
1871	5,094
1872	5,006
1873	3,949
1874	1,581
Total	31,048

The furnace was destroyed by fire in the summer of 1874, and will probably never be rebuilt.

DEER LAKE FURNACE.

In the summer of 1867, a company was organized at Norwich, Connecticut, for the purpose of building a furnace at Deer Lake, and Messrs. E. C. Hungerford and John B. Ward, were sent out to take charge of the work of construction. The company had previously secured a most valuable tract of contiguous hard wood lands, including the present site of the furnace. The first desideratum was to secure an abundance of fuel with a sufficient water power that could be utilized at the smallest possible expense, and this the company found in the purchase of the Deer Lake tract. The Carp, which at that point is a stream of considerable volume, has a perpendicular fall of fifteen or twenty feet, and furnishes a never failing power, which was utilized at a cost comparatively insignificant. It was decided to locate the furnace immediately at the foot of the falls, and work was accordingly commenced about the first of September, 1867. The stones for the stack were quarried so near its base that a derrick was all the appliance necessarily used in transferring them from the quarry to their places in the wall. Though well and substantially built, it was, perhaps, the most cheaply constructed of any furnace in the district. The stack, as originally built, was 38 feet high, with 7 feet diameter of boshes. It was first blown in about the first of September, 1868. In the summer of 1872 the iron broke out through the arch under the tuyere, setting fire to the buildings, which were totally consumed, leaving nothing but the stack and hot blast oven standing. With characteristic energy, Mr. C. H. Hall, then the managing agent, commenced clearing away the *debris* before the flames had ceased to act upon the larger timbers, and having succeeded in drawing the charge without permitting a salamander, he had the buildings reconstructed and the furnace again at work before the expiration of five weeks. Subsequently the stack was raised to a height of 47 feet, and the diameter of the boshes increased to 8 feet. As it now stands, it is what might be termed a hermaphrodite stack, the lower half or two-thirds being of stone, and the upper half or one-third an iron shell. It has a closed top, with bell and hopper.

In 1873, a second stack was built, which went into blast February the 1st, 1874, and continued blowing until the 1st of April last. This stack is 9x47 feet, an iron shell, and while in blast did excellent work, making in a run of fourteen months, on one hearth, 7,863 tons of iron, of which only 311 tons were high grade, and all of which was sold to the North Chicago rolling mill Co., for Bessemer purposes. The blowing cylinders which furnish the blast for both stacks are two in number, 32x60 inches, with five feet stroke. The crusher and hoist are run by power transmitted by common manilla ropes over shieve pulleys.

The landed estate of the company comprises a solid, compact tract of 8,000 acres, upon which there is a large amount of valuable pine, in addition to the hard wood. So far, the consumption of pine has been confined to the lands cut over for furnace purposes, the "pinery" not having been reached.

A wooden tram-road from the furnace to Ishpeming, with T rail on the grades, furnishes cheap transportation of ore to the furnace, and for the pig metal to the railway depot. This tram-road is about one mile and a half in length, and most admirably serves the purpose for which it is intended.

The following is a statement of the product:

YEAR.	GROSS TONS.
1869-'70	5,521
1871	2,809
1872	2,720
1873	3,447
1874	6,524
1875	4,615
Total	25,130

The furnace "location" consists of about 50 buildings of all kinds, the dwellings being particularly neat and comfortable looking. E. R. Hall, the Company's agent, though the youngest furnace manager in the district, has proved himself one of the most competent.

THE FAYETTE FURNACE

is situated on the east shore of Big Bay de Noc, about 25 miles east of Escanaba, in the midst of an immense forest of hard wood, the furnace lands consisting of 16,000 acres. It is owned by the Jackson Iron Company, and runs exclusively on ore from the Company's mine at Negaunee.

The construction of this furnace was commenced in May, 1867, under the direction and management of J. H. Harris, Esq., and the first iron was made on Christmas day of the same year. The furnace is most eligibly located on a small bay named, by the early explorers, Snail Shell Harbor. Aside from being an excellent harbor, it is not far out of the way of vessels plying in the ore trade from Escanaba to lower lake ports, and possesses the best advantages for receiving the ore and shipping the iron after it is smelted.

The furnace commenced operations with a single stack, but a second one, known as "No 2," was completed and put into operation previous to 1870. It was the original design of the company to build two stacks, and with this view the necessary machinery was put in in the beginning.

The following are the figures showing the product since the furnace went into blast.

YEAR.	GROSS TONS.
1868	4,546
1869	4,470
1870	6,450
1871	8,696
1872	10,080
1873	10,696
1874	11,079
1875	14,075
Total	70,092

THE MUNISING FURNACE

was built by the old Schoolcroft Iron Company, making her first iron on the 28th of June, 1868. She was run spasmodically by the original owners till some time in 1870, when the company became an involuntary bankrupt, and the furnace, together with an estate of over 40,000 acres of choice timber lands, passed into the hands of the Munising Iron Company, a new corporation. She was put in blast by the present owners, in June, 1873, but her operations have been irregular, though she has accomplished good work while in blast. Her product since built is given as follows:

YEAR.	GROSS TONS.
1868	1,735
1869	3,013
1870	2,809
1872	2,500
1873	2,237
1874	6,092
1875	4,239
Total	22,625

No. 2 Stack, Bay Furnace, August, 1875.

Date.	No. of Charges.	Lbs. ore Charged.	Total lbs. ore.	Total bus. coal.	Product of Iron. Gross Tons.			Total.
					No. 1.	No. 2.	No. 3.	
1..	117	1,100	128,700	3,510	35	....	....	35
2..	118	1,100	129,800	3,540	35¾	....	....	35¾
3..	116	1,100	127,600	3,480	33½	....	....	33½
4..	116	1,100	127,600	3,480	26¼	8¼	....	34½
5..	116	1,100	127,600	3,480	35	....	....	35
6..	109	1,100	119,900	3,270	15¼	17¾	....	33
7..	110	1,100	121,000	3,300	31	....	....	31
8..	118	1,150	135,700	3,540	35	....	....	35
9..	118	1,150	135,700	3,540	35¾	....	....	35¾
10..	118	1,100	129,800	3,540	24½	11	....	35½
11..	115	1,150	132,250	3,450	24	11½	....	35½
12..	113	1,100	124,300	3,390	23½	8	....	31½
13..	118	1,100	129,800	3,540	25¾	9	....	34¾
14..	117	1,100	128,700	3,510	22½	9¾	....	32¼
15..	115	1,100	126,500	3,450	32¼	....	....	32¼
16..	118	1,100	129,800	3,540	26	6	....	32
17..	124	1,050	130,200	3,720	31	4½	....	35½
18..	126	1,100	138,600	3,780	37	....	....	37
19..	132	1,100	145,200	3,960	38	....	....	38
20..	134	1,100	147,400	4,020	41½	....	....	41½
21..	134	1,100	147,400	4,020	29	9	2	40
22..	130	1,100	143,000	3,900	22	16¼	2¼	40½
23..	130	1,100	143,000	3,900	24¼	13¼	....	37
24..	129	1,100	141,900	3,870	10¼	24¼	4½	39
25..	127	1,100	139,700	3,810	40	....	....	40
26..	124	1,100	136,400	3,720	38½	....	....	38½
27..	125	1,000	125,000	3,750	27	8½	....	35½
28..	126	1,000	126,000	3,780	21¾	13¾	....	35½
29..	127	1,000	127,000	3,810	36	....	....	36
30..	127	1,100	139,700	3,810	29¾	6¾	....	36½
31..	123	1,100	135,300	3,690	27½	8½	....	36
	3770	33,900	4,120,550	113,100	915¼	185¼	8¾	1,109¼

Average yield ore.................................. 60.31
Bushels of coal per ton of iron 101.98
Average make per day 35.78

Proportion of ore used—64 per cent. specular and 36 per cent. McComber hematite.

THE BAY FURNACE

is situated on the main shore opposite Grand Island, six miles west of the Munising, and was first put into blast in the spring of 1870. A second stack was built in 1872, and blown in in December of that year. These stacks worked very unsatisfactorily until the summer of 1873, when the company secured the services of Maj. H. S. Pickards as superintendent, who has since achieved for himself a national reputation as an iron maker. What the Bay has accomplished is shown in the following figures:

CITY OF MARQUETTE IN 1875.

YEAR.	GROSS TONS.
1870	3,498
1871	3,597
1872	4,900
1873	8,760
1874	8,359
1875	9,223
Total	38,337

It is proper to add that the product during the last two years was the work of only one stack (No. 2.), the state of the market not warranting the company in keeping both stacks in blast. The table on the foregoing page is a statement of work done by this stack in the month of August, 1875.

The stack is 45 feet high and 9½ feet diameter of boshes. On the last blast, which commenced May 25th, 1875, and continued till April 8th, 1876, when the furnace was banked for want of ore, the following official report is given:

Blast of No. 2 stack commenced May 25, 1875.
Furnace banked for want of ore April 8th, 1876.
Number of days stopped, 4.
Total number of days run, 316.
Coal consumed, 1,045,440 bushels, ⅓ hemlock and ⅔ hard wood.
Tons of ore used, 15,847.
Gross tons of iron made, 9,695.

GRADE OF IRON MADE.	TONS.
No. 1	7,666¼
No. 2	1,796
No. 3	182
No. 4	36¾
No. 5	14

Bushels of ore per ton of iron, 107.83.
Average yield of ore, 61.18 per cent.
Average make per day, 30.67 tons.

THE MARQUETTE AND PACIFIC ROLLING MILL commenced operation on the 1st of September, 1868. The company under whose auspices this important addition to the manufacturing interest of Marquette was made, was organized under the general law of the State, in October, 1866, with a nominal capital of $500,000. The scheme contemplated the erection of a blast furnace with a capacity of 40 tons per day, and a rolling mill capable of producing from 3,000 to 5,000 tons of merchant iron per annum.

the waste chimney is carried up twelve feet above the top. The gas exit is an iron jacket lined with fire brick, and having an internal diameter of six feet. Its base rests upon a reservoir from which flues lead off to the hot blasts and to the boilers, the flues being provided with valves to regulate the supply of gas, and registers to regulate the supply of air. In this particular the appliances of the furnace are very complete to secure the most perfect combustion.

The hot blast is put up in two compartments, each compartment provided with a combustion chamber twenty-one feet long by five feet wide, and six feet and six inches high, over which are laid in open space, with an arched wall and flame flues intervening, 720 feet of pipe of eight inches internal diameter and one and a half inches thick. The premises occupied by the stack and hot blast and as a casting house, are 50 by 130 feet, the casting floor being 50 by 68 feet. The boilers are located parallel with the casting house. They are three in number, each 26 feet long by 42 inches in diameter, with two 16-inch return flues. They are placed in and surrounded by mason work, but the entire heating surface is exposed in one common chamber. Grate bars are provided for the temporary use of wood or coal, but the space in the rear of the bridge wall is left unfilled, thus affording all the space possible for the combustion of gas. The stack of the boiler furnace is 100 feet 6 inches high—so well elevated as to be above the influence of any wind that may surge over the bluff in the rear of the furnace. Heaters are provided, with 180 feet of 2-inch pipe, and the water is passed into the boilers at almost a steam temperature.

Blast is furnished by a direct acting vertical blowing engine, with a blowing cylinder 7 feet in diameter and $4\frac{1}{2}$ feet stroke, and a steam cylinder 34 inches in diameter and $4\frac{1}{2}$ feet stroke. It is a massive yet compact and powerful piece of machinery. In the same apartment is the blast receiver, the water feeding tank, the heater and two steam pumps—one of the latter to serve the boilers and the other to serve the coolers around the tuyeres, but both fitted so as to be interchangeable and one to do the work of the other, or work together or separately. The stock house is 76x100 feet, with posts 28 feet high. A railway trestle passes through it, with a turn table, from the bank in the rear of the furnace, where the ore is brought in from the M., H. & O, railroad. The fuel is received on the dock in front of the furnace and moved to the stock house in carts.

There are two calcining kilns each 20 tons capacity, in the rear of the stock house, where their contents are readily accessible with the other stock used. Space has been left for two others, should they be required.

The buildings, except the stock house, are constructed of Marquette sandstone and covered with iron roofing. The stock house is a wood and iron frame with iron roofing.

The furnace went into blast under the most cheering auspices, but was obliged to blow out owing to the bad quality of the fire brick, or a faulty construction of the boshes. A new lining was put in and a most successful run followed, the furnace making from 40 to 45 tons per day, running exclusively on second-class ores from the Lake Superior Mine. The furnace made while in operation, iron as follows:

YEAR.	GROSS TONS.
1873	7,800
1874	3,546
Total	11,346

The Grace went out of blast early in the season of 1874, and has not since blown in.

THE ESCANABA FURNACE

is the largest charcoal furnace in the district. It is situated on a forty acre plant on the bay shore, about one mile and a half north of Escanaba. It was built by the Escanaba Furnace Company, of which Joseph Kirkpatrick, Andrew Kloman, Wm. Bagaley, and other prominent Pittsburgh men, were the corporators. Work was commenced on the buildings early in the spring of 1872, and the furnace was blown in the following spring. The stack is an iron shell, lined with fire brick. It is 56 feet high, 12 feet across the boshes, and four-foot hearth, set on columns, and surmounted by a bell and hopper top, with an exit chimney. The funnel of the bosh is encased in an iron jacket and pierced with three tuyere chambers, in which are fitted Taws & Hartman's Philadelphia cooling boxes and water coils. The base is surrounded by a water jacket, and within the foundation are damp chambers and air cells. The gas exit is two feet below the top of the stack, leading down an iron column lined with fire brick of six feet six inches internal diameter, to a reservoir from where gas is distributed to the hot blasts and boilers, and regulated by valves. The blast pipes and tuyeres are to be hung in stirrups, the tuyeres being provided with ball and socket L joint, to avoid the derangement of contraction and expansion. Water is to be supplied to the coolers by gravity from a tank at an elevation on the side of the stack.

The work of this entire structure is of the best character, substantial and complete in every particular. The stack is located in a casting house 71x78½ feet, the space given to it occupying one-half of the narrowest dimensions, the other half being set apart for a second stack to be erected hereafter, and for which the foundation is already constructed. It is a fine building of white brick, on broad foundation walls provided with water sheds, and surmounted by an iron roof of the most approved construction.

The fuel supply is obtained from lands along the line of the Chicago & Northwestern Railway, above and below Escanaba, upon which a sufficient number of kilns for charring purposes have been constructed.

The furnace has not met with the success anticipated. It made an unfortunate commencement, met with a chill, and soon after entering upon a successful run, financial embarrassment compelled a suspension of operations. Its product has been as follows:

YEAR.	GROSS TONS.
1873	2,175
1874	6,335
1875	70
Total	8,580

THE PEAT FURNACE

was built by the Lake Superior Iron Company, for the purpose of experimenting with peat fuel in the smelting of iron ores. It is located at Ishpeming, near the company's mines, and was completed and started up in 1872, but did not prove a success. Some changes were then made, the furnace started again and made some two tons of grey iron; but it was found that the furnace was too small to work effectually, and it was blown out. The next summer, the furnace having been enlarged in height and boshes, and furnished with a larger hot blast, ran very well for some weeks, with a mixed fuel of 80 per cent. peat and 20 per cent. soft wood charcoal. The panic caused a suspension of work, and the furnace has been idle ever since. It made in all 1,150 tons of metal of a very superior quality, and though not wholly successful as an experiment, demonstrated to a certainty the fact that the immense peat beds of the Lake Superior iron region can be utilized for blast furnace purposes.

THE CARP RIVER FURNACE

is the property of the Peninsular Iron Company, and was built in 1873, making her first blast in the spring of 1874. It is situated on the bay shore, at the mouth of Carp River, within the limits of the city of Marquette. It is a stone stack with nine-foot boshes, with kilns convenient, though the wood has to be brought from a considerable distance. After making 1,445 tons, operations were suspended.

THE MENOMINEE FURNACE.

This furnace was built with a view of utilizing, as material for charcoal, the slabs and edgings which are made at the saw mills at Menominee. The furnace is an iron stack, well equipped in every particular, and went into blast about the middle of July, 1873, the first cast being made on the 20th. The experiment of making iron with coal from pine slabs and soft wood, so far as quality and quantity is concerned, has been a decided success, as the following table of products will show:

YEAR.	GROSS TONS.
1873	2,400
1874	4,942
1875	3,510
Total	10,852

It is proper to remark that the furnace was out of blast nearly, if not quite, half the time during the years named, and the figures given do not by any means indicate her actual capacity. This furnace is the property of the Menominee Iron Company, of which M. R. Hunt, Esq., is general manager, with office at Depere, Wis.

TABULAR STATEMENTS.

The following table shows the total shipments of iron ore from the Lake Superior mines in 1875, together with the value at the mines:

NAME OF MINE.	GROSS TONS.	VALUE.
Jackson	90,568	$384,914
New York	70,754	283,016
Cleveland	140,239	560,956
Lake Superior	129,359	463,821
Champion	57,979	231,916
Washington	9,641	38,564
Republic	119,768	509,014
Kloman	8,059	32,236
Palmer (Old Cascade)	4,071	15,267
Barnum	43,209	172,836
Foster	667	1,668
Salisbury	4,330	10,835
Lake Angeline	26,370	98,887
Edwards	12,800	51,200
Spurr Mountain	23,094	92,376
Michigamme	44,763	179,052
Keystone	3,346	13,374
McComber	10,407	26,018
Winthrop	7,502	20,631
Saginaw	55,318	221,272
Goodrich	1,780	7,120
Rolling Mill	37,806	98,295
Excelsior	2,860	7,150
Marquette	3,088	12,352
Grand Central	987	2,468
Iron Mountain	1,035	4,088
Donkersley	282	705
Smith	187	468
Total	910,840	$3,540,499

The following table exhibits the aggregate product of each mine from 1856 to 1875 inclusive:

NAME OF MINE.	GROSS TONS.
Jackson	1,507,285
New York	669,426
Cleveland	1,406,162
Lake Superior	1,690,320
Champion	412,397
Washington	382,504
Republic	363,201
Kloman	64,212
Palmer (Old Cascade)	80,749
Barnum	309,665
Foster	106,157
Salisbury	12,355
Lake Angeline	397,576
Edwards	177,948
Spurr Mountain	97,095
Michigamme	119,164
Keystone	18,999
McComber	96,978
Winthrop	77,303
Saginaw	156,445
Goodrich	8,138
Rolling Mill	72,576
Excelsior	4,681
Marquette	57,980
Grand Central	22,271
Iron Mountain	18,341
Smith	22,960
Pittsburgh & Lake Superior	24,020
Shenango	16,404
Albion	2,228
Carr	2,603
Bagaley	6,243
Howell Hoppock	2,205
Emma	7,863
Home	3,229
Cambria (Old Teal Lake)	2,610
Williams	1,040
Rowland	2,278
Himrod	2,074
Green Bay	8,582
Gribben	4,517
New England (now Superior)	108,990
Allen	9,347
Magnetic	78
Hungerford	145
Parsons	1,896
Negaunee	11,684
Mather	2,228
Franklin	2,007
Michigan	4,439

Quartz	3,108
Stewart	305
Other small and abandoned mines	36,508
Total	8,619,519

The following table shows the shipments of pig iron from Lake Superior furnaces during the year 1875, together with its value:

NAME OF FURNACE.	GROSS TONS.	VALUE.
Pioneer	17,606	$484,165
Michigan	3,098	85,195
Bancroft	5,277	145,177
Morgan	5,377	147,867
Deer Lake	4,615	126,912
Fayette	14,075	387,062
Bay	9,223	253,682
Munising	4,239	116,572
Marquette & Pacific	10,940	300,850
Escanaba	70	1,925
Carp River	70	1,925
Menominee	3,510	96,525
Cliff	2,058	56,595
Greeenwood	1,595	43,862
Total	81,753	$2,248,264

This table shows the aggregate shipments of pig iron from the Lake Superior furnaces up to the close of navigation in 1875:

NAME OF FURNACE.	GROSS TONS.
Pioneer	100,381
Northern	15,059
Collins	41,997
Michigan	41,531
Greenwood	40,202
Bancroft	51,336
Morgan	53,632
Champion	31,048
Deer Lake	25,139
Fayette	70,092
Bay	38,337
Munising	22,625
Grace	11,346
Marquette & Pacific	21,880
Escanaba	8,580
Peat Furnace	1,150
Carp River	1,145
Menominee	10,582
Cliff	6,830
Total	592,892

The following is a statement in gross tons of the aggregate yield of the mines and furnaces of this district from 1856 to 1875, inclusive, together with the value of the same:

Year.	Iron Ore.	Pig Iron.	Ore and Pig Iron.	Value.
1856	7,000	......	7,000	$ 28,000 00
1857	21,000	......	21,000	63,000 00
1858	31,035	1,629	32,664	249,202 00
1859	65,679	7,258	72,937	575,529 00
1860	116,908	5,660	122,568	736,496 00
1861	45,430	7,970	53,400	419,501 00
1862	115,721	8,590	124,311	984,977 00
1863	185,257	9,813	195,070	1,416,935 00
1864	235,123	13,832	248,955	1,867,215 00
1865	196,256	12,283	208,539	1,590,490 00
1866	296,972	18,437	315,409	2,405,960 00
1867	466,076	30,911	496,987	3,475,820 00
1868	507,813	38,246	546,059	3,992,413 00
1869	633,238	39,003	672,241	4,968,435 00
1870	856,471	49,298	905,769	6,300,170 00
1871	813,379	51,225	864,604	6,115,895 00
1872	952,055	63,195	1,015,250	9,188,055 00
1873	1,167,379	71,507	1,238,886	11,395,887 00
1874	935,488	90,494	1,025,982	7,592,811 00
1875	910,840	81,753	992,593	5,788,763 00
Total	8,559,120	601,104	9,160,224	$69,155,494 00

THE MENOMINEE IRON REGION.

The center of this region is about fifty miles north of west from Escanaba; fifty to sixty miles south-west of Marquette, and about fifty miles north of Menominee, in direct air lines. It lies in the northern part of Menominee, and extreme southern portion of Marquette counties, extending across the Menominee river into Wisconsin. It is, as yet, a comparatively new mining field, but the explorations and discoveries made leave no cause to doubt that it will ultimately acquire a value and importance only surpassed, if at all, by the Marquette ranges, which now produce nearly one-third of all the iron made in the United States.

The mines of this region lie apparently not far from the base of the great iron formation of which the mines in Marquette county form a part, and which appears to reach its southern boundary about sixty-five miles north of Menominee village, or the mouth of the river. The geology of the ridges containing the ore is somewhat different from that in Marquette county, in the absence of a limonite rock behind the ore veins, which is here supplied by an iron slate or ore-bearing schist, and the approach to the veins, both hematite and specular, is a clay slate instead of a quartzite. Yet the general features of the formation lead to the belief that the deposits are parts of the same fields in which the mines of Marquette county are located.

Whether these deposits will open with regularity and continue without interruption for some distance, cannot be told, as explorations have not been carried forward to an extent sufficient to determine this point. But the work done at the

Quinesaik mine, through test-pits and a drift across the series of veins composing the ore deposit, shows that considerable dependence can be placed upon an uninterrupted lead of the ores. The soft hematites prevail so far, and their quality is of superior character. Some of the explorations reveal an inferior quality of red specular, and further work will undoubtedly open rich mines of this ore. Very fine specimens are picked up at various points, and are broken from ledges which outcrop north of the present base of operations.

THE BREEN MINE.

This property is located on section 22, town 39, range 28, and the tract consists of 120 acres. It is owned by Messrs. Saxton, Ingalls, B. and T. Breen, and others, of Menominee. Work was commenced upon it some five years since, but at first not enough was done to make the development valuable or the prospect promising. In 1872 work was resumed by the Milwaukee Iron Company, by an agreement which would make that company lessees and proprietors if certain conditions were complied with by both parties to the arrangement. It has since been abandoned temporarily, the Milwaukee Iron Company having changed their base of operations to another quarter.

The deposit outcrops on the south side of a ridge, which has an elevation of nearly eighty feet above a meadow at its base. Into this elevation on the south side, a drift has been driven a distance of about forty feet, through a vein of rich, hard blue hematite, and into a deposit of banded jaspery ore, of little value. Test-pits have also been sunk at various places east and north of this drift, in some of which rich ore has been found: still further west a trench across the formation has exposed a deposit of hard ore seventy-five feet in width, specimens from which have been analyzed and found to contain 68 per cent. of metallic iron. This mine is about fifteen miles distant from the nearest point on the Chicago & Northwestern Railway.

THE BREITUNG MINE.

This mine consists of section 10, town 39, range 29, five and a half miles west and north of the Breen. Its name is derived from the owner of the land, Hon. Edward Breitung, of Negaunee, and all the explorations thus far, have been made by the Milwaukee Iron Company. On the east end of the property a drift has been carried back under the face of the hill, for a distance of over one hundred feet, through a lean specular ore. The rear end of the drift is eighty feet below the surface, and it was expected that here, or before reaching a point so far in the side of the hill, a good deposit of ore would be struck, in the usual way of expecting that a vein will get better as it is worked into. The management was disappointed, however, and the miners were driven out by water and insufficient ventilation.

Several shafts have been sunk on other parts of the property, drifts from the bottom of which across the formation cut a vein of hard ore carrying a width of from 45 to 50 feet, analyses of which show an average of about 55 per cent. of metallic iron. In another place, one of the drifts referred to, revealed a regularly stratified deposit of rich brown hematite ninety feet in width, and which has since been traced a distance of half a mile or more in length. This hematite carries an average of 61 per cent. metallic iron, and lies in such position that it can be mined at a trifling cost. Its discovery fixes an indisputable value upon the mine.

THE QUINESAIK MINE.

This property consists of the southeast quarter of section 34, town 40, range 30, and is five miles north and west of the Breitung mine. It is owned by W. L. Wetmore, of Marquette, Fred L. Lasier, of Detroit, T. W. Edwards and Richard Uren, of Houghton, and J. L. Buell, of Menominee—Messrs. Wetmore and Lasier each owning one-quarter. Operations were commenced early in the summer of 1873, and a valuable mine was opened. The ore is supposed to be in the same range with that of the Breen and Breitung, running from south of east to north of west, along elevations which have been raised in regular succession across the face of the country. Between this and the Breitung mine a heavy ledge of limestone, extending for more than two miles, has been thrown up, but whether it intercepts the ore has not been determined.

The work at the mine is embraced in a cut across a good vein of specular ore, and a series of shafts, drifts and test-pits across the formation at right angles, which reveals the character of the ores very completely. The whole work extends across the formation for a distance of over 500 feet. The veins have a dip to the north, with a hanging wall of lean ore and Potsdam sandstone. Under this wall is a vein of fine-grained, flinty and specular ore, which carries over 50 per cent. of iron in the outcrop, and grows rapidly better as it is worked into. Adjoining this is a thirty-foot vein of soft slate ore, of a blue tinge when first taken out, but a deep brown color when exposed. It powders red, and is in scintillating crystals, assays 63 per cent. of metallic iron, and is as clean and fine a hematite as the Upper Peninsula has yet produced. Next is a vein of specular of some four feet, and then a smaller vein of slate ore, with a foot wall of pesheka schist. Further along are the slates, brown and red, a vein of lean specular and one of brown hematite—the latter being similar to that taken from the Negaunee range—and still further beyond a very strong magnetic attraction. Altogether this mine has great promise, and can be worked to good advantage.

The ore at this mine is a blue hematite, unlike any of the ores found in the Marquette region. It can hardly be called a soft hematite, and yet is not a hard ore, in the common acceptation of the term. It is rather an intermediate between the hard and soft varities of hematite; has been tested in the furnace, yields well, and is pronounced most excellent for Bessemer iron, having scarcely a trace of sulphur or phosphorus. The mine has been leased for a long term of years by the Milwaukee Iron Company, after a long and careful examination, and will be wrought to supply their Milwaukee furnaces as soon as railway communication is secured by the building of the Menominee Range Railroad. This road is almost certain to be completed to the mine on or before the 1st of May, 1877. Escanaba is the natural lake shipping port for the product of these mines.

On the north half of section 32, town 40, range 30, is the

VERMILLION MINE,

owned and opened by Captain Welcome Hyde, of Appleton, Wis. The work done thus far consists of several shafts and a trench across the formation, which show a deposit of soft hematite about 20 feet in width, and in length, so far as opened, about 300 feet. The ore is an unusually rich hematite, the average of several analyses being 60 per cent. of metallic iron. Capt. Hyde has expended about $5,000 on the property, and is now satisfied to await the building of a railroad, when he will be ready to commence active mining operations.

Crossing the Menominee river into Wisconsin, the range has again been opened on sections 20 and 21, township 40, range 18, East, near the dividing line of which sections is located what has been named the

EAGLE IRON MINE,

which was explored and discovered by Fisher & Keyes, of Menasha, Wis. The deposit is in a ridge about eighty feet above the level of Fisher Lake, which lies near its base, and has been opened by the sinking of numerous test-pits, by which a body of hard blue hematite was revealed. This deposit is found to be not less than 125 feet in width, and has been found along a distance of 300 feet on the range. There is certainly every reason to believe that the deposit is a very large one, and the assays which have been made show the ore to contain an average of 56.72 per cent. of metallic iron. Of five assays a trace of phosphorus was found in one only, showing that it will be a very desirable ore for Bessemer pig.

THE ELWOOD MINE

is situated about two miles north of the Eagle, in sections 15 and 16, of the same town and range—on the banks of the Brule River. This location is owned by Elwood Brothers, Decatur, Ill. The outcrop is about se**venty-five feet** above the river, where **may be seen** small veins **of ore, of apparent** good quality. **Test-pits have also been sunk at different** points, but **so far, nothing like ore in** paying **quantity has been develo**ped.

Still **further** west, **on the range in** section 25, town 40, range **17, east, a** heavy **outcrop of** magnetic ore may be seen, and **a few test-**pits encourage **the** belief that the deposit is **not only very** extensive, but the **ore of** a superior quality.

Numerous other outcrops **have** been **found on** the range **east and west of** the river, **but as** yet nothing **has been** done **to prove** the extent **or** value of the **deposits, except at the localities** mentioned. Of the future of the Menominee Iron **Region, all depends upon** the quality **of** the ore **when its mines shall be more fully developed.** That the deposits **rival those of the Marquette region in quality,** there is no **longer a question—nor is it to be disputed that the** blue hematites of **the Quinesaik, Breitung and Breen Mines, are fully** equal, if **not superior, to the best hematites of the** Marquette district. These **alone will be sufficient to give the** district prominence in the **future; but it is by no means improbable that most** valuable deposits **of** specular **and magnetic ores will also be** found in the natural **course of development which is sure to** follow close upon the building **of the Menominee Range** railroad.

RETROSPECTIVE.

The development of the Lake Superior iron interest really **began in** 1856-'7. Like all other enterprises **in** a new country, **the development of** the iron mining interest was attended by **many difficulties which,** at times, seemed almost insurmount**able. The first** discovery **in** 1845 **was met with** many **expressions of doubt** and unbelief, and **when at last** it was **definitely known that our hills contained an** inexhaustible quantity of the richest iron ores, lying in solid masses, the greatest obstacles still remained in the way of their development. The iron hills lay in an unbroken forest, fourteen miles distant from the lake, and means of transportation to the lake side must be provided. This accomplished, the difficulties in the way were by no means entirely overcome. Communication between the Lake Superior country and the cities on the lower lakes was precarious and very expensive. To get the ore to market, it must be shipped at high rates on the few craft that had been brought to Lake Superior over the portage. At the foot of the lake the ore was discharged and hauled over the portage and around the St. Mary's Falls, when it was again loaded in vessels for ports below. This was a tedious process, and its expense made the experiment rather dubious as a remunerative enterprise.

Then, too, the iron had to be introduced into the market and its merits made known; and iron-workers, reluctant to experiment on a material of such different quality from that which they had been accustomed to work, must be induced to try the merits of the new iron. Two objects were necessary to be accomplished before the venture could be successful: the iron must be properly brought before the public, and the facilities for getting it to market must be increased and cheapened. The energetic men who led the forlorn hope went to work in earnest. A road was opened from the lake to the mines, and a tram-way of planks, with strap rails, constructed. A full equipment of tram wagons, mules, and other necessaries, were procured. Docks were built at Marquette, and the greatest part of the paid in capital of the two pioneer companies was expended in making preparations for extensive mining, and the transportation of the ore to market.

In the meantime a large grant of lands had been made to a company to aid in the construction of a canal around the Falls, which would give direct communication between the upper and lower lakes. This project, of such vital importance to the mining interests of Lake Superior, was allowed to lag, and there was well-grounded fears of embarrassing delays, if not ultimate abandonment of the work. Owing in a great measure to the persistent efforts of those interested in the Iron Mining Companies, the work was pushed through to completion, and on the 18th of June, 1855, the canal was opened.

The next thing was to test the value of the ore, and bring it to the favorable attention of iron workers. Rigid tests were made, and proved that while the tenacity of the best Swedish iron was 59 tons to the square inch, English cable bolt 59 tons, and Russian 76 tons, iron manufactured from Lake Superior ore stood at $89\frac{1}{2}$. Its freedom from admixture with sulphur, phosphorus or arsenic, was found to give it a tenacity unequalled by any other iron known to commerce. Quantities of the new iron were introduced into the rolling-mills, car axle factories, boiler plate factories, and other iron works, and the unanimous testimony of all who tried it was that it was preferable to the best iron previously known, both for strength and ease with which it could be worked. Those who tried it were eager to obtain more, and from this time the demand more than kept pace with the facilities for increasing the supply.

The building of the tram-road to the mines, and the subsequent construction of the M. & O. R. R. and afterwards the Peninsula Division C. &. N. W. has already been referred to. The first of these railways was completed in 1857, and the other in 1865.

It is but thirteen years since the first shipments, made from the Cleveland mine, immediately after the opening of the canal, brought the iron district into communication with a market. In that time the mines have been developed into an inexhaustible source of wealth, the neighborhood of the mines improved and built upon, railroad tracks constructed, extensive docks with trestle works, "shoots," "pockets," and other improved conveniences for loading vessels erected, and Marquette itself expanded from a few lonely houses into a large and flourishing town, with an extensive business to which tourists come in crowds, as a delightful summer resort. The total shipment of ore from the two ports of Marquette and Escanaba have increased from less than 1,500 tons in 1855, to over a million of tons in 1873, and but for the panic, which has probably had a more depressing effect upon the iron interest, than any other of our great industries, it is fair to assume that the same ratio of increase in the production of the Lake Superior mines would have been maintained until now.

The larger portion of our ores go to Cleveland, whence they are re-shipped to the coal fields of the Mahoning and Shenango valleys, by railroad. About one hundred furnaces in Ohio and Pennsylvania use Lake Superior ore, while nearly all the charcoal furnaces in the Northwest are supplied from our mines. But the market for our ores is not confined to the furnaces of Ohio and Pennsylvania, though they have hitherto taken the great bulk of the product of our mines. Our market place includes likewise the whole of the great Northwest.

The day is forever past when iron manufacturers east of the Alleghenies will furnish the West with iron. They have ceased to do so. Henceforth 75,000 out of every 100,000 tons of iron ore that goes to the coal fields west of the Alleghenies for manufacture will be from Lake Superior, while 90,000 out of every 100,000 tons of iron used in the West will have been produced west of them. Then consider the present population of the West—some 15,000,000—the rate at which it is being augmented—the commercial facilities which exist to foster and encourage manufactures and the mechanical arts—the numerous railroads that must still be constructed, and the ten thousand other improvements that will ultimately require vast amounts of iron. When we look at these facts, the question of market is forever settled. Then, in the course of human events, Lake Superior iron is going to Europe. With some this may excite a smile, but ere long the fact will be realized, since, for certain important uses, it *has no equal in the world.*

Though now depressed, we doubt whether, in view of all the facts, there is a business interest in the United States which promises better and surer returns for a long series of years, than the mining and smelting of the iron ores of Lake Superior. The panic has been productive of at least one good result; it has brought us down to hard pan; there will be no more speculative iron mining on Lake Superior; the development of our mines will be conducted on legitimate business principles; we have learned a lesson in economy, and though the profits may not be so large in the aggregate, there will be more stability, more real progress, more wealth, and consequently a more enduring prosperity than ever before. And it may safely be said, considering the magnitude of its mineral wealth, that the time is not far distant when the Upper Peninsula of Michigan will take a front rank in the sublime destiny of the great and growing West—if not as a sovereign state, then as a community to which other states must of necessity look for their supply of at least one of the great staple products of the country.

UNDEVELOPED IRON **LANDS.**

For a few years **prior** to the **panic of** 1873 excitement in the Lake Superior Iron District ran high, and the forests of Marquette and Menominee counties were thronged with eager and expectant explorers, armed with compass and needle, and all certain of securing **for** themselves comfortable, if not enormous, fortunes. A great number of **entries were** made at the government land office, embracing **all** the **lands in** the counties named upon which the existence of iron ore was even suspected. Pools were formed in the east, the services **of** veteran explorers secured **on** the co-operative plan, **and the** excitement continued until the panic came and **cast a** cloud **of gloom and** despondency **over the** entire region. Since then **very little has** been done **in the way of** exploration, and the anticipated fortunes of the greedy land lookers are held **in** abeyance. Lands known to possess great mineral value are still undeveloped, and many of them can, to-day, be purchased for the amount originally paid to the government, adding interest and cost **of** exploration. Many **persons** who **were** impelled by the **well-grounded belief that** there could be **no** interruption in **the work of development—that** Lake Superior ores, instead **of going begging in the market,** would **always** be eagerly sought **after by the large number** of new **furnaces then building, and numerous others** to follow—to **invest all** their capital **in new mining** properties, now find themselves so cramped, financially, that they would be **glad to** part with their interests for a consideration equal to that originally paid for them. Not because they are less valuable, intrinsically, but because their necessities are such as to **compel** them **to** sacrifice properties from which large fortunes will ultimately be realized. This being the case, there never has been, in the history of the region, a more favorable time for the investment of capital in iron mining properties than the present. Fortunes, to be realized when "the good times come again," in many cases are begging for takers from those who are unable to weather the storm and await in patience the lifting of the financial cloud which must sooner or later be dispelled, revealing the clear sky beyond. But there are many others more fortunate, who are able to hold on to their purchases, who know the value of their lands, and who will not sell except at a very large advance on the original cost.

Some of the heaviest investments, made in 1871-'2, were in the Menominee Range, to which reference has already been made. Among the purchases of lands in that region were those made by a party of gentlemen of Eastern Ohio and Western Pennsylvania, represented by Geo. C. Reis, trustee. The lands entered by this pool were all closely examined and explored previously to entry, and are known to be among the most valuable undeveloped lands in the district. Some of them are situated near the Quinesaik Mine, and are believed to be equally as valuable; upon other of their lands, in Marquette county, have been found large deposits of first-class red specular ores, and there can be no question that, taken as a whole, the property of this pool will ultimately prove of incalculable value and a source of great profit to the owners.

THE M., H. & O. R. R. COMPANY

own an estate of many thousands of acres, extending along the line of its road from Marquette to L'Anse, embracing in all about 400,000 acres. Some of the best mines in the region, (notably the Champion) are on lands originally owned by this company. The line runs through the heart of the Marquette iron region, there being few mines that are not reached by the main line or its branches, and it is believed that developments yet to be made on the Michigamme and Republic ranges will add a score or more to the paying mines of the district.

Many of the Company's lands are valuable for the timber alone, and in an estate so extensive, extending for more than fifty miles along the great iron range, it would be strange, indeed, if they were not found, ultimately, to embrace hidden deposits of mineral wealth equal to any and all that have heretofore been discovered in the region.

The Company has concluded to place these lands in the market, and, to the capitalist seeking a safe investment, they will be found, on examination, to present many inducements. Notwithstanding the gratifying progress which has marked the history of development in the past, the iron region is yet in its infancy, and it is almost certain that the future will reveal on lands that can now be bought for a song, comparatively, deposits of ore that will rival the famous Republic, or any of the older and most successful mines.

THE TOLEDO IRON, LAND AND LUMBER COMPANY

is possessed of a valuable estate contiguous to the Republic, together with lands in Ontonagon county. Near the Republic, what appears to be a rich deposit of slate ore has been found, but as yet, nothing has been done towards its development. The Company was not organized until after the panic, the continuance of which put an effectual damper on all new enterprises. With a revival of the iron trade, however, will come a renewal of operations in various quarters, and then, it is confidently believed, the earlier anticipations of this company will be fully realized.

MAAS, LONSTORF & MITCHELL,

guided by an outcrop of lean ore, a short distance east of Negaunee, have sunk a shaft to a depth of nearly 100 feet, from the bottom of which they are cross-cutting in the hope of striking the Jackson vein. Some lean ore was encountered in the shaft, but though the indications are favorable nothing of value has yet been found. It is not impossible that the Jackson belt may be found to extend that far east; indeed, the developments at the old Eureka mine, only two miles west of Marquette, would seem to indicate that, the ore belt extends to the lake shore and under the lake itself. It is not improbable, therefore, that new mines may ultimately be discovered at various points between the Jackson mine and Marquette, though it is possible that the deposit may be covered with a greater depth of drift than at either of the places where it has already been opened, and the ore, as at the Eureka mine, may not be fully up to the standard.

There are many other valuable properties in the region which only await the return of prosperous times for their development. To enumerate them would only be tiresome to the reader.

THE PENOKA IRON RANGE.

That the Marquette Iron Range extends westward into Wisconsin is proved by the discovery of iron ore in Ontonagon county, at various points, and the more recent developments on what is known as the Penoka Iron Range, in Ashland county. From the 4th principal meridian this range has been traced south of west to where it crosses the St. Croix river into Minnesota. It first appears in township 45, south, at an elevation of 1,000 feet above Lake Superior, and bearing south 25° west, holds the same general form and course for a distance of twenty miles, when it becomes broken into knobs, and finally, as a mere ridge, crosses the St. Croix, beyond which it has not been traced.

The first discovery and examination of the Penoka Range was made by Col. Charles Whittlesey, of Cleveland, Ohio, who was the assistant of Owen when he made his survey in 1848-'9. Others, not experts, had previously visited the range and found iron, but could not afterwards locate it. These discoveries were made before the territory was surveyed, and numerous parties "squatted" on the lands; but everything supposed to be valuable for iron was entered at the government land office, as fast as surveyed, by Washington rings.

Nothing was done in the way of development until after the completion of the Wisconsin Central Railroad to Penoka

Gap, in 1873, although several companies had been organized prior to 1860. These companies are as follows: The Magnetic Iron Company, organized under the general mining laws of the State of Michigan; capital stock, $500,000, divided into 20,000 shares. This company, of which Col. Whittlesey is President, owns 1,500 acres east of the Gap, but has never done any work worthy of mention. The Wisconsin and Lake Superior Company was organized under a special charter, granted by the Wisconsin legislature, on a basis of 1,000 shares, owns 2,000 acres of land; Angus Smith, Esq., of Milwaukee, President; has never done anything. The Lapointe Iron Company was organized in 1859, under a special charter; owns 6,000 acres of land, just west of the Gap, including that upon which the first discovery was made by Col. Whittlesey; Hon. H. B. Payne, now member of Congress for the Cleveland, Ohio, district, President. In 1873 the Company caused a shaft to be sunk to a depth of nearly 100 feet, in a body of apparently very rich magnetic ore. The panic, however, caused a suspension of operations, and since then nothing has been done. The following analyses will give the reader some idea of the character and value of the ore:

ANALYSIS BY PROF. OWEN, 1850.

Peroxyde and protoxyde of iron.............................. 78.6
Silica.. 18.6
Magnesia... .8
Metallic iron... 58.13

BY CHILTON.

Peroxyde and Protoxyde 89.46
Silica.. 9.65
Magnesia... .85
Metallic iron... 68.08

An analysis of a lot of specimens, from the leanest to the richest, ground together so as to procure an average, made by Prof. Irving, of the Wisconsin State University, in 1874, gave 56.9 of metallic iron. It will be observed that the per centage of silica is unusually large as compared with the ores of the Marquette district; but it is not improbable that

further explorations will reveal deposits not open to this
objection. The work done thus far, if not wholly sufficient
to prove the value of the range, is at least sufficient to encourage a renewal of operations at the earliest day practicable. The running of a drift into the mountain at its base,
from the north side, will reveal all there is of value, or otherwise, at a depth of 600 feet from the bottom of the shaft
alluded to; and that plan will probably be adopted when the
company decide upon a renewal of operations. At present,
the writer, who has been on the ground, prefers not to express a decided opinion as to the merits of the Penoka Range.
He can only hope as he has reason to believe, that the future
will bring to the owners a realization of their most sanguine
expectations.

The Penoka Range is distant from Ashland, the northern
terminus of the Wisconsin Central Railroad, about thirty
miles. The road was completed to the Gap in the expectation that the iron companies would proceed at once with the
work of development, but, as has been stated, the panic rendered such action impossible, and no ore has ever been
shipped over the line. At present, however, the Central
Company is engaged in the completion of its line from
Penoka south to the northern terminus of the Steven's Point
division. This will give a through line from Ashland to
Milwaukee, when the ore from the range can be shipped by
rail to the latter city, or via Ashland to the lower lake ports.

Ashland is, (or was before the panic) a village of about
2,000 inhabitants, which sprang into existence with the
building of the railroad to the range. It is at the head of
Ashland (or Chegwamegon) Bay, enjoys the advantages of a
good harbor, and will ultimately become the chief lake port
west of the Montreal river.

SILVER.

That silver existed in the Iron River region, Ontonagon county, has been known for many years.* A reference to it was made in the Relacions of the early missionaries, and was spoken of by Henry in his history of the first mining enterprise on Lake Superior. Some forty or fifty years ago, when John Jacob Astor and the American Fur Company had a station, or trading post, at the mouth of Iron River, the Indians were known to have constantly in their possession silver in its native state in considerable quantities, and the men are now living who have seen them with large chunks as "big as a man's fist;" but no one ever succeeded in inducing them to tell or show where the hidden treasure lay. A superstitious fear always clung to them, and does even to this day, that if they showed to any white man a deposit of mineral, the great Manitou would punish them with death. Two instances of this kind, proving the superstitious fears of the Indians in this regard, are of comparatively recent date. Several years since, a half-bred Indian brought to Ontonagon some very fine samples of vein rock, carrying considerable quanties of native silver. His report was that his wife had found it on the south range where they were trapping, and to test his story he was sent back for more. In a few days he returned, bringing with him quite a chunk, from which was obtained eleven and one-half ounces of native silver. He returned home, went among the Flambeaux Indians and was killed. His wife, to this day, refuses to listen to any proposals from friend or foe to show the location of the vein,

---

* The author is indebted to Mr. A. Meads, of Ontonagon, for a large part of the information given in this sub-division.

clinging with religious tenacity to the superstitions of her tribe.

The present Nonesuch copper vein was discovered by an Iron River half-breed, and shown to some white men. The poor fellow soon sickened and died. His relatives and friends shook their heads and said they knew it would be so. These instances are mentioned to show the superstition of the red man on the discovery of mineral veins, and to account in some measure for the long delay and failure in tracing up the rich deposits of minerals which have so long been known to exist in the Iron River district.

In 1846 or '47 quite a distinguished party then on the lake exploring, surveying, and examining the wonderful mineral discoveries of Lake Superior, were induced by an Indian to go up Iron River to see a big rock of native silver. They started eager to find the great riches before them. The Indian led them a fearful and useless hunt of several days, but at last the party became tired and disgusted and told the Indian before starting (from their camp in the morning) that if he did not bring them to the silver rock before night they would shoot him. After traveling till noon the Indian brought them to the bank of a small stream and told them to sit down and he would find it. In a short time he returned and told them that the great Manitou had become displeased with him and had turned the great silver rock into a rock of stone. This he showed them and the whole party returned disgusted, weary and ragged, but the Indian was seen no more. From that time to 1855 persistent efforts were made by the early settlers to discover the deposits from which this native silver came, but without success. Vein rock was found in the river bed and on the beach, containing native silver, but its hiding place was not discovered till that year, when Mr. Austin Corser found an outcropping of a vein carrying native silver in Little Iron River, about one mile west of Big Iron River. He continued his examination till he found the vein in place, traced it across the river and became satisfied it was a valuable discovery. The land, however, at that time, could not be obtained, it being one of the odd-numbered sections and reserved in a grant for the Ontonagon and State Line Railroad Company. Nothing daunted, however, Mr. Corser erected a log shanty, and in the fall of the same year removed his family into it, and for many years endured all the hardships and privations of a backwoods life, confident the time would come when the discovery would be valuable. Fortunately for him, and indeed the whole district, the company failed to build the road, the land reverted to the United States, and came into market. Mr. Corser was then able to file a homestead claim upon it, and began at once to prove up the property and make further explorations. His trials, privations, and long waiting were at last rewarded. His homestead, the scene of his first discovery, he sold to a party of eastern capitalists for a large sum, ample to reward him for his trouble and make him and his family comfortable for life. The land is that on which the Scranton Mining Company was organized, being the west half of the west half of section thirteen, town fifty-one, range forty-two west. After long and carefull explorations Mr. Corser found a vein outcropping on Big Iron River similar in appearance to that on Little Iron River, and upon close examinations he found it to be rich in native silver. Being on Government land, he presented the facts to some parties who immediately purchased it. This was the southeast quarter of section thirteen, town fifty-one, north, of range fifty-two west. This was the commencement of the land excitement. All the government land within several miles was quickly purchased, but winter set in soon after and prevented any very thorough examination of the country. Examinations were, however, made by a few mining men, of the vein that outcropped on Iron River, at the point above mentioned. It was found to be partly on the southeast quarter of section thirteen, and partly on the northeast quarter of section twenty-four, by the government survey lines. Its course to an ordinary observer was due east and west, but further and more accurate examinations proved its actual course at this point to be a few degrees north of west and south of east.

At this time excitement began to run high. Every fortunate owner of land in the district penciled out in his own imagination the course of the vein through his property, and considerable land was entered wild, without any reference to its mineral value. Companies were organized and stock sold in several instances at good figures (for the seller), and it is only charitable to suppose that all these transactions were in good faith. Specimens were eagerly sought for, and assays made by parties in various parts of the country, and without a single exception, found to be rich in silver. One of the first assays made after the discovery of the vein was made by Prof. Jenney, of Marquette, the assayer attached to the State geological surveying party, and yielded $206.40 of silver per ton of rock. Another assay was made at the United States mint, at Philadelphia, and yielded $185 silver per ton of rock, with traces of gold and lead. Three assays were also made by Mr. Ropes, analytical chemist of Ishpeming, Marquette county, the first of which yielded $296.86, the second $116.69, and the third $57.38 silver per ton of rock. Another assay was made from thirteen pounds of vein rock and yielded $1,702.45 of silver per ton. This was certainly a very large yield, and encouraged the owners of property. Of course, there were plenty that doubted the value and even existence of the vein, but the facts were too plain even for the most stubborn. Its friends rightly claimed that these assays were the only criterion they had to go by of the actual value of the vein, and these certainly could not be doubted or gainsaid. The next important assay was from a shipment of several tons of rock from the vein on the Superior mining company's property, on the northeast quarter of section twenty-four, town 51, range 42, to the Wyandotte silver works, at Wyandotte, near Detroit, in this State. The following is the

OFFICIAL CERTIFICATE:

ASSAY OFFICE OF WYANDOTTE SILVER
SMELTING AND REFINING COMPANY,
WYANDOTTE, Mich., Aug. 9, 1873.

We hereby certify that the ore said to be taken from the Superior mine, assayed for Mr. Moore, yields:

No. 1, silver 159 oz. fine, $206.72 coin value per ton of 2,000 pounds.
No. 2, silver 9 oz. fine, $11.70 coin value per ton of 2,000 pounds.
No. 3, silver 458.8 oz. fine, $596.44 coin value per ton of 2,000 pounds.
No. 4, silver 1,320 oz. fine, $1,716 coin value per ton of 2,000 pounds.

REMARKS.—No gold in Nos. 1 and 2; others not examined for gold.

J. B. CLEVELAND, Assayer.   W. M. CURTIS, Supt.

These results were most gratifying and attracted the attention of capitalists and mining men from all parts of the country. Since then the vein has been examined by miners and experts who have had considerable experience with silver veins in the west, in South America, Mexico and Germany, and all agree that it is a true silver vein or stratification, and are unanimous in the opinion that it will increase in richness as greater depth is attained. This opinion so far has been verified by the work done on the vein at the several mines.

The location of this silver discovery is on Iron River, one of whose branches is an outlet for Lake A-go-ge-bic; its general course is northeast and southwest, and its waters rapid. The stream passes through some wild and picturesque scenery, its waters running over the different stratification of rocks which are exposed in several parts of the river. It empties into Lake Superior in section 12, township 51, north range 52 west. At the mouth the water is deep, allowing boats drawing five feet of water to enter. Above this the river is not navigable even for canoes. The slate formation near its mouth takes a serpentine course, and has given rise to many theories and queries. To the east and west of the river the formations all seem to be regular; the sandstone, conglomerate, slates and trap all follow the formation in regular order. The land near the mouth where the silver mines are located is heavily timbered with birch, maple, hemlock, pine and fir, and the soil good, capable of producing all the necessaries of

COZZENS HOTEL, MARQUETTE.

life. To the west of Iron River rises the Porcupine Mountains, attaining an elevation of one thousand three hundred and eighty feet. The district is rich in copper veins, and was the scene of some of the earliest mining on Lake Superior; but all discoveries of copper veins were discarded, as the work was carried on exclusively for silver. Several large spar veins were discovered and worked, but as far as known have yielded no metal. The copper veins, however, discovered and worked by the early miners, and by those of more recent date, are among the most valuable discovered on the Upper Peninsula, and are only waiting the advent of capital and a more easy, certain and cheaper mode of ingress and egress to the district to be developed. This day, from present appearances, is now close at hand. The remarkable severity of the fall of 1872, and the early setting in of winter, prevented the commencement of work on any of the properties. Nothing daunted, however, a few capitalists of Marquette concluded to venture the commencement of work in the month of March, 1873, on the north half of the northwest quarter of section 19, town 51, range 41, on which a company was organized, styled the

ONTONAGON SILVER MINING COMPANY.

Work was commenced on the ground when it was covered with four feet of snow, in a section of country perfectly isolated, no roads to reach it, and not a single person living there. All their supplies, provisions, tools and camping material had to be hauled from Ontonagon on dog trains, or packed up on men's backs. The men were made as comfortable as circumstances would admit, in a brush camp. The point selected for their operations was the extreme northwest corner of the property, near the dividing line of sections 18, 19, 13 and 24. Three test-pits were sunk to the slate, which proved that they were too far north. At length, however, in four weeks from the time they commenced work, they struck the vein about twenty rods south from the east and west line and near the north and south line of their property. It occupied the same geological position as at the outcrop on Iron River, at the junction of the slate and sandstone, having the slate for the north wall and the sandstone for the south or foot wall. Its dip, apparently, was about the same, being about 28° to the north and a little east of north. The width of the vein was the same, being about eighteen inches wide, and fully as rich in native silver as the specimens obtained in Iron River. The fact of the vein being found some fifteen rods to the east of its outcropping in Iron River, seemed to prove conclusively that it was a continuous one.

In that year land was cleared, roads made and buildings erected for the accommodation of the miners. Capt. Thos. Hooper was placed in charge of the mine, and under his direction a working shaft was sunk to a depth of about 125 feet on the vein. From the bottom of this shaft drifts were made east and west on the vein, and some two or three hundred tons of silver bearing rock taken out. In 1873 the company believing that they had sufficiently proved the value of their property, abandoned work until such time as they might be able to secure the erection of a mill for the treatment of the vein rock. A small stamp mill was erected in 1874-'5 and a practical test was made in June or July of that year, resulting most satisfactorily to all concerned. About 22 tons of rock mined in 1873 was treated, from which a brick weighing 36 pounds was obtained, equal to $33 per ton of rock. The following is the official report of Prof. Crosby, the gentleman who put the mill in operation and made the first tests:

ONTONAGON SILVER WORKS,
IRON RIVER, July 22, 1875

TERRENCE MOORE, ESQ., Pres't Ontonagon Silver Co.:

Dear Sir:—I respectfully submit the following brief report of the trial run just finished at the company's mill. The mill was put in motion on the 5th inst., but owing to difficulties incident to the starting of new machinery, the run was not completed till the 20th. The rock treated was a lot of twenty-two tons taken as it came from the mine. The result was 523 ounces of fine bullion, nearly 24 ounces per ton. Not having proper assay fixtures I could not determine its fineness and coin value, but I estimate it at 950 fine, and its currency value at $734.00. The mill is now in good condition, the only drawback to its efficiency being its small capacity. A twenty-stamp mill could reduce the ore at less than half the cost per ton that this five-stamp mill can treat it for. Respectfully yours, F. W. CROSBY.

Mr. Crosby is a gentleman of rare experience and ability, having been engaged for many years in the treatment of the silver ores of Colorado and other western districts.

Mr. Crosby has also furnished the following detailed estimate of the "cost of treating such ores as those of the Ontonagon district," with works having a capacity of 40 tons per day of 24 hours. To reduce, he says, forty tons per day will require a 20-stamp mill. The cost of operating such a mill would be as follows:

LABOR.

One superintendent	$ 5 00
One foreman	3 50
One machinist	3 00
One retorter and smelter	3 00
Two engineers, $2.50 each	5 00
Two amalgamators $3 each	6 00
Two assistant amalgamators $2 each	4 00
Two stamp feeders, $2 each	4 00
Two rock breakers, $2 each	4 00
Two roustabouts, $2 each	4 00
Total for labor	$ 41 50

OTHER EXPENSES.

Four cords wood	$ 8 00
Oil, lights, etc	2 00
Salt and chemicals	25 00
Loss of mercury, ¾ lb. per ton ore	30 00
Charcoal	1 00
Wear and incidentals	5 00
Total	$113 50

Which would be $2.80 per ton! "This," says Mr. Crosby, "seems like a low estimate, but it covers every item except interest on capital."

The cost of mining will not necessarily exceed $2.50 per ton, and this being the case it is easy for any one to arrive at a conclusion as to whether silver bearing rock which can be made to yield from $30 to $50 per ton will pay to work. Taking the average of the 8 tests which have been made—

$40 per ton—and it will be seen that the net earnings of a twenty-stamp mill would be over $1,400 per day, or over half a million a year. Mr. Crosby's estimate further shows that the veins would pay handsomely if the average yield of silver was not over $15 per ton.

The next test made was of rock from the Scranton mine, which is situated nearly two miles west of the Ontonagon. Four and a half tons of rock were put through the mill, giving a yield of 163 ounces of silver, 950 fine—equal to $45.27 per ton coin value. At this mine a perpendicular shaft strikes the vein at a depth of 300 feet on the dip or incline, from the bottom of which shaft was taken the rock treated at the mill.

The Collins mine is on the north half of the northeast quarter of section 25. Here the vein was found outcropping in the river near the northwest corner of the tract. The general appearance of the vein is precisely the same as on sections thirteen and nineteen, one mile to the north, occupying the same geological position in the formation, but its course is entirely different, being northeast and southwest, and the dip southeast. After an examination of the vein at the outcrop a shaft was sunk away from the bank of the river perpendicularly through the overlying formation till it reached the vein, which looked well, carrying considerable native silver. During the past year considerable work has been done on this property, with the most gratifying results, so far as proving the extent and value of the deposit is concerned. The vein matter is, apparently, very rich in native silver, but owing to a lack of means the company was compelled to abandon operations.

South of the Collins, on the south half of the northeast quarter of section 25, is the Cleveland silver mine, at which point more practical mining work has been done than at any other place in the district. A perpendicular or downright shaft cut the vein at a depth of 136 feet, at a point considerably over 300 feet from the outcrop, on the dip or incline. Specimens of vein matter from the bottom of this shaft are very rich in native silver—apparently much richer than any that has been tested at the mill. The company have shipped ten tons of this rock to be treated by specific gravity in Frues' improved vanning machines, at Silver Islet. It is believed by many that this is the only proper plan for treating the Iron River silver bearing rock, and should the test prove successful it is highly probable that the amalgamating process will be abandoned. There can be no question as to the presence of silver in paying quantities, at every point where the vein, or veins, have been opened—the problem is how to extract it. This problem solved, it is confidently believed all doubts as to the future of the district will have been put to rest.

The other properties upon which the vein has been opened, is the Superior mine, which embraces the northeast quarter of section 24, the Mammoth, on the east half of the west half of section 13, and the Pittsburg Silver Co.'s mine, on the southwest quarter of section 34, town 50, north of range 42 west.

The work at the Superior is embraced in an adit into the hill from the river bank, from which adit was taken the rock treated at the Wyandotte works, the report of which has been given. A subsequent test of vein matter from the Superior adit, made at the Ontonagon Company's mill, gave as the result from five tons of rock 224 ounces, Troy, equal to $56 per ton.

Very little work has been done at the Mammoth—only enough to show that the vein crosses the tract.

The Pittsburgh, which lies some six or seven miles south of the others, was discovered in June, 1873, by an outcrop in a small stream. The vein does not have the appearance of a mineral bearing rock but from its relation to the other rocks, and its partial conformation with those of the Iron River district, the party by whom it was discovered was led to believe that the matrix contained silver, which belief was afterwards confirmed. The direction of the vein is about 35° south of east, and it has a dip of 80° to the southwest. The average width as far as opened is about 6½ feet. The first analyses of the rock were made by Prof. A. B. Prescott, of Ann Arbor, and gave from $17 to $119. In the summer of 1875, a test was made at the Ontonagon Co.'s mill, which gave $27.38 per ton from unassorted rock, taken from the whole width of the vein, over a space of it 20 feet in length. There have been several opinions advanced in respect to this formation, but probably the most reliable is that of Charles E. Wright, M. E., who claims that the matrix is an argillaceous plumbaginous slate, the hanging wall being the Pottsdam sandstone. He is not certain of its origin, but thinks that it is an older formation than the overlying sand rock—that is, instead of being on the Pottsdam sandstone, it lies under it. The only work done at the mine was the driving of an adit about 20 feet, from which about five tons of rock was mined.

Prof. Charles Rominger, of the State Geological survey, made an examination of the Iron River district in the fall of 1875, and made the following written report:

"The silver-bearing rock, generally termed a vein, is actually a sedimentary rock stratum, spreading uniformly over a wide space of ground which forms the less elevated belt of land in front of the Porcupine mountains, and the higher trap range of the Ontonagon copper mining district. The age of the silver bearing beds is decidedly younger than that of the copper belt, but it has participated in the upheavals of that period, and the originally horizontal beds have been elevated into a complicated chaos of more or less inclined positions, keeping a general conformity with the strike and dip of the higher ranges, but locally subject to a great many minor disturbances, which cause it to be found dipping in various opposite directions, with abrupt breaks in the strike, or bending in large curves out of the straight course. The out-crops of the formation are almost exclusively confined to the river beds or deep ravines; on the rest of the surface heavy drift deposits are hiding the rock ledges from view, and prevent their discovery except by expensive exploring ditches; however, there is not the least doubt of finding the rock beds under consideration, in every portion of the radicated district, if we undertake to dig deep enough to uncover it. The silver-bearing rock is a gray, compact, well-stratified sandstone, interlaminated with undulating thin seams of a black, shaly material, which contains the principal part of the silver in metallic condition. The sand-rock itself is also silver-bearing, but much poorer than the shaly seams, so that only in rare instances silver can be detected in it by the naked eye. The thickness of the strata is from two to six feet. Their footwall is formed by a brown sandstone of great thickness, often having the character of a conglomerate. The hanging wall of the metalliferous beds is formed by a blue arginaceo-arenaceous rock generally termed slate, but not of the fissile structure of true slate. Usually it has the form of thin-bedded, easy decaying flag-stone. Some beds are more compact, and often contain a large proportion of calcareous cement. The visible thickness of this overlying so-called slate rock amounts in many places to over one thousand feet. Only a few feet above the silver-bearing sand-rock there is another series of metalliferous beds, containing finely comminuted metallic copper in astonishing quantity. The Nonesuch mine is working these, and if it were not for the great loss of metal in working the stamped rock, I should consider this mine even wealthier than the famous Calumet & Hecla mines, which are unsurpassed in the world. In all the exploring shafts of the silver mining companies this same bed has been noticed, but not everywhere equally rich in copper.

"It is stated above that the silver in the rock is contained in metallic condition; but a not inconsiderable additional quantity of the precious metal is combined in the sulphur, and makes part of the black, shaly substance pervading the rock in linear seams. Several tests on a large scale have been made with the silver-bearing rock mass, taking for the experiments, without selection, the entire thickness of the so-called vein, and the results have been very favorable. In each experiment several tons of the rock have been stamped and subjected to the amalgamating process, which evidently was not carried out to perfection, but still the results proved very satisfactory. The rock of three different localities, treated in this way, yielded from forty to forty-five dollars' worth of silver for every ton of rock.

"The brown sandstone forming the footwall, if found in the vicinity of the blue-colored slate-like rock of the hanging wall, serves always as a good guide for the explorer; more risky it is to rely on the explorations to follow the direction of the strike of the strata from places of outcrops into territories where the rock is covered by drift, on account of the frequent disturbances and breaks in the strata. The mining of the rock is neither difficult nor expensive, and if carried on with reasonable economy and circumspection will certainly return a large margin of profits to those engaged in its development; otherwise, the history of our mining districts have clearly shown that even the richest deposits of mineral wealth are not sufficient to prevent disastrous consequences and total failures of companies, if speculation and mismanagement are exerting their deleterious force."

Work was continued at the Ontonagon mine during a part of the winter of 1875, but the results at the mill were not satisfactory, and operations were suspended. There has been a difference of opinion as to the cause of the failure; some insist that those in charge of the mill were incapable of achieving a true result, while others give the credit to the mine and the absence of silver. However this may be, the true friends of the district are not despondent, and the Cleveland and Collins companies have continued the work of development, as if certain of future rewards. The writer does not venture an opinion other than that enough has been done to warrant still further research and experiment, believing that the only problem to be solved is the best and most effective process for treating the vein rock.

SLATE.

Among the material and most valuable resources of the Lake Superior country, slate is now taking rank. Long since it was known that large deposits of slate were lying in the hills east of Huron Bay, but the country being almost inaccessible, except by water, and explorers being attracted by what was considered the more valuable products of iron and copper, were not tempted to investigate the resources of the slate country. But by and by a few adventurous and courageous men concluded that if copper found in a wilderness, or iron found in a wilderness, could be so manipulated, with the aid of transportation facilities, as to bring wealth to those who were first to present these minerals to the market, and wealth to the scores who were led to follow the lead of the pioneers, that slate might also be made a medium of prosperity. But it was not with a full knowledge of the character of the slate, or of the quality which they had discovered, that those men commenced their movements. They scarcely knew what they had found—whether it was a slate of an indifferent or of a superior character. But they resolved upon a test, and accordingly Thos. J. Brown, of Marquette, accompanied by Wm. T. Kennedy, of Pittsburgh, and an Indian, as a man of all work, attempted, in November, 1871, to pack out a few hundred pounds of the slate and have it submitted to test. S. C. Smith, the veteran explorer, had previously, in July, 1868, visited the locality and carried away a quantity of the slate, which he shipped to Vermont for the inspection of those posted in such matters.

Geographically, the belt lies midway between the copper and iron deposits; geologically, it is a later deposit than the copper measures and older than the iron of the Marquette range. No estimate of the length, depth and breadth of the belt can at present be satisfactorily made. In township 51 north of range 31 west, the breadth of the belt is believed to be two and a half miles, but the length has not been fully explored. It is evident that the same belt appears in the Ontonagon silver district, while outcrops have been discovered twelve miles to the east of the present quarries. It does not, however, follow that all the slate covering this wide stretch of country can be denominated good roofing slates; on the contrary, slates free from joints and impurities are not easy to find.

Meanwhile, the lands had been purchased, and subsequently a company was organized to quarry slate in township 51, range 31. The company is organized as follows:

President, W. L. WETMORE, Marquette; *Secretary and Treasurer*, H. A. DOWNS, Marquette; *Superintendent*, JOHN THOMAS; *Directors*, PETER WHITE, S. L. SMITH, THOS. J. BROWN, Marquette, D. W. C. WHEELER, JAS. McDONALD, New York.

The organization was effected in October, 1872. Toward the last part of that month, Mr. Williams, the first superintendent, reported for duty, and with a brush shanty, and eighteen miles of primitive forest through which to haul his supplies, commenced the development of what is now acknowledged to be the finest slate quarry in the world.

Operations were first commenced on a bed of slate which seemed to be inexhaustible, and of finest working quality, but which was found to be laminated with mundic, or arsenical pyrites—an ingredient which does not injure the value of the slate any farther than the appearance of the light flakes might affect the sale.

Further explorations were made on the same vein in an adjoining neighborhood, where a clear, pure, beautiful slate was found, and this is the quarry which is now being principally worked. Details as to location are of no interest to the general reader, therefore we omit distances and points of compass in the several explorations and openings.

Of the quality of this slate, little need be said, since it is now so well known and appreciated, that architects in nearly all the western cities insert it in their specifications. It is blasted out in angular shape, without reference to regularity as to cubes or slabs, and afterward broken into tablets of convenient size for splitting. As it comes from the quarry it is uniformly of the same quality, and the proportion of it which is used depends altogether upon the shape it assumes whilst being broken into tablets. The cleavers say they have never handled a slate, in Wales or the United States, upon which they could make as good wages, for instead of being compelled to crease or trench the edge of a tablet to split off a shingle, but one movement and one position of the chisel, with a few taps of the mallet, is necessary to separate a plate, like separating two panes of glass which have been but slightly pasted together. The surface of the sheets is almost as regular and smooth as if they had been planed; and the sheets, however thin, will stand very rough handling without breaking, and are pitched about like wooden shingles. It is of a blue-black color, and gives off a sound, upon being tapped, like hollow crockery.

The product of the quarry is shipped over a three-foot tramrailway to Huron Bay, a distance of 4½ miles. At the bay, the company have a dock which extends 600 feet into the water and has a front of 100 feet.

The company is employing from 40 to 60 men, and commenced shipments this season from a stock of 500 squares of roofing slate, and with orders for 3,000 squares. They make 24 sizes, and find a ready market for their entire product, in St. Paul, Minneapolis, Chicago, Milwaukee and Detroit. Some of the best buildings in Chicago and Milwaukee are covered with the Huron Bay slate, among them the Chicago and Northwestern Railway shops, the new club house, and several churches.

It is not roofing slate alone for which this material is useful, but every purpose for which slate is used. The waste from the quarry in the production of roofing slate could be so utilized for the manufacture of tiles, lamp bottoms, and the like, to pay all expenses of the quarry. And for mantels, fire fronts, table tops, imposing slabs, and such purposes, it is only second to marble. That a large business in these lines will be done at these quarries when machinery has been placed to handle the material, there is no doubt. The Company is considering the question of putting in such machinery, and it will probably be added at an early day.

THE CLINTON SLATE AND IRON COMPANY'S

quarry is situated on a tract which embraces the west half of section 8, and the northwest quarter of section 33, town 51, north of range 31 west. The Company was organized in 1874, with a capital of $500,000, divided into 20,000 shares of $25 each. *President*, DeWitt C. Wheeler, of New York; *Secretary and Treasurer*, James H. Seager, Houghton, and *Superintendent*, R. R. Williams. The quarry, as now opened, lies on the township line between sections 28 and 33. To the north and east, about 1,000 feet, is the Huron Bay Slate Company's quarry, and the slate out-crops here and there between the two.

A shaft has been sunk in the slate at the Clinton to a depth of forty feet. The shaft—or, as the slaters or scalpers call it, "the loose side and back"—is about fifty feet square at present, and it is being constantly enlarged and deepened. It is the intention to carry this loose side and back down into the slate a sufficient depth to admit of a goodly number of stoping parties on the several layers or strata of slate. When once down, a large force may be employed in quarrying out the slate, in steps. During the time consumed in working out the loose side and back, quite a large quantity of slate has been made, and is now ready for shipment. In quality, the slate is pronounced by competent judges, to be equal to the best slate products of Maine. It is a dark, indelible blue, free from mundic and sulphate of iron, and the joints are far apart. As the shaft descends, the slate grows denser and purer. So far, the slate at the Clinton is pronounced the softest yet found, which permits a freer cleavage and thinner slates.

An erroneous impression has obtained heretofore, concerning the dip of the beds, by confounding the dip with the cleavage. On sinking, it has been ascertained that the beds slightly incline to the north, while the cleavage is to the south. It is now believed that the bed lies in a basin. At the northern boundary of the bed a vein of lean iron ore outcrops; and a rock, identical in appearance to the wall-rock of the Ontonagon silver vein, has been found, from which fact, it is believed it may not be impossible to discover somewhere in the vicinity of the slate formation, on the transverse veins, a prolific silver lode. Explorations, with this aim in view, will be made, and it is not at all improbable that the efforts of the faithful in this regard, will be crowned with success.

The tram-road spoken of in connection with the Huron Bay quarry, has been extended to the Clinton, and a force of men has been kept constantly employed in the quarry ever since the first opening was made. Up to the close of navigation in 1875, the Clinton Company had made and shipped about 1,000 squares.

HURLEYS' HURON MOUNTAIN

quarry is owned by a company of that name, and though more remote from water communication, is esteemed a most valuable property. Considerable work has been done at this quarry, though as yet little in the way of making slate, owing to the absence of a suitable road for its transportation to the lake side. The financial depression has had the effect to retard the work of development, otherwise the quarry would no doubt long since have been ready with its product for the market.

THE SUPERIOR SLATE AND MINING COMPANY

is the owner of a large acreage on the slate belt, which will no doubt be opened when the market demands an increased product.

Several other parties have purchased lands, among them

the original discoverers of the belt, S. C. Smith, Esq., Henry H. Stafford, and others, of Marquette.

The soil on the shore of Huron Bay is especially adapted to agricultural purposes. It is a sandy loam, very deep, warm and rich. All sorts of root and grain crops grow exceedingly well. The vegetables are especially fine, and we were shown some spring wheat which cannot well be excelled. The bay is fourteen miles long, with nearly forty miles of shore line, including the inlets and points, with a good depth of water on every mile of the shore. The timber is hard wood, and stands thick and heavy. The bay is absolutely land-locked, as points extend from either shore so far into the bay as to break off all influence of rough weather from the lake.

The superior quality of the slate in this district warrants the prediction that within a few years the entire west will be supplied from Lake Superior. Wherever introduced it attains a celebrity over any and all slates brought from the east, and it will soon be in request like our copper and iron, and its purity, durability, and unfading color, will command for it a better price than eastern slates. The out-put this year will reach several thousand squares, and it will be annually increased as the product becomes better known. In the near future the Huron Bay slate district will become as populous and enterprising as any of her sister Lake Superior communities.

BUILDING MATERIAL.

BROWN SANDSTONE.

The brown sandstone which was quarried at Marquette for some years, without attracting the especial attention of men who have been prominently engaged in this line of industry and utility, has of late years been given particular prominence by being introduced for building purposes through the best architects and builders, and it is found to surpass, in every particular, all other qualities of building stone here in use. It is well known that the mass of most quarries from which building stone is obtained—and especially sandstone and granite—is interseamed with thin strata of limestone, trap, conglomerate, semi-limestone, clay-slate and other substances, which detract greatly from the uniformity of the material taken out. But the stone which is found in the Marquette Quarries, is as uniform in quality and as easily manipulated in a mass of any size—to an especial pattern, if desirable—as if moulded out of soap, aside from the trifle of additional labor required to work the harder substance. This may seem like exaggeration, but operations on the ground, at the quarries, show, that by the usual method of trenching and underseaming, any size of stone may be taken out in as perfect a form as it is possible to obtain it without the use of saw and chisel. Then it is easily worked; so easily, in fact, that the most experienced stone cutters decide that from twenty to fifty per cent. can be saved by carving it to occupy any place which may be desired in a building. And last of all, it is found that as it is exposed to the atmosphere and its moisture is evaporated, it becomes harder than any other stone in use, and when laid up in a wall in the same horizontal position it was taken from the quarry, it will not scale, crack or expand, as is the case with much of the stone used for building purposes. It resembles, as near as possible, in grain, color and texture, the Portland, Connecticut stone, and is much easier worked. It is finer and more compact than the Ohio building stone, and has been pronounced just as good as the New England granites, while it is far less expensive, thus having every advantage of all the best building stones. There are within the city limits of Marquette two of these quarries, from which have been furnished the material for some of the handsomest and most substantial business blocks in Chicago. The

MARQUETTE BROWN STONE COMPANY

owns 126 acres, just back of the rolling mill, which have been worked quite profitably for several years past. It is not deemed necessary to describe the quarry in detail, nor to say more than that there appears to be an immense bed of the stone. The upper layers are white and variegated, under which lies the pure brown stone which is so eagerly sought after, not only because of its beautiful uniform color, but because of its invaluable fire-proof qualities. It is owned exclusively by Marquette men.

THE BURT FREE STONE COMPANY'S

quarry adjoins that of the Marquette Brown Stone Company, and has been wrought for several years, though not very successfully. The stone does not appear to be of quite as good quality as that of its neighbor, and the quarry has been partially abandoned.

At Portage Entry another bed of fine red sandstone has been secured by Jay. C. Morse, Esq., and other Marquette men, upon which it is proposed to organize a joint stock company. Indeed, but for the occurrence of the panic, it is more than probable that the company would have been successfully organized, and work long since commenced. The development of the quarry is only a question of time.

The newest and most important enterprise of the kind is,

however, near L'Anse, where a new quarry was opened by the
L'ANSE BROWN STONE COMPANY,
in the summer of 1875. At this quarry the stone outcrops 400 feet on the bay shore, is of a dark brown color, somewhat harder than that of the Marquette quarries, and it is believed will stand a much greater pressure, while its fireproof qualities are equally as good. The bed of pure brown stone is about nine feet thick at the point where quarrying has been commenced, and test-pits show that it extends back from the water front some four or five thousand feet. It is covered by a drift which does not average more than two feet in thickness, and its situation on the bay is such that it can be quarried and loaded upon vessels at a cost at least 25 per cent. below that of quarries situated at a distance from navigable waters, and in the operation of which teams have to be employed to haul the product to the water's side.

A crib dock has been built into sixteen feet of water, which depth is reached in less than 200 feet from the shore line. The cribs are placed just north of the quarry and are strong and substantial enough to answer the purposes of a breakwater, thus enabling vessels to land in almost any stress of weather. The cribs were all filled with rubble from the quarry, and cost little more than the timber used in their construction. A tram-road extends on a slight incline from the quarry along the whole length of the dock, upon which the product of the quarry is conveyed along side the vessel without the aid of steam or horse power. A small engine is employed in hoisting the stone upon the cars, and in transferring it from the dock into the vessels.

The first "break" at this quarry detached a solid block of stone containing 2,400 cubic feet. The working face on the first bed, or layer, is nine feet in height, or thickness, and as may be inferred, can be extended 400 feet along the shore. These 400 feet cover the front of ten acres, all of which are under-laid with the same quality of stone, as has been proved by a close examination. The ground rises to a height of about 50 feet, about the same distance back from the shore, and there is every reason to believe that the bed increases in thickness—unless, indeed, it conforms most closely to the topography, in which case the facilities for quarrying will, at least, be greatly enhanced.

T. T. Hurley, Esq., of Marquette, is the moving spirit in this enterprise, as he has been in many others that have redounded to the credit and advantage of the Lake Superior region. E. M. Wood, Esq., a competent man, is superintendent.

Near Bayfield, on one of the islands of the Apostle group, a quarry was opened some years ago, and from it was obtained the stone of which the elegant Milwaukee court house is built. In fact, all along the south shore of the lake are situated beds of this brown stone of the very finest quality, which in years to come will be developed and made to yield the material for the building up, in a more substantial manner, of our great lake cities. Indeed, such is the acknowledged value of our Lake Superior brown sandstone as a building material, that we may confidently expect our quarries, in a few years, to become one of the most important elements of substantial wealth.

LUMBER.

It was the desire of the writer to present in this volume full statistics of the lumber trade of the Lake Superior country, but he regrets to say that his requests for information were not generally responded to. Reports were received from twenty-two mills, having an annual aggregate capacity of one hundred and seventy-five million feet: These twenty-two mills cut in 1875, 95,000,000 feet of lumber, 21,200,000 lath, 20,650,000 shingles, and 12,298 bundles of pickets, the total value of which in the market was about $1,500,000. These returns do not include all the mills, and the writer is therefore precluded from making as detailed a statement as he desired to do. The figures show, however, that lumber is not the least important of the many natural resources of the Upper Peninsula of Michigan. In one county alone, (Chippewa,) there is pine timber enough to keep fifty mills at work for as many years, and the whole peninsula, except where it has been burned over, is little less than a vast forest of pine and hard wood.

AGRICULTURE.

The idea commonly held by strangers to Lake Superior is. that it is a barren, sterile region, the surface of the country consisting of rocky ledges, cliffs and hills, with here and there a stunted fir or spruce tree, maintaining a precarious existence in the shallow soil which has collected in cracks in the rocks or in small valleys between the ridges. This idea, which was probably derived from the accounts given by the early voyagers, explorers and missionaries who first visited this region, and rarely, if ever, penetrated the forests far enough to lose sight of the lake, is certainly erroneous. In consequence of these popular fallacies, strangers visiting this region are almost invariably astonished, when they learn that there are farms at various points on the lake, that pay larger dividends to the proprietors than the best farms in the most fertile parts of the country; and they are inclined to doubt their senses when they find farmers actually getting rich on their Lake Superior farms.

There are large tracts of fertile land lying at various points along the south shore of Lake Superior, and all over the Upper Peninsula of Michigan, in such proximity to the mining and lumbering settlements that their products would always be in good demand, and bring the highest cash prices. The soil is either a dark sandy loam, or clay, principally the former—well watered with numerous small streams of clear spring water, and an occasional small lake of remarkable clearness and beauty, well stocked with excellent fish—principally the popular speckled trout. One peculiarity of this locality is that the great depth of snow (from three to seven feet) which falls during the winter, usually prevents the ground from being frozen in the slightest material degree. In many instances, potatoes have been left in the ground during the winter without sustaining injury from frost. A home-steader remarks: "I have been on my location five years, and have planted no potatoes since the first year, allowing them to 'seed' themselves; but," said he, "I suppose I shall have to plant some more, for they get smaller every year; and they'll get so small I can't find 'em in two or three years more. The first two years they were the best potatoes I ever saw."

Farmers from the old settled regions of New York, Ohio, and even of Southern Michigan, Wisconsin, and other near localities, while visiting this region for the first time, are greatly astonished on learning that though the winters usually last from six to seven months, agriculture can be successfully carried on. It would scarcely be profitable to raise live stock for the market, as the length of time for winter feeding is so great, and corn is not a successful crop. The principal crops raised here are hay, oats and potatoes, and other common root crops. Strawberries, and other small fruits, grow luxuriantly and yield abundantly. Wheat would doubtless do well, but as yet there are no mills for grinding, and the cereal is not regularly grown. As soon, however, as the farming communities become extensive enough to warrant it, mills will, of course, be erected. The deep snows, it is contended by some, will smother the wheat; but in the month of June, 1872, the writer traveled from the southern part of Michigan to the Straits of Mackinaw, at the northern extremity of the Lower Peninsula, a distance of upwards of two hundred miles, and the best piece of winter wheat he saw in the State was in Cheboygan county, on the Black river, within six miles of the Straits, where the snow had been from three to seven feet deep for several months during the preceding winter—which is about the depth the snow reaches in the hardest winters on the south shore of Lake Superior. Hay, is probably the easiest and most remunerative crop the agriculturist can raise in this region, as grass attains a rank growth, and when cured, commands a high price from the various mining and lumbering companies. During the season of 1873-'4, hay was sold at $35 and upward per ton. We have seen "blue joint" grass growing in the beaver meadows along the small streams in this region, which stood from four to five feet in height in the month of June—equivalent to May in the latitude of central and western New York. Those meadows, which are accessible from the lumber camps or mines, are mowed every year by the companies nearest adjacent, and indeed much of the land on which they are situated has been purchased by them in order to secure the grass. There is no danger of overstocking the hay market, because, even now, large quantities are annually shipped to this country from those agricultural districts which are the most accessible, and the mineral development of this country has but just commenced. Oats are always in demand at high prices, and yield well. The large number of horses employed in lumbering and mining operations require thousands of bushels of oats every year, which are shipped from as far south as Illinois, and never bring less than fifty cents per bushel, and usually the prices are much higher. Potatoes yield well, and bring strong prices—$1.00 and upwards per bushel—with ready sales.

The timber growing on the agricultural lands usually consists of sugar, or hard maple, yellow birch, basswood, elm, and on the low lands along the streams and near the lakes, white cedar, fir, hemlock, and soft maple, with some pine timber. The numerous charcoal furnaces already built, and others soon to be, will make this timber valuable; in fact, large tracts of the lands covered with this hard wood have been located by speculators, in anticipation of the demand for the wood sure to be created by these furnaces, and large sums of money have already been realized by comparatively small investments in this class of lands, located near enough to the railroads, before they were built, or soon after they were finished, to render them accessible to the charcoal burners.

One furnace company has constructed a wooden railroad of about eleven miles in length, on which to draw charcoal, wood having become scarce in the vicinity of the furnace. Other furnaces have been abandoned wholly on account of the difficulty in obtaining a supply of charcoal. Thus a scarcity of wood may be created even in a "wooden country."

The desirable lands lying near the railroads already built are probably nearly all bought up, but along the line of one or two projected roads, (the Mackinaw & Marquette, and Menominee Range) which must, in the nature of things, soon be built, there are still considerable state and government lands that can be bought for $1.25, $2.50, and $4.00 per acre; or, any one desiring to settle on the land can, by payment of a small fee at the government land office, "pre-empt" 160 acres of the $1.25 land, or 80 acres of the $2.50 land. In buying $4 state lands, the purchaser can, by making oath that it is principally valuable for agricultural purposes, secure the title on payment of $1.00 per acre, and have almost unlimited time in which to pay the balance, with seven per cent. interest, payable annually.

This volume would not be complete without a reference to Lake Superior as a summer resort for the tourist pleasure seeker and invalid; and the writer feels that he cannot do better than quote the words of one who can hardly be considered an interested party. In 1864, M. J. R. St. John visited this region, and was so enraptured with the climate and scenery that he was led to write and publish a small volume, giving an account of the country and its many attractions. In it he says:

"To the traveler for pleasure, let me say a few words. When you shall have read the round upon which I have taken the coaster, you will probably shrink from the toils of following the shore, and wish to go direct, and quick, from place to place, or tarry a time at one place and then go to another—in either case there will be ample provision next season. * *

If you are in pursuit of pleasure, whether lady or gentleman, you can find it in the Lake Superior region, provided you can be pleased with grand scenery, water-falls, lakes and mountains. You can ramble in search of agates and carnelians, in which, of all I have seen engaged, I have never known one to tire of the amusement. * * Or, tired of this, you can wander away with hook and line, to the bright and beautiful lakes that lie among the hills; or take your gun, for

> The Pigeon and the Pheasant's there,
> The wild Duck, and the timid Hare—

but no snakes! I have never heard of any in the country. Or take a bark canoe, which two or three trials will make you at home in, for they are much easier to get the 'hang' of, than most persons suppose; go to the adjacent islands, run into the caverns and grottoes, which cannot be reached in any other way. You may find rare agates there after a gale, and when you return keep along the shore and examine the bottom marked by white spar veins, discernible at thirty or forty feet deep, * * and when you get back you will have an appetite; the tonic air of that region, and the water, will make a new being of you in a few weeks. The air is bracing, yet soft, and is pleasant in 'dog days,' without producing that faintness and lassitude of the warm weather you have been used to; and the water—well, you will not be singular, you will then say you have never drank any water before, and when you return whence you came, and again drink of that you once thought delicious, you will condemn it as an adulteration, or spurious. To the invalid I have a few words to say: I am not 'cracking' up the country; for I shall write nothing that all who go will not find as I represent it, or all who have been will not confirm, either on this or any other subject of their acquaintance which I treat upon. To you I say, go, then; although your health is impaired you cannot be injured, and I know one gentleman who had been south, and to Havana, without benefit, and one season on Lake Superior restored him, as he said, to comparative health. I don't know why it should not relieve consumptives as well as others—all who go there declare they *feel* much better, and I *know* I did."

This was written at a time when the only settlements were at Sault ste. Marie and at Copper Harbor, when the building of such towns as Marquette, Negaunee, Ishpeming, Houghton, Hancock and others of less note, were not dreamt of. Now, we have handsome and flourishing cities and villages, where then stood the primeval forest; palatial steamers plow the great lake; railways connect us with all parts of the Union; we have churches, schools—all the adjuncts of civilization—and yet the clear, babbling brooks and beautiful lakes remain to charm the tourist and afford recreation for the sporting Nimrod.

Come and see us!

THE END.

IRON BAY FOUNDRY AND MACHINE SHOPS, MARQUETTE.

www.ingramcontent.com/pod-product-compliance
Lightning Source LLC
Chambersburg PA
CBHW021623250426
43672CB00037B/1381